# The Artifice of Affect

Modern American Literature and the New Twentieth Century
Series Editors: Martin Halliwell and Mark Whalan

**Published Titles**

*Writing Nature in Cold War American Literature*
Sarah Daw

*F. Scott Fitzgerald's Short Fiction: From Ragtime to Swing Time*
Jade Broughton Adams

*The Labour of Laziness in Twentieth-Century American Literature*
Zuzanna Ladyga

*The Literature of Suburban Change: Narrating Spatial Complexity in Metropolitan America*
Martin Dines

*The Literary Afterlife of Raymond Carver: Influence and Craftsmanship in the Neoliberal Era*
Jonathan Pountney

*Living Jim Crow: The Segregated Town in Mid-Century Southern Fiction*
Gavan Lennon

*The Little Art Colony and US Modernism: Carmel, Provincetown, Taos*
Geneva M. Gano

*Sensing Willa Cather: The Writer and the Body in Transition*
Guy J. Reynolds

*Gertrude Stein and the Politics of Participation: Democracy, Rights and Modernist Authorship, 1909–1933*
Isabelle Parkinson

*The Regional Development of the American Bildungsroman, 1900–1960*
Tamlyn Avery

*Exoteric Modernisms: Progressive Era Realism and the Aesthetics of Everyday Life*
Michael J. Collins

*The Artifice of Affect: American Realist Literature and Emotional Truth*
Nicholas Manning

**Forthcoming Titles**

*The Big Red Little Magazine: New Masses, 1926–1948*
Susan Currell

*The Reproductive Politics of American Literature and Film, 1959–1973*
Sophie Jones

*Ordinary Pursuits in American Writing after Modernism*
Rachel Malkin

*The Plastic Theatre of Tennessee Williams: Expressionist Drama and the Visual Arts*
Henry I. Schvey

*Black Childhood in Modern African American Fiction*
Nicole King

*Keeping It Real: Authenticity and the Confessional Turn in Post-War US Literature and Culture*
David Brauner

*David Foster Wallace and the Question of Scepticism*
Matt Prout

*The Midcentury Minor Novel: American Fiction, 1945–1965*
Michael Kalisch

*Girlhood in the Contemporary American Novel*
Angelica De Vido

Visit our website at www.edinburghuniversitypress.com/series/MALTNTC

# The Artifice of Affect

## American Realist Literature and Emotional Truth

NICHOLAS MANNING

EDINBURGH
University Press

Edinburgh University Press is one of the leading university presses in the UK. We publish academic books and journals in our selected subject areas across the humanities and social sciences, combining cutting-edge scholarship with high editorial and production values to produce academic works of lasting importance. For more information visit our website: edinburghuniversitypress.com

© Nicholas Manning, 2024, 2025

Research for this book was conducted with funding from the Institut universitaire de France (IUF) and the Institut des langues et cultures d'Europe, Amérique, Afrique, Asie et Australie (Univ. Grenoble Alpes, ILCEA4, 38000 Grenoble, France).

Edinburgh University Press Ltd
13 Infirmary Street,
Edinburgh, EH1 1LT

First published in hardback by Edinburgh University Press 2024

Typeset in 10/13 ITC Giovanni Std Book by
Cheshire Typesetting Ltd, Cuddington, Cheshire

A CIP record for this book is available from the British Library

ISBN 978 1 3995 0799 8 (hardback)
ISBN 978 1 3995 0800 1 (paperback)
ISBN 978 1 3995 0801 8 (webready PDF)
ISBN 978 1 3995 0802 5 (epub)

The right of Nicholas Manning to be identified as the author of this work has been asserted in accordance with the Copyright, Designs and Patents Act 1988, and the Copyright and Related Rights Regulations 2003 (SI No. 2498).

# CONTENTS

| | |
|---|---|
| *List of Figures* | vi |
| *Acknowledgements* | vii |
| Introduction: Against True Feeling | 1 |
| 1. Can Realism Speak of Affect? | 47 |
| 2. Beyond Natural Feeling: The Body as Artifice | 81 |
| 3. Inimitable Affect: On the Mimesis of Emotion | 115 |
| 4. Myths of Emotional Equilibrium | 154 |
| 5. Medicalisation, Pathologisation and the Intoxicated Self | 186 |
| Conclusion: The Theatre of the Affective Mind | 218 |
| *Notes* | 238 |
| *Bibliography* | 261 |
| *Index* | 274 |

# FIGURES

1 Guillaume-Benjamin Duchenne (de Boulogne), *Mécanisme de la physionomie humaine ou analyse électro-physiologique de l'expression des passions* (Paris: Renouard, 1862), Plates 31 and 32, unnumbered page. Source: Wellcome Collection. Attribution 4.0 International (CC BY 4.0), https://wellcomecollection.org/works/vr8cb8u5     28

2 Duchenne (de Boulogne), *Mécanisme de la physionomie humaine*, frontispiece. Source: Wellcome Collection. Attribution 4.0 International, https://wellcomecollection.org/works/m33y9ucc     29

## ACKNOWLEDGEMENTS

Over the decade of its gestation, extracts of this book appeared in previous versions – here expanded, significantly modified and in some cases adapted from the original French – in the *Revue française d'études américaines*, *Transatlantica* and *L'Atelier*, as well as in the collective volumes *L'Artifice dans les lettres et les arts* (Presses universitaires de Rennes, 2016) and *Le Comparatisme comme approche critique* (vol. 6, Classiques Garnier, 2018). My warm thanks to Marc Amfreville, Peter Boxall, Antoine Cazé, Mathieu Duplay, Adam Frank and Sophie Vallas, who were among my first readers and whose always incisive remarks helped to forge more fully these arguments; as well as to Lauren Berlant, Rachel Greenwald Smith and Sianne Ngai, with whom my interviews in the *Revue française d'études américaines* allowed me to rethink many of this work's thorniest cruxes. I am also grateful to the reviewers at Edinburgh University Press, whose generous and stimulating remarks contributed significantly to the improvement of this book, as well as to Martin Halliwell and Mark Whalan, editors of the series 'Modern American Literature and the New Twentieth Century', which I am proud to join. Time and research funding provided by my fellowship at the Institut universitaire de France made possible the revision and finalisation of the manuscript in a climate of privileged peace. Céline is always my first and most enlightening reader: our own artifice lies in the shared fashioning of an affective world, of which our children Johan and Nora are the newest, brightest buds. This book is dedicated to them.

*For Johan and Nora*

# Introduction: Against True Feeling

This book argues that when we insist that emotions be true we are often in reality implying that they be limited, homogenised and made to comply with established moral beliefs. Similarly, when we erect emotional truth as a value in literature, whether of authors, characters or literary works, we risk making literature an agent of social and affective conformity. True feeling is frequently a trap.[1] To ask of emotions that they be true is to demand that they attune to an orthodox spectrum: that of the unified, normalised individual in an entrenched communal role, whose affective authenticity is at the service of defined ideological and socioeconomic ends. Furthermore, when we ask of emotions that they be expressible, understandable or balanced – terms which all depend on the implicit presence of a hierarchical truth – we are often employing a range of restrictive categories masquerading as positive ideals.

Throughout the following chapters I propose that much American realist fiction from the Cold War to the close of the twentieth century formulates a trenchant critique of the aesthetic and social imperatives of true, authentic and natural feeling. These three terms moreover became intricately interwoven in an era whose climate of cultural beliefs tended to equate truth with, on the one hand, subjective authenticity, and on the other, an elemental physiological source. This cultural parallelism of terms which have important conceptual differences leads to an extensive overlap, and even amalgamation, of artifice understood as a negative ontological property, as an absence of truth content and as the willed deception of a moral act.

On a theoretical level, I attempt to demonstrate that the intense questioning of the value of emotional truth in modern American literary realism comes to indicate the artificial nature of all affective force. Analysis of the fiction at the heart of this book leads me to propose that all emotional processes, as living visceral constructions, should not be held to the standards of static adequational properties such as accuracy, legitimacy or veracity.[2] *The Artifice of Affect* is thus opposed to the imperative that we should, consciously or unconsciously, feel social or self-imposed pressure to determine the truth of our own feelings, thereby conforming to hypothetically natural affective standards. This is why I will argue against the tripartite concepts of emotional nature, normality and balance – concepts which, commonly employed to support the unstable notional edifice of true feeling, are too often covert mechanisms of limitation and repression, aimed at suppressing troublesome outliers on a continuum of emotional norms.

The post-war era of 1945 to 2000 has been chosen as the focus of this study because it represents a marked intensification, in American realist fiction, in the revolt against cultural demands for affective authenticity, which became increasingly dominant from the Cold War on. In authors as varied as James Baldwin or Richard Yates in the 1950s, to Paula Fox or Richard Ford towards the end of the century, we witness distinct but related critiques, each targeting specific inadequacies and injustices, of restrictive visions of emotional truth to which subjects and citizens are expected to conform. Indeed, one crucial feature that distinguishes post-war American fiction from its realist forebears of the late nineteenth and early twentieth centuries – encompassing such figures as Stephen Crane, Theodor Dreiser, Charlotte Perkins Gilman, William Dean Howells, Henry James, John Steinbeck or Edith Wharton – may indeed be its recurrent denunciation of affective authenticity as a fundamentally oppressive ideal.

## On the Dangers of True Feeling

What is so bad, however, about true feeling as aesthetic principle, cultural touchstone or moral imperative? The following chapters will explore a range of negative consequences related to the ideal or requirement that one live one's life in concordance with the values of emotional truth. We will see that, in spite of these dangers, true feeling is recurrently posed, in a variety of cultural contexts, as a powerful solution and even panacea to the dilemmas of modern affective life. Rather than bypassing the reductive dualism of emotion and cognition, the appeal to true feeling consecrates this binary by implying that, when reflection hits an impenetrable roadblock, true feeling can dissolve the tension at the heart of conceptual paradoxes, cultural aporia or personal moral crises. This situating of true feeling as a higher arbiter – as an ersatz voice of God which indicates the way to lost Reason – effectively establishes it as a subjective circuit-breaker, which kicks in whenever currents of dissent, pain, protest or confusion become overwhelmingly strong. In breaking such circuits, true feeling is, in essence, deployed as a normalising apparatus which seeks to explain away those aspects of experience which remain troublesomely incoherent. For if we believe that we have come to be in possession of an emotional truth which is truly ours, then why search further – for additional objections, disturbances or disquiet – beyond the comfort of a known interior conviction, which so often corresponds to that of an exterior status quo?

This search for harmonisation tends to make of true feeling, as it is commonly used throughout American modernity, a necessarily generic criterion of value, so that in imagining emotional truth we inevitably create an amalgam of the feeling of others: an abstraction which, based on a mean of ambient affective responses, is inherently essentialistic. Indeed, true feeling as both concept and social mechanism has trouble integrating paradoxical emotional states – those which do not make sense or which refuse to conform – for the reason that certain dominant, rationalistic conceptions of truth tend to prefer unity and harmony over paradox and discord. If unity is preferred, then so too is stasis: for the appeal to true feeling tends to set in place a range of emotional processes which are by definition mobile. In seeking to ground emotionality in a truth imagined as subjective anchorage, we risk depriving emotion of the intersubjective dynamism that shapes its being; for in implicitly categorising expressions, modes and states, true feeling establishes an immobile reference point for affect's interplays of vital force.

This indicates another serious problem with the criterion, which has to do with the self and its surrounding world: namely, true feeling is a highly self-centred evaluation, which seeks to determine not if an emotion is true in an abstract sense – though, as we shall see, it is unclear what such a judgement might entail – but whether it is true to me. In a case of intense solipsism posed as an innate subjective right, the self-reflexive subject becomes the ultimate arbiter for the truth of his or her own emotional states. Who else has the right to tell me if my own inner feelings are true? Am I not the ultimate judge presiding over inner emotional trials? Others cannot easily prove that my feelings are false for the reason that, not being the ones feeling them, they have little epistemological or ethical claim to my own visceral processes. This creates a marked disparity: if I am the only evaluator of my feelings' truth, I am essentially living in a hall of self-confirming mirrors – I have become an affective singularity who risks excluding the challenges of alterity at every turn.

Frustration and disillusionment are the by-products of such unfeasible efforts to live up to the hypothetical standards of the true emotional life. For to 'look inside oneself' in an effort to locate one's 'heart of truth', and to find no true feeling there at all – no unchanging point of anchorage for the moving fluidity of affective experience – is the terrifying risk incurred by those who attempt to live according to this dominant myth. The response to such a frustrated search is often a violent rejection, not of the category of true feeling, but of one's own inadequacy to live up to the exacting standards of its ideal. This engenders a terrible equation: if my feelings are untrue, my life too may be fake, inauthentic, without meaning. How then can I trust myself, let alone the world?

If these dangers inherent in the concept of true feeling are not often culturally broached, the same applies to what is presented as its contrary. For we are rarely invited to consider the potential value of feelings deemed to be 'false': that they provide a field of ludic performativity to test out possibilities, alternate identities and modes of dynamic being. Though their 'falseness' is itself a construct, it may precisely be the performative valuing of emotional artifice which allows us to critique, and ultimately transcend, the binarity of this restrictive orthodoxy. To break from such logic, the valuing of the neglected side of this dualism may represent a powerful mechanism of revolt. 'False' feeling – though, as we shall see, we may prefer to speak of the artifice of all affect – can lead to an epistemological expansion, via the play of projection, of the range and richness of our emotional worlds. Exploring feeling's artifice may indeed liberate us: from the need to judge our own emotions with reference to an abstract legitimacy, rendering us freer to explore the full breadth of an affective spectrum rather than censoring its 'distorted' extremes.

In seeking to accord renewed recognition to our desire, and even need, for false, fake, counterfeit and sham affects in all their variety, this book extends the reflection of theorists such as Sianne Ngai in her defence of 'ugly feelings' which do not fit conventional moulds; of Rachel Greenwald Smith in her valuing of impersonal feelings in our thinking of literature; and of Lauren Berlant or Sara Ahmed in their analyses of the perils of positive emotions of the fantasised good life.[3] It is inscribed in a contemporary movement against the notion that ugly or excessive emotions would simply be anomalous disturbances, which must be corrected in order to re-establish inner affective peace. Seeing in the forged or inauthentic a range of new standards of admissible feeling is to propose the existence of affective fictions which, like fiction itself, present an imaginative realm of vivid expansion and unfolding semiosis, rather than an increasing confinement within a hegemonic truth deployed as a normalising force.

For crucially, the avowed preference for unity and harmony recurrent in articulations of the criterion of true feeling is frequently based on concealed structures of political violence, which persist as undercurrents in much cultural arbitration of what is considered to be emotionally true. The risk is that emotional falsity be deemed merely a regrettable exception in a regime of dominant verities, one that must, in a Foucauldian sense, be identified, extracted and ultimately controlled.[4] The supposedly instinctive nature of such feeling – its 'obviousness' precluding other options – is based on the extent to which it seems to come either from the subject's corporal make-up (the 'gut') or from an essential moral constitution (the true self). In either case, true feeling is depoliticised for the reason that it is seen as subjective, private, formed of intimate values, and therefore closed off from the conjectures of others who may dispute it. As Lauren Berlant asks:

> What does it mean for the struggle to shape collective life when a politics of true feeling organizes so much analysis, discussion, fantasy, and policy? When feeling, the most subjective thing, the thing that makes persons public and marks their location, takes the temperature of power, mediates personhood, experience, and history, takes over the space of ethics and truth? When the shock of pain is said only to produce *clarity* when shock can as powerfully be said to produce panic, misrecognition, the shakiness of perception's ground?[5]

True feeling as it is most often conceived – true to me, as autonomous, inscrutable subject – thus excludes other modes of truth, including those specific to historical uncertainties, difficult rhetorical mediations and the dialectics of conflictual interpersonal exchange. To argue for the artificiality of affect is not to somehow argue against truth, but to search for other ways of understanding the notion beyond that of an authoritarian pole.

## What Lies Beyond Emotional Truth?

By the term 'truth' then is understood not an overarching category but rather, as Michel Foucault puts it, 'the ensemble of rules according to which the true and false are separated and specific effects of power are attached to the true'.[6] This struggle holds as much for emotionality as it does for any other ideological engagement. For Theodor Adorno's 'truth content' or William James's vision of truth as a process of validation may be applied not only to works of art or ideas, but to interplays of affective force.[7] As James puts it: 'The truth of an idea is not a stagnant property inherent in it. Truth happens to an idea. It *becomes* true, is *made* true by events. Its verity *is* in fact an event, a process: the process namely of its verifying itself.'[8]

Moving beyond reductive criteria of truth in thinking about issues of emotionality in both culture and literature does not mean that emotions cannot be evaluated, appraised and negotiated between feeling individuals. On the contrary, it may greatly improve the clarity of emotional communication and arbitration if subjects decided to disregard true feeling as an ethically harmful, or at least practically unworkable, category. If no feeling is *a priori* granted a higher rung on the speculative ladder of authentic life, then a range of other qualities in emotional evaluation may take pride of place. Rather than asking if love were true love, its effects on the world would become paramount: we may instead value if such love makes one's life richer, more meaningful – and perhaps most importantly, if it improves not just one's own life but those of others as well. Emotional value is thereby turned from a centripetal, potentially egotistical self-verification – 'Do *I* really love?' – towards a questioning of intersubjective effects, of the order: 'Does my love do good in the world?' What matter if love is deemed true, after all, if it leads to the deaths of myriad Montagues, Werthers, Kareninas and Bovarys, if it causes not just the launching of a thousand ships but the pillage and fall of Troy.

This critique of true feeling as an autocratic category does not aim at preventing us from wondering, in quotidian contexts, if a smile is sincere or feigned. Though the ubiquity of emotional dissimulation may make us interrogate true feeling's legitimacy, the problem is related less to the pragmatic acting of everyday existence than to an internalised pressure to determine if one's own smile is indeed 'true'. The distinction is similar to Jean Baudrillard's between *dissimulating* and *simulating*, with the latter involving a deeper engagement with the status of what is real: 'Pretending, or dissimulating, leaves the principle of reality intact: the difference is always clear, it is simply masked; whereas simulation threatens the difference between the "true" and the "false", the "real" and the "imaginary".'[9] It is thus less the inevitable masks of social life which may incite our concern than the suffering and inner turmoil which can emerge when a stable emotional truth proves elusive. For when doubt emerges as to the emotional sincerity of a particular affective sign, it is one thing to attribute blame to a specific emoting subject, and quite another to the evaluative concept of hierarchical truth itself.

When applied as a moral category of the self, truth of feeling risks becoming the ultimate arbiter of the tenor and value of that self's unstable, and necessarily contradictory, emotional being. To oppose this logic is to participate in a contemporary struggle against affective hegemonies, which notably opposes the demand to display and incarnate 'positive' feelings in an effort to avoid the entanglements of depression, mourning, shame or loss.[10] Like other positively connoted notions such as well-being, positive thinking, happiness and health, true feeling incessantly implies its unspoken other, namely a negative alterity equated with living a lie.[11] Like many ambient pressures regarding wellness, to feel truly is a tacit constraint, entailing accordance not only with an outer social body but with an internally unified self. Divergences from this mode are therefore seen as manipulative feigning, and truth used as a tool of exclusion from accepted norms.

Indeed, if truth is permitted as a criterion for affective states, a spiral of tightening conformity is perhaps inevitable. For in the sociocultural context at the heart of this book, to possess true emotions, and thus to be true to oneself, is by extension to be true to society: to feel true love for family (as families are commonly defined), true grief for national tragedies (as collectively decreed), true regret for transgressions (as deemed by moral codes). In affirming that truth is among emotions' most laudable qualities, the paradigm comes to imply not merely sincerity in social exchanges but a demand for an inner authenticity which, because generic, guarantees one's allegiance to communal ideals. The thinking which associates socially objectionable feeling with this feeling being false is a moral reductionism which undermines the right of subjects to experience affective attitudes running counter to prohibitive collectivist strains.

For the love, pain or grief of the modern subject, truth is a criterion which determines not only the utilitarian value of such affects, but their transcendent moral quality. This entrenches individuals within an impossible standard of torturous self-analysis: if one is forever analysing the truth of one's own feeling, one is confronted with the dilemma that feeling is self-verifying, providing, in a navigational paradigm, both its own earthly vessel and higher star. Though it may not be entirely deprived of referential objects, feeling refers always to other feelings, turning and returning back upon itself in increasingly complex semiotic loops. As we shall see, to equate this process with a quest for 'correspondence' is similar to reductively naturalist visions of literature as the mimetic reproduction of an immovable real.

## Against Affective Epiphany

From the vision of Ishmael as a character who embarks on a dauntless quest for self-realisation with the precept 'I want to see the world!'[12] to that of Jay Gatsby as a tragic hero animated by a noble striving for impossible love, American literature – at least according to a dominant cultural myth – may seem populated with figures who make affective revelation their ultimate end. Such long journeys of subjective becoming supposedly result in moments of ultimate epiphany. Saul Bellow's Augie March's famous affirmation – 'That's the struggle of humanity, to recruit others to your version of what's real' – is thus read not as a highly ambivalent dictum in a novel of omnipresent performativity, but as a movement towards a singular telos: the inner truth of the self.[13]

Though they are frequently presented, in curricula and much popular media, as incarnations of romantic affirmation and self-realisation, such characters – especially given their tragic outcomes – are more cogently viewed in a tradition of errant scepticism and epistemological fracture. For what if such moments of apparent emotional insight were more often than not a mere ruse? What if they indicated the road not to happiness and fulfilment, but to suffering and unsatisfied despair?

An initial case may help us to see the nature of this mythology more clearly. In Ralph Ellison's 1952 novel *Invisible Man*, the passion of the unnamed narrator – his anger, for instance, at the ejection of an elderly Black couple from their apartment, or his fiery speeches to the collectivist movement named the Brotherhood – is the impetus that drives the picaresque action.[14] If the text's ubiquitous irony and paradoxes have long been recognised by Ellisonian literary scholarship, the same may not be said of the way *Invisible Man* is recurrently used in various political, pedagogical and didactic contexts. To take just one example: in the Penguin 'Teacher's Guide' with recommendations on how to integrate the novel into school syllabi, the publisher affirms that the narrator ultimately 'chooses to reject cynicism and hatred and to embrace a philosophy of hope. Ellison wanted his novel to transcend the rage and hopelessness of the protest novel and assert a world of possibility.'[15] Thus identified as a teleological narrative in a melioristic vision of American history, *Invisible Man* is treated in such cultural discourse as a hero's journey from indignation at injustice towards positive emotion and self-knowledge. Evidence against such readings abounds, as when, following another scene of rejection and exclusion, the narrator gives us an almost clichéd version of the emotional awakening that we may expect from a traditional *Bildungsroman*:

> I had no doubt that I could do something, but what, and how? I had no contacts and I believed in nothing. And the obsession with my identity . . . returned with a vengeance. Who was I, how had I come to be? . . . I wanted peace and quiet, tranquillity, but was too much aboil inside. Somewhere beneath the load of the emotion-freezing ice which my life had conditioned my brain to produce, a spot of black anger glowed and threw off a hot red light of such intensity that had Lord Kelvin known of its existence, he would have had to revise his measurements. A remote explosion had occurred somewhere . . . and it had caused the ice cap to melt and shift the slightest bit. But that bit, that fraction, was irrevocable.[16]

Indeed, if *Invisible Man* were a simpler work, and if we did not know the novel's epilogue and end, we may be tempted to believe that this were a story simply of the liberating power of this spark, that this heat – the intensity of true feeling – had the power to be truly transformative. But Ellison's protagonist leads us on a more sinuous path, in which we witness how his affects are ceaselessly used by others for their own moral and political ends, not because they cynically do not believe in the authenticity or legitimacy of the narrator's feeling, but precisely because they do. Their appropriation of his rage is made possible because they see in such powerful affect the ring of truth which, in its desire to persist in autocratic self-affirmation, will always be vulnerable both to usurpation and to the integrating demands of conformity.

Ellison's narrator's grief and resentment may very well be subjectively 'true', and infinitely historically justified – but so what? What does it accomplish in terms of either subjective or social progress if it is all the more easily expropriated due to its purportedly authentic status? For true feeling, rather than a spark towards liberating rebellion, is so often an imperilled criterion which, especially for oppressed and minority voices, is forever on the verge of being labelled false. As we see throughout Ellison's work, the apparent power of true feeling is in fact eminently vulnerable, a vulnerability based moreover on terrible historical precedents. We may think, for instance, of the racist trope of anti-abolitionist ideologies regarding the unreal suffering and false feelings of enslaved persons – made infamous notably by Thomas Jefferson's claims that 'their griefs are transient . . . less felt, and sooner forgotten with them'.[17] In many respects, this claim is not the opposite of Ellison's hero's 'spot of black anger' but its extension: for if we think only in dichotomous terms, then false suffering is true anger's distorted mirror, with each threatening to become the other in a logic of exchange. This schema moreover denies affective experience the status of an infinite spectrum, which can never confine itself to opposing modes. For in the vision presented by Ellison's narrator, such anger is neither mutable nor self-reflexive; instead, described in pseudo-scientific terms of temperature and measurement, it is affect reduced to atomised process, somatic only in the sense that it presents the body as a materialist machine.

The risk that such anger, in claiming its unquestionable truth, will always be accused of falsity in an endless binary is constantly played out in *Invisible Man*, where we are confronted with the fact that true feeling, far from leading to the self's visibility and unity, leads incessantly to its invisibility and division when it is usurped for others' ends. A more convincing argument can thus be made that the novel traces the disturbing recognition that such revelatory anger was not, as the narrator puts it, a way towards epiphany but a 'passion toward conformity'.[18] For though Ellison's invisible hero initially believes that truth of feeling justifies his speeches, they are also a vector of the failed integration of his ever-fragile social self.

Convinced that such feelings are both abstractly true and historically legitimate, it is this perceived truth which allows him to justify his accomplishing of primarily self-serving actions, justified by the need to palliate real moral suffering in the world. Others – whether the revolutionary Brotherhood or the White supremacist majority – will harness the 'truth' of these discourses for their own causes, whether cynical or for righteous progress, but demonstrating always how adaptable their affective authenticity is to any number of utilitarian ends, subjugating passion to the will of various dominant ideologies.

By the time we reach the novel's epilogue, our unnamed protagonist provides a vision not of truth revealed by epiphanic anger, but of such affect's resultant conformity: 'Whence all this passion toward conformity anyway? – diversity is the word. Let man keep his many parts and you'll have no tyrant states.'[19] Paradoxically, the constant divided struggle within the self is the ambivalent 'revelation' of the novel's end, instituting a claim to dynamic change over any statically authentic being:

> There is, by the way, an area in which a man's feelings are more rational than his mind, and it is precisely in that area that his will is pulled in several directions at the same time. You might sneer at this, but I know now. I was pulled this way and that for longer than I can remember. And my problem was that I always tried to go in everyone's way but my own. I have also been called one thing and then another while no one really wished to hear what I called myself.[20]

Far more than the ecstatic truth of a singular identity or of the role of true feeling in its formation, we witness here the danger of seeing in the narrator's prior rage a Messianic quest. For as Ellison's protagonist puts it, his achievement – if we may claim such a term – consists not in having found his way but in having 'learned to live without direction'.[21] To see *Invisible Man* as a journey toward affective epiphany is thus to misread the negative value of such sceptical errancy. And indeed, rather than an affirmation of truth, Ellison in his correspondence frames the novel as one of expansive artifice, in a quasi-folkloric tradition:

> For me it's just a big fat ole Negro lie, meant to be told during cotton picking time over a water bucket full of corn, with a dipper passing back and forth at a good fast clip so that no one, not even the narrator himself, will realize how utterly preposterous the lie actually is. I just hope someone points out that aspect of it.[22]

At this point, the passage from Jefferson mentioned above merits quotation in its entirety, as it establishes the long history of Black exclusion – and that of minority communities in general – from true feeling's privileged embrace:

> Their griefs are transient. Those numberless afflictions, which render it doubtful whether Heaven has given life to us in mercy or in wrath, are less felt, and sooner forgotten with them. In general, their existence appears to participate more of sensation than reflection.[23]

It is not unimportant that later in the same text Jefferson observes that, due to such supposed affective limitation, 'in imagination they are dull, tasteless, and anomalous', incapable of art, aesthetic production or of uttering 'a thought above the level of plain narration'. It is for this reason, according to Jefferson, that affect may indeed exist among enslaved people, but will forever be divided from artifice: 'Among the blacks is misery enough, God knows, but no poetry.'[24]

Enslaved people are here situated beyond affective artifice as a tool of emotional agency. They are exiled not necessarily from all affect, but in particular from the imaginative shaping of affective forces needed to integrate emotion with one's identity, whether personal, cultural or historical. In this lineage, *Invisible Man*, far from a glorious quest towards self-realisation through the epiphany of justified anger, constantly demonstrates the extent to which true feeling is weaponised by privileged groups, in their appropriation of the pain and anger of marginalised others. In support of this, we need only look to the fact that, at the novel's end, and after its 'inspiring' coda, the narrator emerges from his literal hole to a world in which racial and social injustice still reign supreme. This is, of course, a less uplifting reading than those who would seek to present *Invisible Man* as an affirmational paragon in the supposedly resolved struggles of civil rights.

### Towards the Artifice of Affect: Knowable and Unknowable Force

To be thus excluded from affective artifice is to be both historically and linguistically proscribed from the active shaping of one's own emotional world. Language and the body – language's rootedness in embodiment – is an integral part of this history, and is moreover the reason why, before we continue to explore true feeling's inherent risks, a word must be said on the critical vocabulary at play in this book. In particular, it is necessary to pause a moment on what may at first seem an indiscriminate use of an analytic lexis that some affect theorists have worked to make increasingly distinct. Since efforts to establish distinctions between emotion and affect as, broadly, conscious and pre-conscious, assimilated and unassimilated, subjective and pre-subjective force, the tendency in some recent writing on affect has been not only to accept the limits of this distinction as axiomatic, but to widen the gaps in its binary.[25]

This propensity is all the more concerning when we consider affect's unnameable condition, which establishes it as opposed to the potentiality of categorical reductivism *in essence*. Overemphasising the hermeticism of this divide risks perpetuating a heritage of Cartesian mind-body dualism, in which affect would be merely situated on the side of corporality and autonomic reaction, and emotion as a 'later' or 'higher' stage of intellectual integration and conscious awareness.[26] Affect may in this sense be divested both of its representational qualities and of its semiotic capabilities, being ultimately dissociated from the possibility to truly mean. Both linear and hierarchical, such a model risks distorting the extent to which affective and emotional processes occur in causal, evolutionary and simultaneous relationships. The passing affective force which causes my sadness may become momentarily emotionally identified, only to slip away again into the moving flux of an ambient affective field. Aspects of it may endure, emerge to precarious consciousness within the subject, losing a measure of their obscurity; but their delimitations are not fixed. Porous membranes, instead of walls, branch through rather than divide them, and are the sites of their interactions, assimilations and correlative dispersions.

In Brian Massumi's lexical distinction, for instance, though the term 'emotion' is seen to refer to feelings' subjectively anchored modes – which nevertheless remain profoundly proteiform – the subject is nevertheless able to associate such states, in a meaningful semiology, with a slate of socially identifiable categories of sense.

Affect, however, as disembodied, extra-subjective intensity, is seen to present a more radical epistemological trial:

> Affect is most often used loosely as a synonym for emotion. But ... emotion and affect – if affect is intensity – follow different logics and pertain to different orders. An emotion is a subjective content, the sociolinguistic fixing of the quality of an experience which is from that point onward defined as personal. Emotion is qualified intensity, the conventional, consensual point of insertion of intensity into semantically and semiotically formed progressions, into narrativizable action-reaction circuits, into function and meaning. It is intensity owned and recognized.[27]

It is this extra-subjective range of intensities which is seen to constitute affective force, engendering an epistemological, phenomenological and subjective divide between the terms 'emotion' and 'affect', which precludes their confusion as synonyms.

While recognising the potential value of this distinction for our theoretical vocabularies, we must be cautious of the possibility that it become a fixed or established binary, somehow existing stably 'within us' or 'out there' in the world. We are, after all, dealing ineluctably with the realm of semiotics, and may profit from continually recalling the supremely artificial nature of our analytic apparatus. For just as Russian Formalism and various Structuralisms sought to forge a critical lexis for dynamic textual mechanisms at the risk of frequent reductivism, so too may we be sceptical of our own claims to be able to clearly distinguish between affect, emotion, feeling, sentiment or sense. And indeed, if we take affect and emotion to be purely non-subjective or subjective, pre-conscious or conscious poles, there is something curiously Structuralist about their binary pairing, which seeks to layer the body's moving membranes – rather than mechanisms – into overlapping hermetic tiers. Given the anti-naturalist arguments at the heart of this book, we may doubt that there exist 'hard-wired' physiological differences between assimilated or non-assimilated affects at the neurochemical level, which is nevertheless suggested in the categorical delineation of affects as 'autonomic, bodily reactions occurring in the brain but outside consciousness'.[28] For what are the established limits of consciousness? For affect to be entirely 'pre-conscious', or for emotion to be considered as entirely 'integrated' into the subject's inner weft, are we not forced to concede to a categorical conception of consciousness itself?

Affective forces may begin as affects, only to lose aspects of their power at moments of subjective assimilation; they may resist this process of subjective integration; conversely, they may themselves become transformed. In doing so, they are potentially integrated – or not, or to an indeterminable degree – within the energetic strata of that self's becoming, including at the levels of its imagination, projections and representational self-awareness. To imply any differently – to suggest for instance that each lexical use of the term 'emotion' or 'affect' in literary criticism should refer to a distinct corporal phenomenon – is at best optimistic, at worst a severe distortion of the true mobility of the intersubjective forces here at play.

A moving spectrum rather than binary is thus posed, with the constant recognition that there is usually far more lexical and conceptual overlap than we may care to admit. In this context, the forging of strict divisions in a territory of utter fluidity retains something of the ratiocentric: as though we believed in the absolute divisibility not only of our critical categories, but of the objects they sought to 'describe' – while the world's vital movement works incessantly against such static architectures. For indeed, affect and emotion are often indistinguishable, both subjectively and in the domain of their teleological effects. Who can ever say, after all, if a force is purely and utterly 'unassimilated' by us, if it does not exist, somehow, at a level of being somewhere between unconsciousness and a latent but still present awareness? Awareness is not, after all, a light switch of meaning and unmeaning, conscious clarity and pre-conscious dark.[29]

For all these reasons, throughout this book I use the terms 'affect', 'emotion' and 'feeling' if not interchangeably, at least in a fluid sense. I am not disturbed by instances when my usage of such terms may seem to overlap, or indicate kinetics of weave and weft. This fluidity is to my mind integral to a refusal to erect new semantic barriers between 'affective' and 'emotional' energies in a state of permeable exchange. In seeking to go beyond the true-false dynamic in thinking about emotionality, *The Artifice of Affect* is an extension of Eve Kosofsky Sedgwick's call to forge nondualist modes of thinking affectivity. As Sedgwick observes, however, 'it's far easier to deprecate the confounding, tendentious effects of binary modes of thinking – and to expose their often stultifying perseveration – than it is to articulate or model other structures of thought'.[30] Here, as elsewhere, fiction is a key tool in attempting to articulate such new structures. To true feeling is opposed then a fundamental artifice of all affect. Following postulates of affect's autonomy – the concept's resistance to being contained within the feeling subject's delineated frontiers – a similar defiance to traditional registers of truth may now take centre stage.[31] Affect may be seen as freer not only of subjective ties, but also of the ties which bind it to hegemonic notions of a restrictive binary truth.

Though we may want to identify it as less conscious or subjectively possessed, affect, because it is mediated by individuals and their internalised representational devices, is by definition artificial: its circulation through various corporal porosities implies its shared construction by a range of subjects, existing in relationships which are by turns participatory and cooperative, dissonant and antagonistic. Insisting on the artifice of affect is a way of recognising affect's disruptive potentialities, all the while avoiding associating such disruption with a reified return to Nature or to the intensities of an 'uncorrupted' force. As vital artifice, all affect is by definition theoretical and ideational: it exists according to the corporalities and subjectivities which it *affects*, but may not, because of this quality, be conceived as a force of primeval purity. Literature itself, like a range of other aesthetic forms and processes, may be seen as a literal enactment of this quality, made especially relevant due to its efforts not merely to embody, but also to express. How to speak of the unspeakable is, especially in the post-war American fiction at the heart of this book, a familiar way to frame this question, though the way to envision such paradoxical speech is certainly not with an overly categorical lexis, which implies that we can easily distinguish between what within us is conscious or pre-conscious, pure alterity or subjectively owned. For in truth, these fabricated categories are as dynamic as the moving (in all senses of the term) objects which they seek to trace. In this vision, maintaining affect's speculative status – which means not claiming, in our critical lexis, to possess a scientific precision which, for emotionality, is as impossible as it is unproductive – is central to its potential value as liberating force.

## True Feeling as Philosophical Concept, Social Category and Moral Precept

It is also crucial to underline at the outset that my argument is concerned less with contemporary discussions in logic and epistemology about whether we may abstractly apply the concept of truth to emotional states, than with the deleterious effects of moral ideologies of true feeling in the context of modern and contemporary culture and aesthetics, and especially in the late twentieth-century United States. For it is one thing to interrogate emotional truth as a philosophical parameter, and quite another to object to it as a sociocultural mechanism and moral ideal. While I am careful not to imply that such models exist in an environment uncontaminated, so to speak, by sociopolitical norms, there are reasons for not interpreting this distinction as an attempt to isolate philosophical logic within an asocial realm of pure ideas. The primary reason is that the conceptions of truth that such epistemological inquiries put forth are generally far more flexible, inclusive and heterodoxical than the implied notion of truth as it is culturally deployed as a form of moral oppression.

Indeed, contemporary philosophers who argue for the ultimate applicability of the term 'truth' to emotions – and most notably Ronald de Sousa – tend to establish a complex and fluctuating concept largely at odds with hierarchical archetypes.[32] This cautiousness in part derives from an acute awareness of the controversy that has tended to surround the concept of emotional truth in the specific disciplines of modern epistemology and logic.[33] In spite of these challenges, a variety of thinkers have argued that emotions may nevertheless, under certain conditions, be considered as 'truth-apt mental states, even if they cannot be reduced to propositional attitudes'.[34] Whatever our reaction to these debates, such prolegomena are testament to a heightened wariness regarding the dangers of the concept. These conceptions are in many ways so far from the repressive exemplars of domineering truth under discussion in this book that they seem to describe a different principle, with utterly divergent moral aims.

Deliberations over the validity of emotional truth as a concept in recent epistemological inquiries are thus very different to the use of the criterion in the literary and sociopolitical environment of the American post-war period. In foregrounding such scepticism, these contemporary philosophies seek to inoculate more measured proposals against the risk of affective hegemonies. Moreover, these models generally highlight what is often ignored in broader literary and cultural contexts, namely the specificity, and always latent invalidity, of the notion of truth when applied to emotional states. As de Sousa puts it:

> Insofar as the notion of truth is applicable to emotions, the sense of that notion is indeed significantly different from that of 'truth' as traditionally ascribed to propositional or 'factual' beliefs. The main reason is that each emotion provides its own conditions of appropriateness, or 'formal object', in terms of which its success or failure should be assessed.[35]

It follows that emotional truth is 'quite distinct from the notion of truth ordinarily dealt with in epistemology', and that all efforts to apply it to affective contexts must involve great methodological care.[36] Though we may be tempted to debate the system of adequation they imply, attributing a value such as 'epistemic warrant' to emotions appears an eminently reasonable gesture.[37] When I use the term 'true feeling' or 'emotional truth', I am therefore referring not primarily to these epistemological contentions, but to the moral understanding and implications of these categories in the context of modern political ideations.

For in contrast to its usage in these epistemologies, true feeling as a sociocultural and aesthetic criterion almost invariably implies a transparently referential ideology. Whatever their position regarding the validity of the term 'truth' when applied to emotional states, the philosophical positions mentioned above stress the spurious nature of uncritically realist conceptions which, based on naïve notions of reference, search to locate, for unstable feelings, solid points of anchorage within the self or the noumenal real. In depending on conjectures of an adequational nature, such visions inevitably conflate the question of whether emotions are true to the self with whether they are true in the abstract, and whether they are socially germane.

When the American realist writers under discussion in this book interrogate and critique models of true feeling in fictional contexts, they are rebelling against a specific framework of restrictive, moralised verities, with a concomitant demand for subjective integrity. There is here an explicit but crucial irony, revelatory of the contrasting logics of modern philosophy and literary history, in arguing that 'realist' authors (in the literary sense) of post-war America argue for 'anti-realist' philosophical conceptions of truth that are not based on models of reference. This is, however, in line with my argument regarding the implicit project of many of these literatures, namely an effort to make use of the tropes of realism to counteract a hegemonic vision of the stable constitution of both the 'real' and the 'true'.

The undermining of a rational hegemonic truth is central to this epistemological project. My reticence to systematically distinguish between terms such as 'true', 'natural', 'authentic' and 'real', or 'false', 'artificial', 'inauthentic' and 'unreal', is in this way intentional. It is an overlap which is not only everywhere present in the fiction under discussion, as well as in the culture at large, but which reflects a basic presumption that true feeling constitutes an encompassing ideological creed. In brief, this confluence reflects usages wherein to be affectively false is to be at once inauthentic, artificial and unreal, in an amalgamated series of ontological associations. There is a reason, then, why I resist formulating static distinctions between such apparently distinct qualities as truth, authenticity and reality: not because there is no debatable conceptual distinction to be made, but because such terms' interchangeable usage in the rhetorical contexts at play reflects a higher conviction, namely that emotion, in the end, is to be justified with reference to an exterior axiological pole. Whether we term such anchorages truth, nature, authenticity or the real, the value of feeling is established with regard to an ontological foundation – one which, unsurprisingly, tends to conflate the transcendent categories of the true, the natural, the authentic and the real.

## Truth as Commodity: On the Commercial Attraction of the Natural

In the context of the American post-war period, the association between emotions being unnatural, inauthentic and thus untrue stems in part from a commercialisation and commodification of feeling common across modern liberal economies. As has been explored both in Arlie Hochschild's forging of the concept of emotional labour and in much feminist theory on the ethics of care, the commodification of emotional processes is concomitant with their social valuing or neglect.[38] Moreover, such valuing is supported by a range of presumptions related to feelings' supposed ontological qualities as natural, inherent, instinctive or innate, providing an unstable grounding for emotions' perceived authenticity or truth.

As Hochschild observes, in modern democratic economies 'the value placed on authentic or "natural" feeling has increased dramatically with the full emergence of its opposite – the managed heart'.[39] As though in proof of the insidiousness of truth paradigms in thinking about emotional value, Hochschild's work has precisely been criticised for implying that emotions which are 'managed' – that is, filtered through the infrastructures of commerce – are somehow less authentic than those which remain protected from mercantile ends. 'We are intrigued', Hochschild writes, 'by the unmanaged heart and what it can tell us.'[40] As Sarah Tracy and Angela Trethewey have observed, 'this point of view presumes that emotion is more authentic and pristine before it enters the realm of organizations, where it is "transmuted" and thus "processed, standardized" for organizational ends'.[41]

The use of truth as a criterion of value for emotionality thus often contaminates those very efforts to free emotion from the limiting bounds of adequational thinking, of which capitalistic pragmatism is a prime incarnation. Even critiques of 'the managed heart' have trouble avoiding the essentialism of a natural-artificial binary. This is hardly surprising given that modern liberal societies tend to evaluate claims to emotional truth as though emotions were material products, whose authenticity needed to be proven as a sign of their reliability and durability. In such an affective marketplace, 'real' anger is superior to 'fake' anger, regardless of their real-world effects, because it is what it pretends to be: real.

In a solipsistic process, authenticity's aura is self-justifying: just as for marketable goods, true emotions are made of more natural, more visceral, better-quality materials, because they derive from a better source – in this case, the unified feeling subject as certified manufacturer. Rather than being the chaotic product of circulating beliefs or abstract ideas, they are seen to emanate directly from the subject's biological weft: from the organic life and vital quiddity of gritty corporal workings. It follows that it is better for emotions to be artisanal – the product of individuals or small feeling communities – than mass-produced. We are sceptical of the truth of large-scale circulating affects, instead preferring the solitary emotion of the isolated heart. Needless to say, such beliefs fail to interrogate the fabricated quality of the very organic life which they take as affective integrity's ontological guarantor.

## In Search of Incoherence: Troubling Defences of Emotional Truth

In spite of these difficulties, defences of emotional truth as a criterion for literary and cultural value have, from the post-war era until today, been manifold. Such true feeling is frequently posited not as a future ideal, but as a lost or degraded touchstone, more luminously present within past eras and now approached from a perspective of wan nostalgia. To begin with one example, from Edward F. Mooney's *Lost Intimacy in American Thought*:

> Why not propose that cognitions and passions each incline toward propriety or truth? ... We have true friends, true grief, and true prayer, as well as true opinion. In matters of truth, of whatever sort, we seek the rather abstract *desiderata* of coherence, appropriateness of fit, and proper causal and cultural antecedents. A person's grief should cohere with what we know of a wider narrative of her history; it should have a fittingness to the situation of its expression; and it should not be induced by drugs or threats or brainwashing. Otherwise, we'd face false grief. The daunting problem is to fill in what concretely would satisfy these *desiderata* in

contested instances where it is urgent to know of friends if they are true, or of grief or opinion, if it is true or false.[42]

For Mooney, there is no ethical problem in judging, in the abstract, that a person's grief does not 'fit' her narrative; the question is rather about determining between true and false feeling only in specific 'contested instances'. What is implied is that the vast majority of cases of emotional interrogation in our lives are not open to contestation: that in most instances we intuitively and unproblematically tell the difference between true and false feeling, based on an ensemble of standardised norms.

This is, however, simply not the case. The ambiguities of emotional experience do not intervene merely in fringe situations of abnormal perception or anomalous doubt. Why then should a person's grief 'cohere' to 'a wider narrative of her history'? Who determines such a narrative? Is it singular? Open to change? To internal paradoxes? What if its very incoherency – its performative artifice – were precisely what is needed to broach grief's tenacious hold? In this context, it is unsurprising that the phrase 'proper causal and cultural antecedents' is presented as though its agglomerating logic were an issue of communal accord. Finding such antecedents risks imprisoning grief within a cage of set cultural parameters. To take one iteration: grief 'induced by drugs' is implicitly compared to a hypothetical natural grief issuing from an uncorrupted corporal state. Does this mean that any individual consuming 'drugs' – with no sense here of a multivalent *pharmakon* – is in the throes of fake feeling? This rhetoric of purity and incorruptibility is not only ideologically troubling, but does not correspond to the messiness of human affective experiences, wherein clear lines between normality and abnormality rarely exist.[43]

We may indeed judge, in particular cases, that the anger or sadness engendered by an 'altered' state is not preferable, and seek to actively avoid it; but in labelling it lesser and false, or heightened and true, we are effectively promoting a hierarchy of experiential value which tends towards the neutral and the pure. In this framework, it is difficult to see how one's relationship to emotional experience could be anything less than a dialectic of conformity and rebellion with regard to essentialistic norms. This moreover entails a vision of the subject which, geared towards its normalisation, leaves little place for the valuing of affects as iconoclastic force.

A study such as Robert Charles Solomon's *True to our Feelings* represents another questionable case. After equating subjectivity with emotional experience – 'we *are* our emotions, as much as we are our thoughts and actions' – Solomon seeks to 'defend a concept of *emotional integrity*, or what one might call, "being true to one's feelings"'.[44] Although he then rejects what he calls reductive conceptions of 'basic' emotions as 'discrete physiological syndromes', we learn just how ideologically restrictive the apparently positive project of 'emotional integrity' can be:

> What makes us human is our collective emotional imagination and our individual ability to learn and cultivate our emotions. I am not for a moment denying that there are primitive physiological responses that may well be more or less universal across our species, but what makes us human is our ability to embellish, refine, and arise above such 'basic' responses, which is not to deny that, even in the most refined and civilized context, these crude emotions may have a very powerful and impressive effect. But like profanity in a play, it is their rarity that accounts for their power. A steady diet of crude emotions makes a person hardly worthy of our company, and this has nothing to do with manners.[45]

In a conception, and an accompanying lexis, where being 'human' depends on the ability to 'embellish', 'refine' and 'arise above' our 'basic' emotions, a distinctly stratified vision of emotional integrity is endorsed. In a linear chain of command, 'crude' emotions may be admissible, provided that their 'rarity' preserves their power to disrupt – in what is by far the passage's most troubling turn of phrase – the 'civilized context' of their exposure.

In denying complex value to the lower rungs of this classificatory ladder, such projects, though aiming to delineate emotional integrity, tend to import and apply pre-established hierarchies to a moralised affective world. 'Truly understanding', Solomon states, 'the nature of our emotions and how they express and embody our deepest values is the beginning of emotional integrity.'[46] But what about when these 'deepest values' need to be, not emotionally 'expressed' and 'embodied', but rather changed, challenged, rejected or denounced? If, as is the case here, we simply *are* our feelings (and therefore seek to be true to them), how may we ever shift and sculpt them without denouncing ourselves?

## Self-Help Dualisms: Real and Fake Selves, True and False Smiles

My argument is thus that the use of truth as a moral criterion for emotional value is perilous, for the reason that it tends to inflict a violence of normalisation on subjects' dynamic emotional lives. It is revealing, however, that we rarely encounter, throughout the last half-century, explicit questioning of the criterion of emotional truth within a wider cultural context. Myriad self-help books advise readers to distinguish between true and false feelings, to push through fake happiness into true joy. Beneath these popularised outgrowths are modern heritages of Freudian and Jungian psychotherapeutics which, from Freud's *Verdrängung* to Jung's *persona* – conceived of as 'a kind of mask' which, deployed in social contexts, serves 'to conceal the true nature of the individual' – establish dichotomous logics of the authentic and inauthentic self.[47] In advocating true feeling, psychology as a nascent discipline was reacting against the spectre of a manipulating sentimentality, with false emotion being specifically linked to the rise of twentieth-century totalitarianisms, present for instance in Jung's well-known affirmation: 'Sentimentality is the superstructure erected upon brutality. Unfeelingness is the counter-position and inevitably suffers from the same defects.'[48]

And indeed, one of the key heritages behind the category of true and false feeling is that of the true and false self. Such positions became increasingly widespread, both throughout the general culture and within academic discourse, precisely during the post-war period.[49] Following such logic, the binary of emotional truth and falsity becomes connected, causally and symbolically, to a dualistic vision of subjectivity, conceived, in the face of social imperatives, as a site of recurrent dissimulation. As Tracy and Trethewey have argued, 'the self is largely dichotomized as either real/authentic or fake/false in popular renditions of identity in self-help books, organizational members' everyday talk, and even remnants of scholarly theories such as emotion labor'.[50] The dominant characteristic of such positions is an implied exclusivity: either the self conforms to an authentic image or it does not. Such positions propagate the idea that identity, rather than 'a product or an effect of competing, fragmentary, and contradictory discourses', is an essentialist entity: 'fixed, stable, or "real"'.[51] This essentialism produces not only pressure to conform to preconceived notions of true selfhood, but an immobilism which eschews fluctuation and negotiation in favour of a statically legitimised ideal.

A specific tradition of psychotherapy has undertaken the legitimisation of these convictions within the history of modern psychology. To mention merely one of the most well-known cases, that of D. W. Winnicott's influential distinction between the True and False Self: 'Only the True Self can be creative and only the True Self can feel real. Whereas a True Self feels real, the existence of a False Self results in a feeling unreal [sic] or a sense of futility.'[52] Even more disturbing than this categorical dualism, psychoanalysis becomes for Winnicott an epiphanic maturation which seeks to reveal the self's ecstatic but hidden truth. In so doing, the process of analysis can effectively degrade all existence and selfhood prior to the True Self's revelation to the status of corrupted distortion. Winnicott, in a rhetoric which echoes the language of Messianic apocalypse and Evangelical conversion, thus describes a patient's life before analysis, and her shedding of her False Self, in the following terms: 'She contains no true experience, she has no past. She starts with fifty years of wasted life, but at last she feels real, and therefore she now wants to live.'[53]

Such heritages gave rise to an array of psychotherapies in search of subjects' true selves beneath dissimulation, as well as the true feelings which helped lead to this self's rapturous discovery. To take a contemporary example: writing on emotional trauma, Donald E. Kalsched and Daniela F. Sieff argue that 'the conviction of being a victim' is 'a false grief', for the reason that it is 'a story created by the self-care system to give meaning to our pain and to prevent the deeper, original pain from surfacing'.[54] The equation between falsity and 'a story' is telling: stories are not coded as symbolically vital engagements with the real, but as the inventions of a divided psyche seeking to delude itself. Kalsched and Sieff go on to introduce a binary vision of good and bad, innocent and calculating aspects of emotional life: 'When the innocent parts of us are able to emerge from hiding and enter into consciousness we start to suffer "true grief". True grief is feeling the pain held in the innocent parts themselves.'[55]

Such an argument is nothing less than a dichotomous moralisation of the mind. It is the application of didactic categories to fluid emotional states, distributing them according to a dualistic schema wherein the quest for meaning through adopted roles, fantasies or projections is seen to take one 'further' from a mythologised 'original pain' which 'hides' in mere 'stories'. In a rhetoric of dissimulation and display, this 'innocence' further implies the existence of a base impurity and treacherousness within the self, effectively turning individuals against themselves in an effort to flush out the enemy within. In a rhetoric which recalls both Freudian theory and Cold War exclusionist paranoia, we are witness to an inner civil war between the true and false self, the inner angel and its dissimulated demon. There is often at the basis of this postulate a naïve conception of the innocent subject which exists *a priori*, before the corrupting effects of traumatic division. A subject's efforts to discover 'true grief' are subsequently fraught with peril. For what could be the ultimate proof that a subject's false grief has now become true? Is this visible in external alterations? Is it a purely subjective conviction? And what occurs if an individual feels herself to be forever distant from this ideal?

In a revealing and particularly disturbing example of the paradigm, psychologist Martin Seligman, in his *New York Times* bestseller entitled *Authentic Happiness*, mobilises a strict binary opposition between what he terms true and false smiles:

> There are two kinds of smiles. The first, called a Duchenne smile (after its discoverer, Guillaume Duchenne), is genuine. The other smile, called the Pan American smile (after the flight attendants in television ads for the now-defunct airline), is inauthentic, with none of the Duchenne features.[56]

The fact that Seligman would choose the French nineteenth-century neurologist Duchenne de Boulogne (1806–1875) as the medical validation of this so-called 'authentic' smile is telling.[57] Indeed, though no commentary nor gloss is given, it is harder to think of an individual more representative of the artifice – the aesthetic performativity – of a certain nineteenth-century medicine than Duchenne who, known for his experiments with electricity and its effects on human physiognomy, famously hesitated between medicine and a career in the *beaux-arts*.[58] Duchenne becomes here, moreover, the 'discoverer' of this smile, as though it were a pre-existing object of rational experimentation and scientific episteme, to be 'detected' rather than performatively invented.

For what is ironic when contemplating the photographs of Duchenne's allegedly authentic expressions is precisely how theatrical they appear.[59] Plate 32 (Figure 1B) below is what Duchenne presents, for instance, as true laughter – in contrast to the 'false and lying laughter' produced by medical manipulation in Plate 31 (Figure 1A) – though he admits that he does intentionally 'excite the gaiety' of his posing subject in order to photograph such 'frank and communicative laughter'.[60] In both these cases, external stimuli – whether communicative and social, or electrical – are used to elicit a contrived response. Neither, however, is in any way 'natural', though at times Duchenne chooses to highlight his own

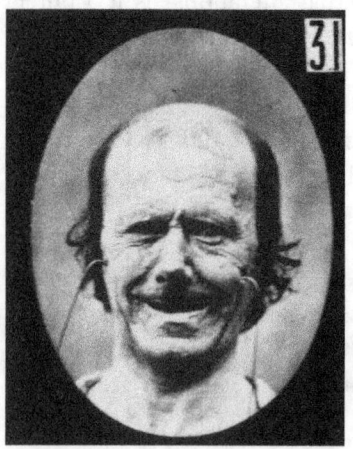 

Figure 1 Guillaume-Benjamin Duchenne (de Boulogne), *Mécanisme de la physionomie humaine ou analyse électro-physiologique de l'expression des passions* (Paris: Renouard, 1862), Plates 31 and 32, unnumbered page. Source: Wellcome Collection. Attribution 4.0 International (CC BY 4.0), https://wellcomecollection.org/works/vr8cb8u5

presence and the processes of artificial influence, while at others he downplays them altogether. In Figure 2, the presence both of the doctor and of electrical implements as the origins of 'fake' displays of the passions are notably foregrounded.

Rather than interrogating this performative heritage, Seligman, like a variety of other authors who refer to Duchenne, presumes the reality of an inherited medical binary.[61] The notion that there exists an easy and obvious distinction between 'voluntary' natural smiles and 'involuntary' artificial smiles, which moreover translates into distinct regional brain activity, persists in much contemporary

Figure 2 Duchenne (de Boulogne), *Mécanisme de la physionomie humaine*, frontispiece. Source: Wellcome Collection. Attribution 4.0 International, https://wellcomecollection. org/works/m33y9ucc

literature in the neurosciences.[62] My contention is not that such brain imaging is in no way revelatory but rather that, in many interpretations of such images, the pre-defined categories of voluntary and involuntary, natural and artificial are taken as static givens. Filtering down from a supposedly stable biological source, Duchenne's true smiles come to be associated with a physiological basis, while the fake smiles of flight attendants are seen as social masks of interested economic gain.[63]

In a rhetoric of internalised anxiety, this veritable inquisition seeks to eke out the traitors of fake feeling via recourse to the informants of inherent corporal codes. In order to understand just how pernicious this distinction is, we need only remark on Seligman's insistence that individuals with clinical experience can easily tell the difference between true and false emotional displays. Faced with a catalogue of various smiles, educated professionals become true feeling's guardians at the gates: 'When trained psychologists look through collections of photos, they can at a glance separate out the Duchenne smilers.'[64] Seligman proceeds to recount a 1960 study at the University of California in which psychology researchers 'studied 141 senior-class photos from the 1960 yearbook of Mills College' and then contacted these women at different periods of their life to ask 'about their marriages and their life satisfaction':

> When Harker and Keltner inherited the study in the 1990s, they wondered if they could predict from the senior-year smile alone what these women's married lives would turn out to be like. Astonishingly, Duchenne women, on average, were more likely to be married, or stay married, and to experience more personal well-being over the next thirty years. Those indicators of happiness were predicted by a mere crinkling of the eyes.[65]

The underlying moral lesson is disturbingly clear: for modern women, true feeling leads to happy marriages, within standardised domestic existences, and the 'personal well-being' of a satisfied life. In other words: feel truly if you want to find a man, keep him, be happy and reproduce this ideal. It matters little to Seligman that the study in question concerns a singular moment, captured in one photograph on one specific day of one specific year. In this essentialist ideology, even if one were having a bad day, one's true

Duchenne smile or fake Pan-American smile would nevertheless shine through. If one is unfortunate enough to smile 'falsely' in one image, for whatever reason, one's entire negative future is apparently traced out. In an instance of supreme determinism, a muscular contraction in the examined bodies of women is seen to map out all future sexual, relational and emotional teleologies.[66]

This is because, in such a vision, there is something subjectively essential about false affect: it is the sign of a fake individual, who always, in essence, is deceptive to others and to herself. The lesson is that true feeling is not an infinitely modifiable spectrum – wherein all affect is more or less opaque to all of us at different moments – but that some of us live in a state of authentic emotion, expressed by a true self, while others simply do not. Some women are Duchenne smilers, some Pan-American smilers – *by nature*. Their moral reward or punishment will depend on this distinction, for what is being qualified are ultimately the smilers, not the smiles:

> Questioning their results, Harker and Keltner considered whether Duchenne women were prettier, and their good looks rather than the genuineness of their smile predicted more life satisfaction. So the investigators went back and rated how pretty each of the women seemed, and they found that looks had nothing to do with good marriages or life satisfaction. A genuinely smiling woman, it turned out, was simply more likely to be well-wed and happy.[67]

Beyond the startling process of judging 'how pretty each of the women seemed' under the auspices of scientific method, the message contained in the notion that 'the genuineness of their smile predicted more life satisfaction' is worryingly complex. Did the fake Pan-American smilers of 1960 'know' that they were emotional manipulators, and paid the price for their emotional deception by poor marriages down the line? Or, in a deeper paradigm of spies among us, did they too remain unaware that their own outward displays of happiness were somehow internally 'false'?

We see the extent to which such projected true feeling and visions of a rigid social conformity go hand in hand. These passages set up a miniature morality play wherein certain women are effectively punished for their untrue feeling by unhappy marriages and lives.

In a vision of conformist congruity, being 'well-wed' is equated, both causally and structurally, with being 'happy' – though at no point does Seligman interrogate what he or other researchers mean by the terms 'happiness', 'life satisfaction' or 'personal well-being'. With marriage ranked so high on the list of what makes a modern woman's life 'successful', true feeling is both a predictor and an expression of this future normative union. The absence of any other evaluative criteria is telling: for one may be entirely 'satisfied' with one's life all the while acting in a manner which, to others, appears utterly ethically reprobate.

## The Spectre of True Feeling after Modernism

How then did we get to this point? What has led to the ready approval, in cultural and literary contexts, of true feeling as an undisputed value? To trace this modern historiography we need to briefly return to the context of European and Anglo-American modernism; for indeed, the extent of modernist anti-sentimentalism is by now a critical commonplace. As Jonathan Greenberg has observed, 'the narrative of early modernism begins to look like an effort of each new splinter movement to surpass the previous in the completeness of its antisentimentality'.[68] Dogmatically anti-sentimental modernist movements such as Imagism, Vorticism and Futurism were all aggressively geared against a perceived emotional untruth in Romantic and Victorian sentiment.[69] Ezra Pound recurrently railed against prior eras' emotional falsities, and the necessity for modern aesthetics to avoid 'any sham of emotion'.[70] Advocating, in an explicitly anti-Romantic crusade, his famous 'escape from feeling', T. S. Eliot championed the objectivising language of scientific positivism and disinterested contemplation: 'The end of the enjoyment of poetry is a pure contemplation from which all the accidents of personal emotion are removed.'[71] In continental Europe, but also on English soil, F. T. Marinetti argued, regarding both politics and aesthetic form, against the feminine weakness of false sentiment in contrast to true feeling's masculine dynamism and strength, resulting in numerous calls to 'liberate humanity' from 'the great tyranny of sentimentality'.[72] As Hugh Stevens notes, in his condemnation of the modern loss of the 'real individual' in favour of the merely 'social individual', D. H. Lawrence also perpetuated this anti-sentimental campaign: 'The social consciousness can only be analytical, critical, constructive but not creative, sensational but not passionate, emotional but without true feeling.'[73]

'An attack on sentimentality was one of the few threads uniting the internal variety of modernisms,' Michael Bell has observed. 'Yet the modernist generation also continued the transformation of sentiment into an implicit criterion of true feeling, a development which even now largely escapes recognition whether in the common language of feeling or in the specialist practice of literary criticism.'[74] The extent to which anti-sentimentalist positions had contaminated the atmosphere of modernist literary production can hardly be underestimated, with the quality of emotional truth being seen as the surest litmus for both moral probity and aesthetic force. Writing in the *Paris Review* in 1955, a novelist such as Joyce Cary was thus able to argue that 'a novel should be an experience and convey an emotional truth rather than arguments'.[75] In a formulation wherein the concept of emotional truth is opposed to the novel of ideas, Cary's remarks take aim at the traditions of nineteenth-century realisms, with their claims not only of representation and mimesis, but of sociopolitical engagement.

The category of experience is in this way eloquent: what is defended is an experiential aesthetics opposed to a literature of rhetorical *agon*. The irony, however, is that true feeling, for the modernist generation as for today, was and always will be an inherently political category. The supposed isolation of the feeling subject in a privileged aestheticised space is, of course, itself a political gesture, a fact underlined by recent efforts – especially among feminist critics – to insist on alternate currents of a 'sentimental modernism'.[76] Seeing modernism as, in its own way, highly sentimental is in part about revising its minority- and gender-exclusionary canon: about recognising that the anti-sentimentalism of Eliot, Pound, Lewis, Marinetti or Brecht does not, in spite of a long-held dominance, constitute the era's final say.

Nevertheless, in the context of modernism's post-war inheritance, it was this anti-sentimental legacy which most impacted those American realist writers otherwise at odds with such traditions. At the same time, it was no longer possible – as anti-sentimental modernists had done for the Romantics, and many Romantics before them with regard to Enlightenment rationalism – to merely repeat the gesture of casting aspersions on the authenticity of prior generations' emotional attitudes.[77] It will become clear throughout this book that while the cultural demand for true feeling only intensified throughout the post-war years, there occurred an increasing exhaustion of its value as a literary, aesthetic and ultimately moral criterion. This new generation of realist writers were less determined to prove that they, as a privileged minority, had finally gained access to emotional truth, than to show that the very concept must be denounced as a violent social and aesthetic mechanism.

## Enemies from Within: Post-War America and Emotional Control

There are many reasons to begin this study in post-war America and to choose realist fiction as its focus. Firstly, these literatures frequently posit a deeply rooted link between the cultural demand for true feeling and the repression – emotional, sexual, political and socioeconomic – of the modern liberal subject. Indeed, the Cold War, McCarthyism, anti-civil rights reactionism and shifts in gender politics created a climate wherein emotional restraint was seen to guarantee the cohesiveness of the social order, shoring up a unified resistance of stable values in the face of countercultural attacks. In this environment, to foster an agreed standard of emotional truth is nothing less than to participate, at a private and domestic level, in the larger structures of a unified community and nation state. In post-war ideology, true feeling is what often ensures the smooth passage from micro to macro political contexts, for as Marga Vicedo observes, 'the construction of a nexus between mother love, emotional maturity, and the stability of a democratic order was a Cold War affair'.[78] It is hardly surprising that true feeling, as an extrapolated value, came to be associated with other such dominant and mythologised categories as Whiteness, heterosexuality, bourgeois respectability and traditional gender roles. The affective control of a predominantly suburban WASP majority was seen not only to create consensus regarding emotional truth, but to maintain the strength of a social order able to call on true feeling as a universal principle of cohesion in cases of both interior and exterior threat.

True feeling in this way becomes one of the primary moral qualities of the balanced, productive, resilient – not to mention White, middle-class and heteronormative – post-war subject. Crucially, the appeal to truth of feeling, omnipresent in cultural discourses as diverse as advertising, sports, corporate organisation and self-help, was not just an unpremeditated upwelling, but constituted a highly intentional political strategy. Guy Oakes, tracing the affective ideologies of emotional control through such Cold War programmes as Project East River and the Psychological Strategy Board, describes what came to be termed 'emotion management':

> Emotion management may be understood as a strategy for the mobilization, administration, and control of emotional life ... Emotion management defines standards that tell us what it is possible to feel, how far the horizon of emotional experience extends, and what our feelings mean. It also defines norms that tell us what is expected of us emotionally, what the limits of acceptable emotional expression are, what we ought to feel in specific circumstances, and how these feelings should be expressed.[79]

What was unique about the post-war period was not so much that a government should set about overseeing or influencing the emotions of its citizens – a common executive *modus operandi* – but that such influence should so strongly focus on a superior truth of feeling. In a dominant post-war rhetoric, American society was presented as exceptional not only for its faith in God, its economic prosperity, its democratic freedom and its moral values, but for the overarching power of its transcendent affective truth. In his 'Enemies from Within' speech on 9 February 1950 in Wheeling, West Virginia, Senator Joseph McCarthy characterised the United States as a country which cherished affective precepts decried by Communist nations. Alongside the exclusion of God, McCarthy mentioned another value denied by Communist ideology, namely love:

> Karl Marx dismissed God as a hoax, and Lenin and Stalin have added in clear-cut, unmistakable language their resolve that no nation, no people who believe in a god, can exist side by side with their communistic state.

Karl Marx, for example, expelled people from his Communist Party for mentioning such things as love, justice, humanity or morality. He called this 'soulful ravings' and 'sloppy sentimentality'.[80]

In this final comparison between soul and sentiment, the equation between the exclusion of a true God and true feeling is complete. Modern American capitalism, McCarthy and others imply, embodies affective universals which have been forsaken by Communism's apathetic rationalism. This claim to possess emotions which are not only more valuable, but more human and more true than those of one's enemies – true to the self, to nature and ultimately to God – establishes true feeling as a touchstone of national allegiance, familial prosperity and psychosocial cohesion.

In proffering intense suspicion regarding subjective identities, anti-Communist distrust spread to the passions and affective dispositions seen to underlie such ideological allegiances. If the effort to not create 'fake' affects is the concept's commercial incarnation, to not be a traitor to one's own feelings is the political level of this emotional espionage. In both cases, truth translates values of socialised normality and control. With defectors in the midst, can one still count on the emotional cohesion of American patriotism, seen as an ensemble of strong and communally identifiable affective ties? In such a climate, it is logical that anxieties about criteria of truth and authenticity should come to concern not merely social identities, but the affective forces which traverse them. Moreover, with affects being more dynamic and uncontrollable than sociopolitical institutions, efforts to limit their excessive vectors must be even stricter.

This climate – wherein intense doubt is seen to hang over all identities, but especially those of society's marginalised outliers – was of course not dispersed by 1960s countercultures and the sociopolitical upheavals of the civil rights movement. Indeed, it is possible to contend that the hold over the cultural discourse of proponents of true feeling only strengthened, throughout the following decades, in response to reactionary backlash. For the concept, rather than being abandoned in rebellion against repressive Cold War universals, became central to countercultural demands, throughout the 1960s and 1970s, for authentic subjective experiences.[81]

Throughout the post-war years both nominally reactionary and revolutionary currents thus called upon true feeling to caution their claims to a broader legitimacy. There were, however, notable dissidents to the conceptual hegemony of emotional truth. Writing in 1962, Gore Vidal railed not against the prevalence of false feeling in American culture, but rather against the fact that true feeling had itself become a repressive regime. Writing on the theatre, and attributing the dominance of the idea to a milieu where psychoanalytic theory and Stanislavsky reigned supreme, Vidal observed:

> The cult of feeling has not only undone much of our theater writing, it has also peculiarly victimized those gentles, the actors. They have been taught that 'truth' is everything. And what is 'truth'? Feeling. And what is feeling? Their own secret core, to which the character they are to interpret must be related. To listen to actors talk about 'truth' is a chilling experience. They employ a kind of solemn baby talk compounded of analysts' jargon and the arcane prose of the late Stanislavsky.[82]

That American fiction more generally is tightly bound up in the knotted problems of this climate is unsurprising. What may appear more remarkable, in the pages that follow, is the strength of the literary revolt against the growing dominance of emotional truth as aesthetic theory and social exemplar. We may even posit that at no time in the history of the novel has the repressive potential of true feeling been perceived so viscerally as in the mid to late twentieth-century United States. For the narrator of George Eliot's *Middlemarch*, written in an era before true feeling's modern sway, 'our good depends on the quality and breadth of our emotion': on an affective capaciousness where quotients of veracity are not yet evoked.[83] Indeed, Victorian insistences on the intensity or breadth of feelings, rather than on their authenticity or truth, are mainstays of much nineteenth-century criticism, in spite of Romantic claims to a contested equivalence between intensity and affective truth. If Emma Bovary can question Rodolphe's love, or if suspicions are expressed regarding Dmitri Karamazov's filial devotion, such uncertainty does not extend – or not in the same radical sense – to the intimation that love or devotion *cannot* be true, only that their sincerity, in such and such a particular case, is in doubt.

Such characters are not concerned with true feeling as a categorical imperative. Rather, the search for concordance, in specific instances, between outer surface and inner depth does not seek to penetrate to a point, in the inner workings of the self, where true feeling is expected to resolve the tensions of a necessarily uncertain emotional life. If, in such prior contexts, the sense of particular emotional expressions is always open to doubt, this is a very different concern to widescale scepticism of the category of truth of feeling itself – a scepticism which, I argue, comes to be the norm in American realist fiction from the 1950s until the century's end.

## Emotions of Privilege: Cultural Anxieties for the Ebb of Emotional Truth

As we see throughout this book, the obsession with true feeling often appears to stem from a fundamental anxiety about the solidity or permanence of established structures of dominance. This anxiety is related to the nominally 'threatened' status of such traits as masculinity, heterosexuality and Whiteness – concepts which were, of course, focuses of intense disquietude for the modernist and post-war generations, with their jeopardised status revealingly accompanied by the perceived erosion of true feeling: a point consistently returned to, in both eras, in recurrent critical movements of anti-sentimentalism.

Is the conviction that one is in touch with true feeling thus more accessible if one occupies a position of social privilege? For to have one's anger, fear or pain constantly suspected, doubted or impugned is the reality of many groups – women, people of colour, LGBTQ+ communities – who frequently remain excluded from true feeling as powerful epiphany. In this sense, the impression in much American literature of the twentieth century that true feeling is always on the decline begins to resemble the creeping loss of the conceit that there is an obvious *a priori* validity to the affects of a dominant class. To understand this point, we need only remark that, at a time – the 1950s and 1960s – when suburban WASP writers increasingly discoursed on the steady seeping of a consecrated emotional authenticity from their world, feminist, gay and lesbian, Chicano, Asian and African American literatures, while challenging the status quo of accepted truth-regimes, were not staking similar claims to either true feeling or its supposed decay.[84]

In the anxiety that true feeling must be preserved against attack and the intuition that it may suffocate divergent forms of emotional being, we witness the decline of dominant modes of affect that previously went unquestioned. For in many cases, both true feeling and the anxiety for its loss emerge from what Keith Wilhite, writing on the American post-war years, terms 'a double crisis: the perceived waning of WASP cultural authority in the face of increasing racial and ethnic heterogeneity, and an untenable commitment to the insular domestic sphere in an era of political unrest'.[85]

Though it has historically been framed by White heterosexual men as a transparent or neutral ideation, true feeling is in this sense a highly gendered and racialised construct, in that it tends to consecrate its famed authenticity on an altar of social exclusion.[86] Since the era of Stephen Crane, Theodore Dreiser and Henry James, and despite the critical reclaiming of works by Edith Wharton, Kate Chopin or Charlotte Perkins Gilmore, the tradition of American literary realism was long framed by critics as a White-male dominant tradition. With this lens enduring into the post-war period, the realist questioning of emotional truth became bound up in many ways with the sense of an imperilled hegemony, in which such apparently stable values as Whiteness or masculinity no longer seemed quite so reliable as firm anchors for the affective self. For in much of the fiction considered in this book, we encounter explicit critiques of the limiting restriction and pain that demands for true feeling can produce, coupled with a sense of frustration on the part of characters who can no longer claim transparent access to such affective privilege. This tension is of course complex, and not a simple relation of affective oppressor to affective oppressed. Feeling oneself unjustly deprived of emotional truth, however, remains a privileged position, firstly because we must feel that we deserve access to it as a fundamental right, and secondly because we must agree with the consensus as to what emotional truth actually is.

Supported by a heteronormative WASP majority committed to authenticity, unity and containment at a subjective as well as national and transnational level, post-war affect frequently comes to resemble a type of involuntary regulation enacted by dominant factions upon their own communities and themselves. Unsurprisingly, many of the paradoxical critiques of true feeling analysed in the chapters that follow occur within the picket fences of suburbia, among writers who, while ambiguously perpetuating the centrality of emotional truth as a concept, attempt to work against it in order to delegitimise its cultural hold.

It is no doubt for this reason, among many others, that a variety of post-war realist writers who are exterior, but adjacent, to a mythologised White 'normality' depict individuals able to 'pass' – socially, racially, emotionally – for a member of this dominant identity. In creating avatars who attempt to problematically assimilate with a normative majority, queer, African American or Jewish characters (to consider just these examples) adopt the codes of true feeling as an extension of standardising social masks. Such masking, perhaps most evidently in Ellison's *Invisible Man*, is all the more detrimental when it serves only to ratify the existence of an unmovable binary between the true and false self: between a sham surface of social integration and a supposedly true inner depth, both of which poles will necessarily be ideations, which ignore the incessant weave and weft of these inherently artificial dynamics. Such complex affective and identitarian processes are indeed omnipresent in many of the African American protagonists in James Baldwin's or Kathleen Collins's fiction, or in Seymour 'Swede' Levov in Philip Roth's *American Pastoral*, who is able to pass for the idealised WASP athlete only when he shapes his outward emotional identity into one of courage and reserve.[87] It is also a mechanism which plays into the overwhelming presence of frustrated heteronormative characters in the work of a writer such as John Cheever. In this sense, we will come to understand differently the predominant fascination with true feeling among a majority which perceives its affective sovereignty to be both symbolically and socioeconomically jeopardised.

## Why Realism? A 'Restrictive' Mode against Restrictive Truth

It is not by chance then that post-war attacks against true feeling should be most fully formulated within the tradition of modern realist fiction, the literary mode with the strongest and most debated historical claims to pretentions of truth, representation and reference.[88] While we have come to expect opposition to the reductivism of hierarchical truth-regimes in postmodern works, this antagonism is all the more surprising among realist authors due to this contested representational heritage. The resistance with regard to structures of exclusionary truth is all the more compelling when it occurs in texts which maintain an ambiguous relationship to both the abstract values and technical praxis of nineteenth-century realisms and Naturalism. As in the case of the desire, within postmodernism itself, to return to ideals such as transparency or sincerity, the simple equation between formal experimentation and a rebellion against stable truth categories does not hold.

Importantly, throughout *The Artifice of Affect* I do not propose a restrictive definition of realism, but rather consider the term to encompass a wide range of flexible modes, tropes and techniques, which at once express, counter and play with mythologised ideals of narrative coherency, rhetorical transparency, extra-diegetic reference and epistemological omniscience. Even more so than for nineteenth-century antecedents, for the post-war period such a generalised definition would not only be impossible but would effectively exclude texts which reshape realist traditions for specific formal and ideological ends. Many of the authors analysed here produce works which intentionally flout or rebel against realist conventions, making full use of unreliable narrators, temporal disruptions and metatextual layers. Rather than concentrate on these more obvious revolts, my focus is on texts which formulate their critique of emotional truth by way of a simultaneous reflection on literary mimesis.

Though the denouncement of true feeling may seem more evident in literatures deemed to be postmodern, I strive to show the erosion of the principle within a literary tradition – namely modern realism – often seen to reinforce essentialistic conceptions of affective life. For the American realist fiction discussed in this book explores a vacuity at the heart of quests for emotional truth, with the cycle of alternating conformity and rebellion which they frequently cause. Though applicable to other currents, post-war American realism is in many ways the epicentre of this struggle, expressing a scepticism with regard to the criterion of true feeling rarely seen to such an intense degree. My contention is that it is precisely the choice of supposedly neutral representative modes which makes the realist attack against true feeling so compelling, for the reason that they use the very forms of American and European sentimental literature to show that sentimental truth is not a viable modern category. In criticising the sociopolitical strictures of the concept, American realist writers also challenge the reductive vision of realist traditions, especially when they are seen to promote a simplified emotionality for a naïve commercial readership.

The analyses of the following chapters traverse the work of a variety of post-war authors such as James Baldwin, Saul Bellow, Raymond Carver, John Cheever, Kathleen Collins, Ralph Ellison, Richard Ford, Paula Fox, Walker Percy, Philip Roth, John Updike and Richard Yates. In the texts under discussion, characters recurrently forbid themselves 'false' feeling: when it appears – as it inevitably must – they may seek to deny it (as in Baldwin's or Cheever's stories of affective repression); they may melancholically accept its inevitability (as in Ford's Bascombe novels); they may play with ambivalent roles and masks (as in the fiction of Collins or Fox); they may perform internal dialogues to determine the truth of what they feel (as in Yates's *Revolutionary Road*); or they may diabolically abandon themselves to the perversions of affective illusion (as in Roth's *Sabbath's Theater*).[89]

In all these cases, characters' reasons for resisting forays into 'fake' emotionality are manifold. At the same time, their profound dissatisfaction and unease with regard to emotional truth as a criterion are paramount: conceiving it as a terrible restriction, they are not able to dispel the paradoxes inherent in the concept, nor deploy it for valuable personal ends. Those who feel the impossibility of true feeling in turn become staple chroniclers of modern American angst. Once they apply the criterion of truth to dynamic states which cannot possess truth in these terms, a solipsistic interrogation is engendered which returns always back to the questioning self. A result of this process is that many interpret as a moral failing what is in reality a loss of spiritual and philosophical ideals. True feeling thus becomes a replacement for cultural values lacking outside of isolated identities. Rather than interrogate this desert of lost values, with their requisite sociopolitical dimensions, individuals incessantly wonder if their own feelings are true. Instead of seeking to change the objects of their affective fixations, they turn inwards in an attempt to endlessly interrogate the authenticity of their 'private' emotional lives.

Given the historical pretensions of realism to totality, transparency and omniscience, and its supposed resistance to alterity, Chapter 1 asks whether realist modes can be said to 'represent' affect, if affect is understood as that which is most other, both to the inner subject and to narrative diegesis. Reading against the grain of visions of realism as a fundamentally reactionary tradition, analyses of the fiction of Walker Percy and Saul Bellow will demonstrate the extent to which such writing strives precisely to speak of affect's silences, to represent its unrepresentable voids. I will propose that this paradox, which moreover mirrors the disparities of artifice at the heart of the affective self, is in fact integral to modern realist projects. Affect is thus seen not to be beyond the scope of realism, but to be broached in complex ways by realist texts' highlighting of the paradoxes of emotional representation.

Chapter 2 traces the myth of the natural origins of literary affect, arguing that not only does a natural biological emotion – in the sense of a stable *a priori* anchorage – not exist, but its projected role as foundation of literary emotionality confers to literature the role of secondary confirmation of prior affective hierarchies. Basing an alternative vision of literary affect on the artificialisation of corporality in thinkers such as Georges Canguilhem, this chapter explores the denunciation of the quest for natural emotionality in John Cheever and Philip Roth, whose characters both dream of a natural foundation to their feelings and intensely suffer from its absence or loss. Tracing the drastic consequences of such efforts to locate a natural affect at the basis of all actions and beliefs, such fiction elaborates a related condemnation of the cultural valuation, central to American modernity, of the unified and autonomous self.

In an extension of such critiques, Chapter 3 scrutinises claims that true feeling would somehow be 'inimitable': a transcendent essence or epiphanic experience not only beyond realist representation (as in Chapter 1) but perpetually resistant to imitation and mimesis as a whole, within either literature or the self. In the fiction of James Baldwin or Kathleen Collins, the nostalgia for an original emotionality at the basis of identity takes on particularly racialised tones as a fantasy of a White emotional normality. In the work of John Cheever, Richard Ford and Richard Yates, such normalisation by way of the exclusion of 'imitated' feelings is articulated as a further mechanism of often unintentional societal control.

Chapter 4 examines a further criterion of affective value, namely the modern myth of emotional equilibrium in the work of Paula Fox and Richard Yates. These texts interrogate the extent to which emotional balance – as a concept which aims to repress the outliers of a normative spectrum – risks becoming a criterion of conformity, wherein true feeling and affective equilibrium interact as self-verifying constructs. Artifice becomes a potential means to reject such mythologies, though not without the ever-present danger of dissipation of a fractured – because fabricated – self. Torn between the poles of excess and absence, the characters of these fictional worlds evolve in an array of simulated masks and environments which, far from resolving the dangers of an imposed equilibrium, theatricalise both artifice's potential for liberation and its risks.

In the increasingly medicalised context of modernity, Chapter 5 interrogates the pathologisation of emotional alterity throughout the post-war period, asking why emotions experienced under 'altered' states are deemed to be less true than those which originate within a hypothetical bodily purity. The conferral of truth to emotions seen as the product of an intoxicated self posits the existence of a normalised affect meant to act as a baseline for subjective evaluations. The case study of alcohol in post-war American realism, and in particular in the fiction of John Updike and Raymond Carver, highlights the complexity of this dynamic, in which characters do not simplistically penetrate into truth through derangement but rather make use of the artifices of intoxication to rupture an unbearable real.

Finally, the Conclusion delves deeper into the dangers of associating the value of literature with its ability to express, represent or incarnate the true feelings of the self. An alternate model of affect's artifice, based on fluidity and ontological play, comes to replace the stable anchorages of normal, natural and true emotion. Such a vision has its associated risks, existing always on the precipice of emotional entropy. The theatre of the affective mind, as this book's concluding motif, opens on to a new vision of the feeling subject wherein authentic affect is imagined as a spectrum of vibrant representation, expanding outwards from the self's own fictions and fantasies, rather than a ratiocentric or dominating ideal.

## Dynamic, Unstable, Free: 'False' Feeling Opening on to Alterities

Affective truth is not an inherent or stable quality of the subject, not a moment when the self turns inwards to verify its own internal coherence, but a process of spirited negotiation with unstable and interactive alterities. The appropriate response to distress in the face of true feeling's absence is not to restore the extent to which affects belong to subjects – restricting and limiting them in order to guarantee them stable borders – but to explode these frontiers, recognising that their truth is not a fixed quality of their belonging but a vital property of their movement.

In the following chapters, the more characters seek to validate the truth of their own feeling, and the more they seek to prove how much their feelings are their own – and are true because of this subjective integration – the more these feelings seem constructed and exterior, increasingly resembling uncontrollable affects existing beyond the cognisance of the self. Rather than seeing in this exteriorisation a liberating experience of alterity, it is most often an encounter marked by a profound malaise, for the reason that it posits a decentring of the self with regard to its enveloping world.

It is not, however, because emotions are not our own, because they are merely circulating exterior affects, that they may seem untrue, but rather because they appear to be so integrated with the self, so at one with its inward processes, that they are coloured by the same aura of creative artifice as that which shapes that self's inner life. If emotions are utterly fused with us, fundamentally a part of our being, we may have great difficulty altering them: at the mercy of their influence, we may be reduced to passive subjects instead of active agents of change. If they are 'false' then, in the end, so are we.

I argue throughout the following pages that it is in insisting on the extent to which emotions do not always belong to subjects, by emphasising their dynamism over their belonging, that we can confer on them a value far greater than a reductive, hierarchical truth. A central aspect of this value is the ability to change and to be changed; for emotional truth most frequently implies a static category, frozen in the timeless amber of a subject's essential constitution, social enactment and intimate past. Observing, living, experiencing emotions as though they were not us, but passing through us on their way to other worlds, and were none of them more or less true than those artificial worlds themselves, is the extent of this liberation.

CHAPTER 1

# Can Realism Speak of Affect?

Literary realism, as both transhistorical impulse and historicised form, has been a favourite target of modern theoretical attack.[1] From Theodor Adorno's accusations of political reactionism, to Roland Barthes's undermining of a realist 'referential illusion', realism's pretensions to totality, transparency and omniscience received starkly bad press throughout Russian and French Formalisms, heightening with poststructuralist and deconstructionist critiques.[2] Though the causes of such opprobrium are manifold, these negative appraisals focus on perceived realist tendencies to limit the representative possibilities of literary texts. Literary realism is seen to ignore, or at least circumvent, those aspects of experience which, because of their alterity and heterodoxy, refuse to be integrated into a stable textual apparatus, and thus resist typical realist values such as formal cohesion, objectivity and epistemological inclusion (omniscience).

As we will see in this chapter's analyses of the fiction of Saul Bellow and Walker Percy, such indictments centre on the question: what do realist modes hide in the midst of their pretension to show? Bellow and Percy prove to be particularly revealing case studies for this inquiry, as their protagonists' apparent praise of such values as authenticity and emotional sincerity is swathed in recurrent paradoxes and layers of ironic distancing, and is never quite what it seems. In spite of such undermining, the critical canard of realism's inherent conservatism has remained strong, often for primarily political reasons: even when dealing with socially marginalised content, literary realism, by its very diegetic tropes, is seen to implicitly reinforce the dominance of a (most often bourgeois) status quo. At a formal level, and by extension, realist textual devices are believed to tend towards the constraining of semantics within a self-contained referential field. In their claim to express the universality of experience in a neutral discourse, they are reputed to advocate, albeit unwillingly, a naïve lack of critical distancing, as per Flaubert's famous affirmation: 'The artist in his work must be like God in his creation – invisible and all-powerful: he must be everywhere felt, but never seen.'[3]

Alongside such critiques, and concomitant with realism's supposed persistence as modernity's dominant narrative form, arises the aporia of a theoretical tradition which has lauded oppositional counter-attacks. In an institutional context, the hegemony of realism has been rendered fragile, especially given the ironic institutionalisation of a variety of anti-realist campaigns. Literary modernism undoubtedly provides the most well-known example of this paradox, with acts of modernist rebellion given pride of place in the halls of a modern academy wherein Virginia Woolf has come to be read and analysed far more than Arnold Bennett or John Galsworthy.[4]

Against this heritage, many modern defences of realism have been articulated.[5] Lilian Furst, for instance, attempts to 'unmask realism as illusion or deception – or, more broadly, as a literary artifact' in the positive sense.[6] Not only are such texts less influential, however, than more hostile structuralist and poststructuralist invective, they generally occupy a defensive outpost, reading realism against the grain of its detractors in order to prove that it is in fact more ambiguous, polysemous and politically heterodox than it has been deemed.[7] Even when this complexity is proved, and in spite of realism's alleged pre-eminence among readers, its impoverished reputation among theorists has founded a lineage in which 'the unconscious, the foreign, the supernatural . . . are declared "other" to realist narrative'.[8]

It is concerning this specific question of realism's relationship with otherness that affect enters the conceptual fray. We may perhaps epitomise the above excluded terms by a more general category: that is, what is perceived as 'other' to literary realism is any object which escapes its epistemology, refusing to be integrated into the formal totality of realist processes. Given that affect is often seen to refer to such unconscious and unknowable force, the question of realist modes' relation to affect's representability must be posed.

## Affect as Alterity: Literary Realism's Epistemological Divide

Ironically, in the specific context of its nineteenth-century theorisations, realism may not seem uncomfortable with the exclusion of affect from what it seeks to represent. After all, this hypothetical absence is an important aspect of nineteenth-century realist myths of the impersonal, objective narrator, most famously crystallised by Flaubert's dubitable claims of affective authorial distancing:

> Madame Bovary has nothing 'true' in it. It is a totally invented story; into it I put none of my own feelings and nothing from my own life. The illusion (if there is one) comes, on the contrary, from the impersonality of the work. It is a principle of mine that a writer must not be his own theme.[9]

Such a claim – that, as Flaubert goes on to say in a revealing condensation, 'Art must rise above personal emotions and nervous susceptibilities' – does not mean that *Madame Bovary* does not 'speak of' affect, but rather that affect is considered, from an authorial point of view, as consciously alien to realist authorial process.[10] In other words, though it may find various forms of textual incarnation, affect can never be a part of a realist author's conscious intentions, for the reason that it is precisely pre- or extra-intentional, intervening at a point before or beyond authorial cognisance.

The representation of subjectivised feelings may be an appropriate, if controversial, aim for a realist author aiming at scientific objectivity and neutrality; but affect is never neutral – not because 'nothing is neutral', in the terms of a clichéd postmodernism, but more radically because affect is in some respects outside of value, as a force not yet fully judged by the axiological criteria of the self. Indeed, in some sense affects cannot even be said to be 'neutral', for the reason that their neutrality is not yet a question to be posed.

Can realism thus speak of affect? The question may at first appear surprising. Why, after all, should the codes of a specific literary tradition necessarily prevent the exploration of an entire aspect of subjective life? The interrogation takes on greater meaning if we understand affect as ceaselessly eluding, to a greater or lesser extent, the full awareness of the feeling subject. In these versions of the concept, affect not only resists outward presentation in the form of language or descriptive signs, but escapes a totalised representation of the self to itself. The feeling subject is not only unable to fully express such affect to others – for it is, by definition, outside of a representative impulse – but unable to represent it at the initial level of conscious apprehension.

What happens if we apply such modern comprehensions of affect as that which, as Brian Massumi puts it, is never fully 'ownable or recognizable' to the functioning of realist modes?[11] The question must be raised for the reason that realist narrators often strive to create the impression that they both know and recognise, and are in fact able to name and narrate a vast range of affective propensities of characters and their world. Even more crucially: in seeking not to foreground moments of rupture and incoherence, this harmony is frequently the foundation upon which realist structures of omniscience and formal coherency are built.

Does the very fact that one seeks to incarnate affect in literary form immediately imply the adoption of consciously anti-realist techniques? Techniques which, in contrast to rhetorical constriction, would make themselves more flexible, self-referential and self-contradictory, allowing for breakage and perceptive spillage? In literary-historical terms, a curious parallel is created between, on the one hand, realism as a perceived 'dominant' mode – but one which fails to take into account that which is heterodox or refractory in emotional experience – and, on the other, affect as precisely this ensemble of heterodoxical material itself. If affect describes that which is not ownable or recognisable, and realism seeks to gloss over – to render more stable and uniform – this magma of affective force, then must realism be ruptured in order to allow affect to surge forth? Does realism seek always to recognise and to own – to incarnate emotionality within subjects or subjective states? More explicitly: do modernist, postmodernist and other anti-realist insurgents seek to transform what is 'emotional' in literary realism – in the sense of that which is incarnated, subjective and to a certain extent understood – into a disruptive affect of uncontrollable, antagonistic drives?

## Outside of Language? On the Unrepresentability of Affect

Each of these questions encounters a larger paradox, namely the hypothetical impossibility of all language to articulate affect, and not merely a specific, theoretically more 'constrictive' form. As Eric Shouse observes: 'Affect cannot be fully realized in language . . . because affect is always prior to and/or outside consciousness.'[12] As mentioned in the introduction, we may wish to question the radicality of this categorisation, especially considering the risk of essentialism in the definition of the limits of 'consciousness' itself. But 'fully realized' should not be taken to mean 'not realized in any way at all'; nor does it imply that literary texts cannot point towards forces and potentials which lie beyond their scope. On the contrary, they can make felt, in the heart of their unfolding, an unsayable affective absence – like Jean-François Lyotard's affect as 'inarticulate phrase' – which remains beyond their epistemological grasp.[13]

This problem is perhaps simply magnified in realist traditions which attempt to convince us of their far-reaching capacities to know and to say. To take, for instance, the question of representation: if affect is commensurable with what is unrepresentable to the self, how may it ever be represented within the confines of a literary text? Not only does the subject not know parts of itself, but it is unable to fully recognise which parts in particular it does not know. According to this conception, affect is related to the subject's own structures of internal alienation, which seem to preclude any further diegetic integration. In a literary context, we may think of the alienation of a discursive identity which does not fully know its own processes – a limitation which intervenes well before the restricted knowledge of an invented narrator playing the role of expressive guise.

This problem takes on a specific colouration in the context of a realist tradition intimately tied to this representative (if not necessarily mimetic) impulse. Realist literature intervenes at a precarious junction, namely at the point where the representation of affect becomes both inevitable and necessary, at least for a formal lineage historically committed to this idea. The problem is not simply whether realist literatures can represent the unrepresentable. Ron Katwan expresses the complexity of this question when he notes, in relation to Lyotard, that 'it is crucial to realize that the affect must not be understood as an encounter with a transcendent, inexpressible reality . . . To the extent that it is a disruption of discourse, the affect can only manifest itself within the realm of that which it disrupts.'[14] But if affect is fundamentally a disruption of discourse, how can it effectively exist within realist texts that harmonise or gloss over disruptions, favouring the creation of a greater unity of narrative, character and sense?

This may seem an important problem, for the reason that realist modes tend to minimise narrative and representative turmoil, valuing formal coherency and the stability of established codes. First among these is the recourse to omniscient narrators, with their penetration into inner emotional states. In contrast to the early picaresque tradition of the novel in Cervantes or Sterne, high realism from the nineteenth century onwards displays markedly less tendency to ironise or play with such textual devices. Narrative omniscience is treated with far less distancing in Tolstoy or Balzac, and diegetic disturbances are minimised rather than highlighted in self-referential play.

It is thus not only a problem of representing the unrepresentable, but one of affect as that which perturbs established processes of representation itself. In signalling that part of uncontrollability and unknowability in emotional life – as well as textuality's limitations regarding this epistemological 'blank' – affect, we may suspect, will always work against pretensions to reliable apprehension within all aesthetics, and not merely those which aspire to a realist mastery of their world. Affect will, by definition, seek to undo claims to totality or absolute understanding. It will not simply establish new formal rules, but will disrupt any rule which texts internally forge.

Across its diverse definitions, affect always speaks of that which, at least to some extent, is beyond the knowledge and understanding of subjects. Affect may sometimes seem then to have no end. For what is the limit to what we do not know? Is not this border forever expanding, as soon as we take the time to examine the illusion of epistemological stability? Not being bound by language, meaning or the feeling self, affect overflows these borders, describing the ever-moving forces of an agonistic world. How then may we ever hope to contain such an incessant deluge within realism's more static divides?

## Empathy Is Not an Affect: Alienation and Identification in Realist Terms

The controversy appears even more salient when we examine a staple notion of realist technique, namely empathy, or at least emotional identification. Here again, affect may at first seem at odds with realist process. Emotions may very well be integrated into a vision of literature which relies on empathetic equivalence, but as Massumi puts it, affect 'is not about empathy or emotive identification, or any form of identification for that matter'.[15] Affect does not 'care about' identification for the reason that it is, in a sense, beyond it, existing in a realm where emotional adequation or even understanding are not theoretically possible, due to the singularity of the affective forces traversing the self.

According to this idea, as soon as we identify with an affect, as soon as we feel empathy for its effects, it has ceased to be purely affective and has become incarnated within a recognisable identity: one which feels and experiences the feelings of others, adopting congruent modes. This may make of affect an alien and alienating principle; though ironically it is precisely the inability of realism to incorporate the alien which has made it an object of theoretical attack.[16] That which is alien is perhaps by definition disruptive: both of a textual order and of a totalising narrative. When realism is denounced as a limiting tradition unable to encompass heterogeneous experience, such heterogeneity is conceived socially (reinforcing accepted values) as well as phenomenologically (forcing the flux of consciousness into ordered narrative arcs). It is an integral part of the modern reaction against nineteenth-century realist traditions, including Theodor Adorno's well-known reproof that realism resists 'impulses that disturb its order or evoke inner elements of the unconscious that cannot be admitted'. Adorno postulates a rigidity and conformity, a 'hostility to anything alien or alienating' indissociable from realist form.[17] In doing so, he situates realism in a primarily political dimension of docility and orthodoxy. In a critique of socially conscious fiction since the realism of Stephen Crane, William Dean Howells, John Steinbeck or Theodore Dreiser, the conformist power of realist epistemologies – Adorno's 'rigid coordinates' – effectively negates the possibility of their integrating anything alienating or other. Affect is inherently alienating and other in that it implies the impossibility of a subject's simple embodiment, wherein somatic systems would merely express inner emotional states in a hierarchical arborescence. Given the tendency of affect to establish complex feedback loops – wherein the individual subject analyses and reacts to unknown desires in the very midst of their unfolding – we may think that the ideal literary mode to represent affective paradigms would be one which is itself highly solipsistic and self-aware. Archly self-conscious narrators, who ceaselessly demonstrate their awareness of their own internal divisions with regard to themselves – the fact that they are aware that they are *not* their own bodies and minds, not even 'themselves' – may initially seem to provide a better portrait of affective intensities lying forever beyond our control.

## Disrupting a Lack of Disruption, or the Ironic Pretension to Clarity

So much for the prosecution's arguments against literary realism's limitations. We must be careful, however, not to oversimplify realism's famed lack of self-awareness, nor fail to problematise its ironic pretensions to clarity. Such pretensions are just that: theatricalised positions which are not meant to be taken as either literal or complete. They are in many ways rhetorical and symbolic; realist narrators pretend to a certain knowledge and insight, all the while leaving in a state of utter suspension that which gives them the ability to encompass the diversity of the events and emotions being described. As Peter Boxall observes:

> The no doubt proper sense that the novel, over the course of its history, has become increasingly sceptical of the conditions of its own production has perhaps blinded us to two things: both to the fact that the realist novel, so called, was not uncritical of its own mimetic procedures, and

to the fact that neither the modernist nor the postmodernist novel have completely freed themselves from the coils of such procedures.[18]

In this sense, realist texts may appear less 'disrupted', but this apparent lack of disruption is ironically a quality of all texts, which ceaselessly seek to hide their own internal mechanisms. Just as apparent cohesion is not specific to realism, disruption is not specific to affect, but may be seen as a fundamental quality of textuality itself. This is Derrida's position in his well-known opening remarks to 'Plato's Pharmacy': 'A text is not a text unless it hides from the first comer, from the first glance, the law of its composition and the rules of its game.'[19] Derrida underlines the part of unknowability and lack of finitude which define textuality itself. Texts 'disappear' in the process of their own making; this disappearance itself, however, is invisible: it does not manifest at the moment of its unfolding, *'au présent'*, but is only visible by way of a subsequent reconstitution, temporally and analytically abstracted from our moments of textual meeting.

While it is true that realist modes do not highlight this disappearance and even attempt to conceal it, it is not clear that they hide them more or better than narrative texts which reject such supposed complacency. Realism simply frames itself, in a highly performative way, as a more stable form – for this too is an integral aspect of its myth. This does not mean that realist texts are any less adequate as vessels of passing affective force. On the contrary, affect is not merely exemplary of this quality of texts to dissimulate their own rules – it is an extension of it into a realm where affect is irremediably present, whether it happens to be 'disruptive' or not.

## 'A secret sense of wonder': Experiencing Unnameable Affect in Walker Percy

Rather than a base antagonism, affect and realism therefore maintain a relationship of subtle and often mutually revelatory interactions. Indeed, the ways of not speaking of affect, but rather indicating its silent presence, are omnipresent in the realist fiction of post-war America. Instead of the effort to render affects via novel formal inventions, such texts betray numerous strategies of indetermination in order to intimate the weight and valency of affects which remain unnamed. Though existing beyond the bounds of both language and a traditional realist omniscience, these affective forces affirm their ontology – the power of their simple existence – in spite of the inability of realist language to semantically determine their precise nature. It is thus frequently when realism displays its limits – what characters, and even omniscient narrators, do not and cannot know – that the most compelling affects appear.

Walker Percy's 1961 novel *The Moviegoer* presents an ideal case of this capacity of the modern realist novel to silently hint at inscrutable affective presences.[20] The novel follows the unremarkable life of Binx Bolling in mid-century New Orleans. Binx works in his uncle's brokerage firm, has various affairs and watches movies – but beyond the aimless wandering of an unsatisfied existence, Binx, in an effort to avoid 'everydayness', has embarked on what he calls 'the search'. In a motif of indeterminacy, the search remains throughout the text undefined. From its emergence, however, we learn several of its qualities:

> This morning, for the first time in years, there occurred to me the possibility of a search. I dreamed of the war, no, not quite dreamed but woke with the taste of it in my mouth, the queasy-quince taste of 1951 and the Orient. I remembered the first time the search occurred to me. I came to myself under a chindolea bush . . . Six inches from my nose a dung beetle was scratching around under the leaves. As I watched, there awoke in me an immense curiosity. I was onto something. I vowed that if I ever got out of this fix, I would pursue the search. Naturally, as soon as I recovered and got home, I forgot all about it.[21]

Such alternating between revelatory epiphany and a bathetic fall into ordinariness is typical of Binx's life; and indeed, as in Viktor Shklovsky's *ostranenie* – in which one would strive to intentionally disrupt automatic perceptions of the world, creating a renewed vision of reality instead of simple recognition – Binx expends a great deal of effort attempting to preserve this unnamed mystery in the face of its quotidian decay.[22]

This particular affect engendered by the search is not specified further: there is a quality to this experience that either cannot be named or must not in order to consecrate its value. Binx thus speaks around it. We learn only that, in this state, ordinary objects with pragmatic uses – 'pencil, keys, handkerchief, pocket slide rule' – are invested with such strangeness that they suddenly appear 'both unfamiliar and at the same time full of clues'.[23] Ephemera, sensations, images accumulate in a spiralling semantics, where the world becomes charged with hidden meaning. We are presented then with myriad situations – as in the following scene in an old cinema where Binx used to watch movies – where a mysterious affect surges forth:

> There was this: a mockery about the old seats, their plywood split, their bottoms slashed, but enduring nevertheless as if they had waited to see what I had done with my fourteen years. There was this also: a secret sense of wonder about the enduring, about all the nights, the rainy summer nights at twelve and one and two o'clock when the seats endured alone in the empty theatre. The enduring is something which must be accounted for. One cannot simply shrug it off.[24]

What is so compelling to Binx about this presence? This investing of objects with affective weight qualifies the feeling individual as an 'other'. The silent seats, laden with emotional presence, surround him and outnumber him – and the theatre is empty only in the sense that no similar beings to Binx are present within it. There is a mockery to the old seats in part because of their belonging to an alternate temporality: the long time of phenomenal ontology, of evolving and ending worlds. This accumulated duration is far beyond the human sense of 'all the nights, the rainy summer nights'. Ironically, Binx imagines that in spite of the objects existing in this other chronology of substance, quintessence and objecthood, they are nevertheless attentive to the becoming of human lives. The speculative nature of this state – 'as if' – is crucial, for one can never be sure if the outside world is truly invested with feeling, or merely garbed in an affective imitation projected by a human mind. But in Binx's vision, it is as though the distinction did not matter: this affect's potency exists regardless of its subjective or objective origin, and this divergence, in the presence of such enduring, begins to lose all meaning.

If Binx has grown and lived, the seats, not being alive in the same sense – as they are beyond all corporal contracts – may show signs of decay, while 'enduring nevertheless'. As the pronoun makes plain, these spent years 'belong' to Binx only in the ironic sense of his mortality: in reality they belong to the silent congregation of seats become spectators. In spite of their personification, the cinema seats are not in fact entities, but parts of the world which affirm their alterity, their abiding status as non-subjects. Their intense affective charge has its origin partly in their inhumanness: not in their immortality exactly, but in their being outside of both life and death. Seats are 'made' to accommodate human bodies; but once made, they are part of the world. They do not depend on human agency for their affective valency. Their affect has not required a human presence in order to transform it into human emotion: its artifice, as well as its autonomy, is what renders it disturbing, with the world's independence being a source and agent of affect's weight. Crucially, this quality is usually not 'accounted for', but 'shrugged off' by human subjects who all too frequently insist only on the life of active organisms, with their worldly feelings and cares.

Binx's concerns regarding the world have nothing to do with truth. In an instance of his explicit reaction to Kierkegaard's philosophy – and particularly of the concept of truth as subjectivity – the truth of God, for Binx, is a futile interrogation: 'The proofs of God's existence may have been true for all I know, but it didn't make the slightest difference. If God himself had appeared to me, it would have changed nothing.'[25] In this paradigm, truth is not the search. It changes nothing for the reasons that Kierkegaard outlines, namely that any such objective 'proofs' would negate the subjective value of God, who, as Kierkegaard puts it, 'exists only for subjectivity in inwardness'.[26]

This is partly why Binx recurrently contrasts such mysterious affects in the outer world, to which he devotes his life, to the reductive vacuity of scientistic objectivity. It is moreover part of Percy's refusal to accept pragmatic explanations of emotional states, dependent on material circumstances. As he puts it: 'We should be happy when we have achieved our "goals", as they say, and are living well in East Orange, New Jersey. Things should be fine when you come home from work on a Wednesday afternoon, yet they're not fine.'[27] Percy's own opposition to scientific rationalism lies partly in what he perceives as its neglect of subjectivity, and its concentration on the mere interaction 'between things and things'.[28]

This rationalising impulse in post-war society is what Binx repeatedly condemns. His relationship to positivism is complicated however by the fact that, as Michael Kobre has observed, he adopts postures of detached observation which prove, in spite of his railings, 'just how deeply Binx has been affected by the scientific temper of his age'.[29] As both an incarnation of rationalistic epistemologies and a revolt against their hold, Binx's rebellion is all the more poignant for his ambiguous position regarding a culture of classificatory logics. At once dissatisfied with scientific models and inhabiting a realm where objective truth is of no interest to him, Binx posits for himself a new phantasmagoric ontology. 'As a ghost' existing between worlds, he seeks to become receptive to those atmospheres of unclaimed affect with which the world is invested:

> As for hobbies, people with stimulating hobbies suffer from the most noxious of despairs since they are tranquillized in their despair. I muse along as quietly as a ghost. Instead of trying to sleep I try to fathom the mystery of this suburb at dawn. Why do these splendid houses look so defeated at this hour of the day? Other houses, say a 'dobe house in New Mexico or an old frame house in Feliciana, look much the same day or night. But these new houses look haunted. Even the churches out here look haunted. What spirit takes possession of them?[30]

The strong personification is again what produces this 'mystery'. In a reversal of the expected paradigm, where houses may be haunted by events in their past, these new houses are rendered apparitional by their absence of rootedness in the world. They are 'defeated' in that they, like Binx, no longer inhabit time. In contrast, the houses of New Mexico or Feliciana, though existing within history, are trapped in the cycle of sameness which Binx sees everywhere among human subjects who endlessly repeat their limited lives.

In spite of his best efforts, 'I try to fathom the mystery' is the extent of Binx's engagement. Such is the impenetrability of these affects – whether the mysterious defeat of suburban houses or the enduring of empty cinema seats – that he cannot progress very far into the heart of such feeling's enigma. There is no moment of revelation. Indeed, these passages crucially end in an interrogative rhetoric of repeated questions. Not only will such questions not receive a response, but this quality is woven into the fabric of their being. The enduring of cinema seats and the haunting of new houses are affects which are not only unnamed but necessarily unnameable, for the reason that any linguistic imposition would destroy their specific ontology. They are inhabited by spectral presences, affects which are themselves ghost-like because of their existing between a semantic and a non-semantic realm.

This does not mean that the text itself cannot insinuate such unnameability, cannot shift around it, itself like a speaking ghost moving delicately through this material which cannot be subjected to the materialism of prior realist and naturalist theories. And revealingly, there is no formal disruption in Percy's narrative: no knowing metatextuality, no solipsistic self-reference, no diegetic breaks. In spite of this glaze of normality, Binx Bolling's narration – like the surface banality of his job, his projects, his leisure activities – only enhances the mysteriousness of affects being not described, but silently pointed towards in a mime of metaphysical surprise. For Binx, these unknown forces penetrate the world, beaming out in rays from charged places in what he comes to call 'spirit-presence':

> Me, it is my fortune and misfortune to know how the spirit-presence of a strange place can enrich a man or rob a man but never leave him alone, how, if a man travels lightly to a hundred strange cities and cares nothing for the risk he takes, he may find himself No one and Nowhere. Great day in the morning. What will it mean to go moseying down Michigan Avenue in the neighbourhood of five million strangers, each shooting out his own personal ray?[31]

The risk of being in the presence of such unnameable affects is to lose one's own name: one's sense of a privileged, clear subjectivity, along with one's spatiotemporal rootedness, due to the realisation of the multifarious energies traversing the world.

This interpretation of such presences goes against the grain of critics who see Binx's existence as fundamentally lacking in intensity, in a qualitative and quantitative sense: as being structured precisely in order to minimise the disturbance of deep emotional impacts. Brian A. Smith, for instance, poses that Binx's 'quest focuses not on any sense of wonder at the mysteries of his world, but rather evolves around fleeting moments of novelty, excitement, and consumption'.[32] While this may appear to be the case in a life made of intentional banalities, the new modes of affective investment that Binx identifies are not necessarily less intense, but merely less readily assimilable with regard to established affective norms.

Has the strangeness of these presences prevented readers from postulating that the mystery of empty cinema seats may in fact be both emotionally valuable and metaphysically complex? To remain ambivalent, swathed in quotidian pains and cares, is the usual solution, Binx intimates, to the problems of dynamic affect traversing the world. This is why he is always desperate to avoid those moments of emotional conformity that he refers to as 'the malaise'. 'Everydayness is the enemy' for the reason that within everydayness, 'no search is possible'.[33] In moments when such malaise does occur, it descends with the terror of the restricted affect of amiability and politeness:

> We sat frozen in a gelid amiability. Our cheeks ached from smiling. Either would have died for the other. In despair I put my hand under her dress, but even such a homely little gesture as that was received with the same fearful politeness. I longed to stop the car and bang my head against the curb. We were free, moreover, to do that or anything else, but instead on we rushed, a little vortex of despair moving through the world like the still eye of a hurricane.[34]

Here, the artifice of aching smiles does not cover a hypothetically true emotional state beneath: it is rather a social construction woven with the 'fearful politeness' of conservative gentility. Kate, Binx's unstable adoptive cousin who will later become his wife, is similarly tortured by such ordinariness, describing 'the abyss that yawned at their feet even on the most ordinary occasions – especially on the most ordinary occasions'.[35] What is needed is a return, not to a more true emotion, but to the more mysterious (because unknowable) affects which remain divorced from the banality of 'ordinary life'. Any action, from sex to violence, is desperately sought in order to tear the subject from the terror of superficiality, into the richer artifices of affective force. Such energies are at least partly constructed, for Binx's rejection of objectivity – like Kierkegaard's and Percy's own – precludes affects' belonging to a natural or independent ontological realm.

A logic is thus instigated whereby increased knowledge – in the specific sense of the known familiarity of everyday modes of feeling – comes to equal an abolishment of the distance required for affective mystery. The uprootedness of unknowable landscapes, places, objects, is far more preferable than the deadness of the known. For Binx, the power of subjective experience – including the experience of the world itself as subject – replaces the quest for an illusory truth. In such a paradigm, brief moments become laden with untold sense:

> As the train rocks along on its unique voyage through space-time, thousands of tiny thing-events bombard us like cosmic particles. Lying in a ditch outside is a scrap of newspaper with the date May 3, 1954. My Geiger counter clicks away like a teletype. But no one else seems to notice. Everyone is buried in his magazine.[36]

Literally embodying an instrument of scientific apprehension, Binx's attention is riveted on an object which would, in normal conditions, not be considered a worthy focus of epistemic analysis. What captivates him then in this vision? Firstly, dates may appear to be the most precise, fact-based indication imaginable. What they refer to, however, is a fiction, insofar as neither 'May' nor '1954' can be said to objectively exist in the world. Like the newspaper's date, these 'thing-events', in Binx's terms, are not endowed with truth: their mere ontology, their pure being-in-the-world, is what makes them pulse with an energised life.

The newspaper's supreme specificity – which in fact 'means' nothing, refers to nothing 'actual' outside human minds – further increases the object's strange affective hold: one particular day of one particular year, some time ago, is captured in a meeting of invented fictions randomly endowed with sense. Ironically, it is the language of objectifying science, with its technology of 'cosmic particles' and 'teletype', that Binx uses to record this unknowable affect's victory over the very concept of 'facts'. In doing so, he divests such particles of the reductive naming applied to them, in spite of the surrounding apathy of other individuals who remain 'buried in [their] magazine[s]' – pages which, though they are supposed to convey meaning, bear none of the metaphysical weight of an old newspaper fluttering in a ditch.

To be absorbed in easily decoded but spiritually meaningless magazines is to realise the extent of the error of those who value easily identifiable, personal emotions over unidentifiable, impersonal affects. The scope of Binx's project is thus not a mere pleading for the inherent subjectivity of truth, but for the overcoming of the restrictive category of truth altogether in the evaluation of affects and experiences. This places him at direct odds with a surrounding middle-class, conformist culture, which depends on the clear recognition of affective states. This conflict is distilled in Binx's relationship with his aunt. Indeed, Aunt Emily is the embodiment of a genteel Southern lineage: the incarnation of familial heritage and the type of old-world moral values which Binx continually disappoints. Confronted, late in the novel, with her nephew's uninterpretable behaviour, Emily Cutrer strives to resituate Binx's inappropriate conduct within a recognisable affective frame:

> 'Is it not true that in all of past history people who found themselves in difficult situations behaved in certain familiar ways, well or badly, courageously or cowardly, with distinction or mediocrity, with honor or dishonor. They are recognizable. They display courage, pity, fear, embarrassment, joy, sorrow, and so on. Such anyhow has been the funded experience of the race for two or three thousand years, has it not?'[37]

This quasi-Aristotelian list of discrete emotional categories – 'pity, fear, embarrassment, joy, sorrow' – are linked to socially recognisable valuations, as though there were a perfect formal correspondence between specific feelings and principled modes of comportment. Affects, being unrecognisable, are not only beyond Aunt Emily's moral code, but present transgressive danger, as they suggest that this equivalence between morality and emotionality may not always hold true. They thus make emerge what to her is the terrifying spectre of a disordered world, deprived of an immanent ethical sense:

> 'Your discovery, as best as I can determine, is that there is an alternative which no one has hit upon. It is that one finding oneself in one of life's critical situations need not after all respond in one of the traditional ways. No. One may simply default. Pass. Do as one pleases, shrug, turn on one's heel and leave. Exit. Why after all need one act humanly? Like all great discoveries, it is breathtakingly simple.'[38]

What appears absurd to his aunt, in her evident irony, is the supreme subjectivity of Binx's position: the fact that what he searches for, like the affective experiences in which he engages, have no social connectivity or shared historical depth. They are not based on lineages of prior human attitudes which define the notion of what it is to act 'humanly'. On the contrary, in an overturning of established axiologies, they value the atmosphere of old cinema seats or a dirty scrap of newspaper over and above the noble emotional comportment ratified by one's ancestors.

Binx's response to this accusation is telling: 'I try as best I can to appear as she would have me, as being, if not right, then wrong in a recognizable, a right form of wrongness. But I can think of nothing to say.'[39] Giving up on the possibility of ever communicating to his aunt his new, strange scale of values, Binx settles on the possibility of presenting her with a type of strangeness that would at least be 'recognizable' within her ordered categories of moralised beliefs.

Emotional truth matters to Aunt Emily: it is what guarantees the order of her moral universe, for it is what allows for the recognisability of emotional states and their insertion into a historical lineage of communal values equated with truths. Without true or natural emotions – in other words, faced only with Binx's unformed, preternatural affects – there is for her no stable basis for behaviour. This is the motive for her condemnation of what she sees as post-war American culture's valuing of a sentimental sincerity:

> 'We're sentimental people and we horrify easily. True, our moral fiber is rotten . . . But we are kinder than ever. No prostitute ever responded with

a quicker spasm of sentiment when our hearts are touched. Nor is there anything new about thievery, lewdness, lying, adultery. What is new is that in our time liars and thieves and whores and adulterers wish also to be congratulated and are congratulated by the great public, if their confession is sufficiently psychological or strikes a sufficiently heartfelt and authentic note of sincerity.'[40]

Subjective feeling has replaced for her the emotional truth of established 'class', which is now nostalgically seen to belong to a lost and idealised era. This argument is moreover opposed to critics who see in Emily Cutrer's position a retreat from emotionality into the safer world of dispassionate moral principle. Bertram Wyatt-Brown affirms for instance: 'Like so many others in *The Moviegoer*, [Emily] seeks the means to escape authentic feeling', incarnating a 'disembodied barren intellectuality, by which [she] maintains a constricted equipoise'.[41] Such a reading, via the recourse to a postulated 'authentic feeling', risks imposing a reason-emotion dualism, whereby moralising discourse would be somehow free of emotional value. Aunt Emily's principles are indeed defined by a conservative rigidity; but rather than emotionless incarnations of a 'barren intellectuality', they are for her invested with great emotional charge.

Binx is another case altogether. He is not a character questing after a lost moral foundation, but is rather in search of a depersonalised presence lying beyond the human, mediated criterion of emotional truth. It is thus crucial that Binx's only response to Emily's desire to contain him within recognisable feelings is not an outflowing of sincerity, but silence.[42] In such inarticulateness lies one mode of affect's paradoxical revelation, by way of a negative theology: an ability to say only in what the purpose of life does *not* consist, what empty movie seats cannot express, or express only incompletely. Art or culture do not cease to have value for Binx; rather, they are accorded no superiority merely because they are a 'known' form of intensity, in comparison to the mysterious 'thing-events' which, for all their uprootedness, may provide one with just as strong a sense of one's existence in the world. We see that the emergence of such affects is an interruption not only of the metaphysical mundaneness of existence, but also of its social order.

This latter category, concentrating on the tangible aspects of daily life, is ironically what realist fiction has been seen to highlight since its nineteenth-century theorisations.

In his ongoing struggle against a reductive positivism, Percy revealingly identified a devotion to the non-rational among his realist contemporaries: 'I write about these things, Cheever writes about them, Updike writes about them, Bellow writes about them. But are we saying that we're going to leave it to the novelists, that nobody but novelists or maybe theologians can write about these things?'[43] *The Moviegoer* thus turns the eye of realism to those darkened areas of affective experience about which other modes of expression may have very little to say. But in speaking around this darkness, such efforts illuminate it, revealing that which lies beyond 'a set of meanings held in common'.[44] These meanings are, ultimately, not beyond the scope of realist narrative, which is able to say the unsayable only through a conscious demonstration of its own limits.

## Why the Self Is Not its Feelings: Saul Bellow's 'Emotion of Truth'

Like Binx Bolling, Saul Bellow's heroes engage in recurrent rebellions against both social and affective conformities, and in doing so map out zones of hidden affect which escape the full awareness of highly reflexive narrators. At the root of this concern for unspeakable affect is the conviction, shared by almost all of Bellow's protagonists, that they move and exist in a climate of repression which tends to limit an expansive individualism and to command emotional acquiescence. From the opening pages of Bellow's first novel of 1944, *Dangling Man* – whose publication near the war's end heralded the changing winds to come – a credo of emotional expressivity is laid out, conceived as a revolt against structures of American affective conformity:

> Today, the code of the athlete, of the tough boy – an American inheritance, I believe, from the English gentleman – that curious mixture of striving, asceticism, and rigour, the origins of which some trace back to Alexander the Great – is stronger than ever. Do you have feelings?

There are correct and incorrect ways of indicating them. Do you have an inner life? It is nobody's business but your own. Do you have emotions? Strangle them. To a degree, everyone obeys this code. And it does admit of a limited kind of candour, a close-mouthed straightforwardness. But on the truest candour, it has an inhibitory effect.[45]

The novel's narrator Joseph traces these 'correct and incorrect' modes of feeling to historical causes: Protestant reserve, English class structure and a mythologised masculine warrior ethos. As the first in a long line of Bellow's protagonists bent on expansive justification of their lives, Joseph seeks in expressivity a rebellion against truth: 'If you have difficulties, grapple with them silently, goes one of their commandments. To hell with that! I intend to talk about mine, and if I had as many mouths as Siva has arms and kept them going all the time, I still could not do myself justice.'[46] In its accumulative vigour, language must express all aspects of the self regardless of their divergence from a limited affective 'code', enforced by what Moses E. Herzog will later call 'Reality Instructors': 'Reality instructors. They want to teach you – to punish you with – the lessons of the Real.'[47] The Real and Reality are here capitalised criteria of exclusion, which confine the self within a limited existential environment, curtailed by the imposition of a dogmatically restrictive truth.

How to understand this problem of the oppressive nature of the Real when Bellow's fiction, according to a common critical trope, stages modern quests for subjective authenticity? These quests, I argue, must be understood not as a search for a singular truth, but for the self's capacity to embrace its own variety, including its most artificial aspects. Within this epistemological aim lies a need to encompass feeling's panoply, in a cumulative logic not dissimilar to Bellow's expansive prose. 'For Bellow', James Clements affirms, 'the goal is to attain a level of perception in which meaning is found within the world, rather than imposed upon it.'[48] The rejection of a reductive, and thus deceptive, authenticity is part of this project; it is similar to Joseph's distinction between 'a close-mouthed straightforwardness' and 'the truest candour', with the latter embracing those paradoxes of mental life so integral to Bellovian characters' sense of opposing inner intensities.

We may be cautious then of Bellow's reputation as a novelist embarked on ecstatic quests for authenticity of experience and the self. Lionel Trilling in many ways consecrates a tradition of reading Bellow as a valiant opponent to modern scepticism regarding the authentic. Indeed, Trilling sees in Bellow's fiction an effort, against cynical nihilisms, 'to assert the value of the achieved and successful life'.[49] In another representative position, Frank D. McConnell underlines a prevailing post-war view that Bellow above all struggles against 'the besetting disease of contemporary man: his conviction of *inauthenticity* – his sense that he has no real self, no real identity, no real creative life'.[50]

In contrast to such visions is opposed an alternative reading of Bellow's fiction as rhetorically shifty, subjectively solipsistic, with its declarative tonalities often a deceptive ruse. Criticising 'the consensus reading' of *The Adventures of Augie March* (1953) as a triumphant discovery of the authentic self, Michael K. Glenday insists for example on the wide 'discrepancy between the rhetoric and the reality of Augie's existence', and affirms that, in the wake of a waywardness among false idols, 'the reader who goes in search of [Augie's] rehabilitation will be disappointed'.[51] In proposing this reading, we are faced with an evaluation of Augie in binary terms. Operating with reference to an implicit true-false dichotomy, Glenday proposes that Augie's 'voice can now be recognised as belonging to a guileful and self-estranged rather than naive protagonist'.[52]

The problem with such controversies is that they articulate an either/or dilemma, whereby Augie's emotional experience must be judged either true or false, authentic or inauthentic, ultimately successful or failed. 'No wonder then that readers have found Augie lacking in personality and depth of being,'[53] Glenday concludes; again, a verdict of emotional truth soon becomes an appraisal of underlying moral qualities, in a wholly dualist dynamic. Such polarity moreover extends into *ad hominem* critiques of Bellow's own authorial integrity: 'Emotional honesty', declares Brooke Allen, 'is not Bellow's strong suit.'[54]

Such a debate seeks to situate Bellow with regard to an implicit binary of true and false feeling, real and fake existence, authentic and inauthentic selfhood, associating his fiction – and even his life – with one or the other pole. Bellow never ceases, however, to couch his concerns for valuable experience in an awareness that authenticity and artifice are not opposed. Indeed, the quest for authenticity is everywhere accompanied by the omnipresent recognition of the constructed nature of both the self and its world. This accompanies the rejection, via layers of narrative irony, of naturalising foundations to either emotions or experience. 'We live among ideas much more than we live in nature,' Bellow affirms. 'There are more artifacts than natural objects about us.'[55] This statement is not, as it may appear, a despondent observation regarding the inauthenticity of modern American life, but a recognition of the inevitably synthetic nature of those structures which encompass the self. Such artifice is an integral part of Bellow's vision: 'People's lives are already filled with mental design of one sort or another. If you don't have it yourself, your environment has it. If your environment hasn't got it, your government has it.'[56]

The identification of such imposed binaries is not the same as the recognition that there exist structures of vigorous polarity in Bellow's work. Such polarities, as Ellen Pfifer argues, even constitute a critical consensus.[57] This in turn has ramifications for all interpretive methodologies, for it implies that 'any passage selected out of context may reflect, at best, only one pole of the antithesis buried in the structure of the work'.[58] Such is the inclusiveness of Bellow's wide-ranging epistemologies that there is always a risk of finding specific illustrations for any argument within a vast gallery of Bellovian masks. Counter to this, the movement between polarities – which holds true across the expansiveness of Bellow's corpus – works always against rigid binaries, including that of a supposedly true or false feeling. In arguing for such an inclusive approach to affective evaluations, which does not argue for a generalised tendency of either emotional truth or dissimulation, we may even hope to mirror the inclusivity of Bellow's own narrative processes.

Though Bellow's fiction frequently presents the transcendence of spiritual experience – at the close of *Herzog* (1964) or *The Dean's December* (1982) – as an escape from such oscillations, it does not promise a resolution to the questions of necessarily divided minds, surrounded by constructed environments. There is no utopian possibility of breaking out of such fabricated strictures into the purity of the true or natural life; nor is there, on the contrary, the nihilistic promise of unchecked inauthenticity as an amoral dream of anarchic liberty. Instead, irritation is expressed with regard to those who raise authenticity to the status of utopian ideal. Herzog rails for instance against the 'forlorn' obsession with inauthenticity which he sees as characteristic of a narcissistic modernist generation:

> But we mustn't forget how quickly the visions of genius become the canned goods of the intellectuals. The canned sauerkraut of Spengler's 'Prussian Socialism', the commonplaces of the Wasteland outlook, the cheap mental stimulants of Alienation, the cant and rant of pipsqueaks about Inauthenticity and Forlornness. I can't accept this foolish dreariness. We are talking about the whole life of mankind.[59]

In an affirmation where T. S. Eliot's obsessions with false feeling are explicitly decried, inauthenticity is presented as a clichéd complaint against the ills of modern life, and authenticity a ready-made concept, pre-packaged for consumption. Herzog sees such lamentation as profoundly reductive of the 'whole life of mankind', for the reason that it is at heart a criterion of exclusion: it categorises certain aspects of life into true and untrue, making of this ontological concern a neurasthenic 'mental stimulant'.

Such a rejection of nostalgic jeremiads for a lost emotional truth does not, however, make the locating of authentic affective experience any easier. On the contrary, we are recurrently faced in Bellow with the impossible effort to locate an interiorised true feeling, as in Herzog's presence at the trial of a mother who has killed her own child, when he discovers that he is unable to participate in consecrated models of empathetic engagement:

> With all his might – mind and heart – he tried to obtain something for the murdered child. But what? How? He pressed himself with intensity, but 'all his might' could get nothing for the buried boy. Herzog experienced nothing but his own *human feelings*, in which he found nothing of use. What if he felt moved to cry? Or to pray? He pressed hand to hand. And what did he feel? Why he felt himself – his own trembling hands, and eyes that stung.[60]

In a utilitarian rhetoric, the search for mirrored feeling is framed as an effort 'to obtain something', instigating a mercantile symbolism whereby finding 'nothing of use' leads to the inevitable question: use for what? In order to enact change, by way of emotive commitment, in an unjust world? Or, as is more convincing here, to reassure the feeling observer that through his own suffering he has fulfilled an implied affective contract? Dominant conceptions of true feeling often produce just this model of empathy, in which subjects feel internalised pressure to participate in shared epiphanies of emotional union. Rather than insisting on the potential alterity of such encounters – that forms of suffering may not coincide, and that this is not to be condemned – Herzog is here at the mercy of a vision of empathy as emotional coherence.

For the problem is not that Herzog does not feel at all, but rather that his attempts to force feelings of compassion give rise only to an impression of solipsistic humanity. In experiencing 'nothing but his own *human feelings*' – whose emphasis insists on their generic inadequacy – Herzog is reduced to an interiorised awareness of his own 'unfeeling' body, isolated from possible action in the world. And indeed, the insistence on 'mind and heart', which is supposed to allow Herzog access to empathy, is likely to render it impossible, consecrating as it does a heritage of Cartesian dualism. As the passage progresses, the verb 'to feel' comes to refer no longer to interiorised emotions but to sensual perceptions within the body, with Herzog feeling 'his own trembling hands' rather than the empathetic suffering he desires. Were we to move beyond paradigms of required true feeling, Herzog's conclusion regarding his body's self-reflexive reactions may be very different. Rather than an impression of failure and division from the world, the ultimate question and response – 'And what did he feel? Why he felt himself' – could perhaps be recognised as a positive coming to awareness of feelings' embodied construction.

This critique of the domineering pressures of true feeling also takes complex form in Herzog's distinction between two contrasting poles of emotional oppression, namely what he calls, in highly Bellovian rhetoric, 'Reality Instructors' and 'potato love':

> Potato love is a weak emotion that people often have of friendliness and a melting heart toward other people, the real source of which is terror. It's a low-grade emotion, like potato sap. Reality Instructors are people who think they know the score. You don't. They're going to teach you.[61]

At either end of this spectrum – whether melting sentimentality or blind didacticism – is situated an absolute of emotional truth: either a maudlin conviction of heartfelt sympathy or a sententious claim to unique knowledge. Both constitute convictions of true feeling, and both are equally rejected. For crucially, and in contrast to the depressed modernist bemoaning of inauthenticity which he condemns, Herzog is not satisfied with the mere statement of this emotional problem: as though, in rejecting such 'potato love', he would have helped anchor the modern subject in a static authenticity of affect, thereby solving the problems of the self. On the contrary, this realisation is a prototypical stage in a far more important movement, that of the questioning of the very concept of true feeling itself. As we read regarding Herzog:

> Having discovered that everyone must be indulgent with bungling child-men, pure hearts in the burlap of innocence, and willingly accepting the necessary quota of consequent lies, he had set himself up with his emotional goodies – truth, friendship, devotion to children (the regular American worship of kids), and potato love. So much we know now. But this – even this – is not the whole story, either. It only begins to approach the start of true consciousness. The necessary premise is that a man is somehow more than his 'characteristics', all the emotions, strivings, tastes, and constructions which it pleases him to call 'My Life'. We have ground to hope that a Life is something more than such a cloud of particles, mere facticity.[62]

Herzog cannot stop at the recognition of a 'necessary quota of consequent lies' and establish from that point a restricted gamut of reductive 'emotional goodies': feelings which, at least, one can rely on, if on nothing else. Like Aunt Emily's categories in *The Moviegoer*, Herzog's 'goodies' are recognisable, socially valued emotional objects. 'Truth, friendship, devotion to children' are the catchwords of social feelings emptied of subjective engagements, but obeyed mechanistically as tropes of higher cultural ideals. The entire passage is less a condemnation of emotional falsity than a rebellion against the presumption that, if only we were able to distinguish between true and false feeling, we would ultimately know ourselves. It points to an inevitable limitation if we begin to presume that our lives are reducible to our emotions, whether these are deemed to be authentic or not.[63]

Far from defining inner being, emotions are here associated with other extraneous 'characteristics' that make up mere 'facticity'. The feelings of the self are no more that self than the date of its birth, its socialised life-goals, its likes or dislikes – all such 'emotions, strivings, tastes, and constructions' being confused, however, for a reductive essence (the capitalised 'My Life'). Crucially, not only does this quiddity remain undefinable, but Herzog's reflection ends with a negative theology similar to Binx Bolling's, whereby the incomprehensible is the only space of freedom in the face of a comprehensibility that ceaselessly limits and constricts.

As in the Austrian modernist writer Robert Musil's *The Man without Qualities* (1930–32), Bellow frames a quest for subjective definition that would move beyond finite 'qualities' or 'facts'. In this sense, authenticity is not a static anchoring in stable principles but an accretive process of expanding interrogation. Characters are engaged in action and find their sense in action. They are not invested with stable moral 'natures' which underpin and direct their conduct, but come to a sense of dynamic authenticity only through their embracing of difficult alterities. This process is necessarily performative: their actions are not oriented around a hypothetical true feeling, but are motivated by an inverse epistemology wherein 'only the incomprehensible gives any light'.[64]

Rather than emotional truth as the magnetic north which individuals strive to reach, Bellow thus posits the existence of a distinct notion, namely an 'emotion of truth'. As we read in *The Adventures of Augie March*:

> 'One of the things I thought is that you and I are the kind of people other people are always trying to fit into their schemes. So suppose we didn't play along, then what? But we don't have the time to go into it now.'

> To these words that she spoke I responded tremendously, I melted toward her. I was grateful for her plain way of naming a truth that had been hanging around me anonymously for many long years. I did fit into people's schemes. It was an emotion of truth that I had, hearing this. Mainly of truth.[65]

Far from a rational ideal, truth becomes here an affective construct. In a reversal of typical schemas of adequation, it is not emotions that are true, but rather truth which is emotional. To postulate an 'emotion of truth' implies that the equation's priorities have been inverted: feelings are not judged as true or false for the reason that the category of truth is itself conceived as being able to affect the individual without controlling his actions from a hierarchical zenith. In contrast to a ratiocentric criterion, such an emotion is opposed to classifications: it is, in itself, not a 'scheme' devised to convince others of the nature of the real. It does not put others 'on trial', for the reason that it is recognised as a subjective reality which comes into existence only when it is temporarily named and assimilated as a transient state.

In proposing such an inversion, the question, as so frequently in Bellow, is how to preserve and value the intensity of subjective reality without cutting oneself off from the world. The concern is expressed in Augie's fears of his feelings being crushed by accumulated information: 'It doesn't give my feelings enough of a chance if I have to store up and become like an encyclopedia.'[66] Metatextually, this concern positions Bellow's narrative against the categorical approach of prior realisms: of Balzac's intricate stock exchange or Zola's mines and marketplace, wherein emotion may appear less a wilful invention than the inevitable end of social process.

For in spite of critical claims that Bellow's anti-heroes remain in search of the always fleeting authentic life, their self-invention is framed as an endless artificial unfolding. Even in Augie's well-known remonstrances against the dearth of 'genuine' experience, the synthetic formation of the self remains an endeavour of sheer survival:

> All this time nothing genuine is allowed to appear and nobody knows what's real. And that's disfigured, degenerate, dark mankind – mere

> humanity. But then with everyone going around so capable and purposeful in his strong handsome case, can you let yourself limp in feeble and poor, some silly creature, laughing and harmless? No, you have to plot in your heart to come out differently. External life being so mighty, the instruments so huge and terrible, the performances so great, the thoughts so great and threatening, you produce a someone who can exist before it. You invent a man who can stand before the terrible appearances.[67]

Rather than the heart as a tropological source of emotional authenticity, Augie affirms that 'you have to plot in your heart' in order to better invent a self able to confront the immensity of the world's external 'performances'. Similarly, to 'invent a man' able to 'stand before the terrible appearances' is an effort to combat artifice with artifice: to contend with the problems of representation not by seeking a mythologically natural version of the self, but by embracing fabrication as a defensive shield. We glimpse the possibility that letting oneself 'limp in feeble and poor' may not be less of a performance than those who present a 'strong handsome case'.

The opposition is thus not a binary between artifice and its lack. On the contrary, 'nothing [is] genuine' because the desire for the genuine is itself part of human guile and creative make-believe. Mark Greif captures this quality in *Augie March*'s narrative construction in his observation that the novel's greatness 'has to do with its ability to take a put-on mood, a forced boisterousness and energy, and run through it for hundreds of pages until it takes root and seems natural'.[68] There is a grandeur and delusion to this project of mass artifice, for though this vision is presented as a ruse – an immense theatrical project in which all individuals are equally embroiled – it is also at the basis of the ceaseless creativity attributed to human ingenuity. Invention is not reserved for artists, but concerns all selves necessarily involved in their own self-creation, fashioning their own affective beings:

> And this is what mere humanity always does. It's made up of these inventors or artists, millions and millions of them, each in his own way trying to recruit other people to play a supporting role and sustain him in his make-believe . . . Then a huge invention, which is the invention maybe of the world itself, and of nature, becomes the actual world – with cities,

factories, public buildings, railroads, armies, dams, prisons, and movies – becomes the actuality. That's the struggle of humanity, to recruit others to your version of what's real. Then even the flowers and the moss on the stones become the moss and the flowers of a version.[69]

It would be a serious misreading to see in this passage a simple lamentation of the lack of a genuine world. We are rather faced with the concern that, at any moment, a mere image may 'impose its claim to being genuine with more force than others'; the true and the real are thus seen as forces of hierarchical dominance, which instigate dynamics of domination by way of ontological claims.[70] To be 'real' here is to be the best at convincing others of the truth of one's invention. The reversal of this passage's coda is profound: divested of substance, the world itself becomes a subjective 'version', behind which there may be no ultimate real. The ambiguous syntax highlights this problem, for in the phrase 'the invention maybe of the world itself', is the world passive subject or active object? Is it the world doing the inventing, the world which is invented, or – simultaneously and mutually – both?

Like the oppressive power of polemics in favour of the 'actual world', proponents of true feeling attempt to lay claim to the implied unicity of the real. One origin of Augie's relentless wanderlust lies in his inability to settle on a stable self, and thus to recruit others to his version of the real. Such artifice – the invention of the self in order to face a necessarily invented real – is seen to be at the origins of the world: 'I certainly looked like an ideal recruit. But the invented things never became real for me no matter how I urged myself to think they were. My real fault was that I couldn't stay with my purest feelings. This was what tore the greatest hole in me.'[71]

Ironically, the impossibility for Augie to locate or stick to his 'purest feelings' follows his affirmations on the invented nature of identity. Logically, such purest feelings, 'uncontaminated' by processes of internalised representation, cannot exist if all subjectivity is a ceaseless self-invention. We realise the illusory nature of this quest for purity: torn between his desire to remain true to inner feelings and his recognition that everything in the world – including the self – is invented, Augie has set for himself an impossible task.

His explanation of this antinomy is moreover typical of the tortuous paradoxes of his psyche and of the internal artifices of Bellow's anti-heroes more generally:

> As for me personally, not much better than some of the worst, my invention and special thing, was simplicity. I wanted simplicity and denied complexity, and in this I was guileful and suppressed many patents in my secret heart, and was as devising as anybody else. Or why would I long for simplicity?[72]

Simplicity is presented as merely another in a long line of 'guileful' inventions of the self masquerading as a disinterested need. Augie's convincing logic is that the desire for simplicity would not be necessary if one truly possessed this quality. Desiring it is another mode of manoeuvre, a further turn in the self's inner artificial labyrinths.

Crucially, as though to support this admitted exclusion from the simple, the genuine and the true, realist modes – as is the case in Bellow – frequently do not name these 'patents' of a 'secret heart'. They are, it seems, unknowable, for all desire for a 'simple' truth will fall into the trap that Augie has outlined, namely that transparency, simplicity, sincerity, will be types: ready-made concepts every bit as artificial as the feigning they nominally attempt to suppress. 'Personality is unsafe in the first place,' Augie goes on to say. 'It's the types that are safe.'[73] The desire for authenticity is recognised as part of the typologies of human desire, and wanting simplicity is again an artificial effort to protect oneself from the anguishes of being.

And this is where the 'emotion of truth' described by Augie previously intervenes. For as so often occurs in Bellow's fiction, in the face of such inner subjective complexity, powerfully revelatory forces cut through the self's representational layers. As we read in the final pages of *The Dean's December*, which seem at first to describe, in the act of star gazing, just such an epiphanic promise:

> The sky was tense with stars, but not so tense as he was, in his breast. Everything overhead was in equilibrium, kept in place by mutual tensions. What was it that *his* tensions kept in place?
> And what he saw with his eyes was not even the real heavens. No, only white marks, bright vibrations, clouds of sky roe, tokens of the real thing,

only as much as could be taken in through the distortions of the atmosphere. Through these distortions you saw objects, forms, partial realities. The rest was to be felt.[74]

We have not entirely transcended fabrication to a plane where there is only the blinding presence of the real. Instead, these forms remain 'partial realities' – but at the point that such ontology stops, where it is not possible to distinguish any longer the limits between sense perceptions and the object being perceived, feeling emerges in a movement towards completion. At the point where sensual apprehension fails, an affective energy takes control: 'the rest was to be felt'. This unnamed affect, which is described only by its effects, is simultaneously a projection towards the outer world and an internalising spiral within the self. It is sufficiently powerful that it transforms the self into the object of a higher regard, by way of passive structures which posit an external agent: 'you were being informed'. The important thing is not a higher true feeling, but that emotion is at the origin of an active advance: 'It wasn't only that you felt, but that you were drawn to feel and to penetrate further.'[75]

If part of Bellow's project would be 'to recover the world that is buried under the debris of false description or non-experience', the challenge is not to transform this newly discovered world into a hegemonic, capitalised Reality, which subjugates others to its singular whim.[76] Rather, the aim is to foster an *élan vital* towards the 'bright vibrations' of an always invented real. Though 'tokens of the real thing', such visions are no less valuable. For at this passage's end there is no fixed point from which other versions of the world may be rejected or judged, but merely a direction: 'the sense in which you were drawn'. To be drawn towards the real via such feeling is the extent of a new deliverance: not the restriction of Augie's unattainable 'purest feeling', but an artificial affect which leads forever on, in an unending construction where what matters is the movement itself.

### Shattering Realism? The Flood of Affect into the Breach

Are realist traditions somehow limited then with regard to their representation of those affective forces which ceaselessly threaten to overflow established boundaries into aformality, disorder and excess? Is a breaking of realist conventions in fact necessary in order to open up new territories of emotional representation? Can realist modes thus speak of affect without rupturing, in the process becoming other than what they are?

The analyses of the fiction of Bellow and Percy appear to run explicitly counter to this limiting reputation of affect's unrepresentability in realist modes. Importantly, this controversy is at the heart of a variety of modern critiques of the American and European realist heritage, intensifying with modernist and postmodernist explorations of refractory forms. A recurrent tenet of such reproofs was that the old forms were inadequate for new ideas. Such forms were meant to create, by extension, new emotional 'content', with formal inventiveness becoming a *sine qua non* of the forging of new affective material.[77] We must perhaps, however, resist the intuitive tendency of associating 'rebellious' forms with rebellious affects, and 'conservative' forms with a limiting of emotional breadth. For the idea that a fractured formality would better account for affective rupture is tantamount to suggesting that form and content must geometrically coincide. Concerning affective forces, the tendency to argue the superiority of certain aesthetic forms over others, in the abstract, is itself a precarious ideal. Effectively negating rhetorical effects of ironic distance, this presumes a causal relationship between content and form, whereby an apparently excessive material, for instance, would require an equally excessive shape.

It is a problem to think of affect as an emotional content somehow limited by the strictures of realist technique. Affect is so dynamic, existing in a state of such incessant flux, that such a model risks neglecting its constant transformations, which prevent it from ever crystallising into a solid object of sustained contemplation. This is not to minimise the importance of anti-realist experiments, with their invention of new and vital forms. It is, however, an effort to dissociate such novel formalities from the creation of necessarily novel affective content.

For the specific traditions of literary realism are not alone in the semantic problem of how to 'speak' of affective force. Indeed, can literature itself speak of affect? Can language? Can we? If affect's ebullience is always, to some extent, unrepresentable, then literary realism presents a crucial intensification of this question. Critiques of realism may in this way fall into a particularly slippery trap: in attacking realist texts for their limitation of a hypothetical emotional content, they risk implying that affect is far more stable and identifiable than it can ever be.

Here lies then a final irony: affect, in its unknowability, is perhaps neither more nor less difficult to incarnate in realist traditions, for the reason that it is precisely not defined by its norms of representation. It escapes, disrupts and undoes these forms, no matter how stable or coherent they may appear. It is not a question of which formal processes, or which stylistic codes, may 'better' represent unknowable affective force. These affects will always, by definition, work against such rules, and it is in part their disruptive power which constitutes their enduring value for literary texts.

CHAPTER 2

# Beyond Natural Feeling: The Body as Artifice

A fundamental misunderstanding persists in much thinking about literary emotion's purportedly natural origins. Aristotle's formulations of mimesis may seem to found a tradition in which aesthetic emotions, being artificial and secondary, would take as their model the primary corporal emotions aroused in material bodies by lived events. This would appear to imply that the value of aesthetic feelings may be determined by the degree of their resemblance with emotions 'truly felt' outside of the diegetic confines of literary works. According to this notion, Nestor's artificial sadness in the *Iliad* would be based on an organic prototype, namely the original sadness of a substantive living body, or at least this body's imagined avatar.

For Aristotle, however, emotions are not the original representable 'objects' of mimesis, to be found in a prior stable 'nature' and subsequently mimetically reproduced; they are on the contrary mimesis's artificial, aestheticised *products*, engendered via catharsis in the predisposed spectators of tragic form.[1] Aristotelian mimesis is to be understood, in its primary sense, as *mimêsis praxeos*: the imitation of an action. What Aristotle claims is not that the artificial emotions of art must be based on the natural emotions of 'real' bodies, but rather that powerful emotions be elicited by suitable aestheticised actions within tragic aetiologies: 'Tragedy is a representation not of persons but of action and life, and happiness and unhappiness consist in action. The point is action, not character.'[2] It is never emotion, as a coherent corporal or character-incarnated 'object', which is imitated, but rather the sequence of actions seen to lead to the climax of a causal chain.

Far from remaining enclosed within a representational model which opposes nature and artifice, aesthetic emotion, at the origins of its Aristotelian formulations, is a mobile product of artificial works. This important distinction is moreover eluded by naturalising traditions which base their quests for affective mimeticism on more simplistic – because more deterministic – conceptions of the relationship between aesthetic feelings and an organic body 'beneath'. It will be of crucial importance in this chapter's analyses of the fiction of John Cheever and Philip Roth, whose work both undermines reductive visions of a stable nature at the root of emotionality or the self, and proposes an alternative model of affect as an often distressing play of competing manufactured masks. Indeed, the novels and stories of both Roth and Cheever recurrently present us with characters who, in the painful throes of an unresolvable dilemma, strive to locate the natural origins of their feelings and identities only to penetrate deeper, with a terrible frustration, into the tortuous labyrinths of the non-natural self. Such a quest moreover reflects a dominant philosophical tradition, for although affect may seem one of the most nebulous aspects of both bodily and aesthetic experience, it is a frequent target, precisely because of its instability, for a range of naturalising approaches. Such methodologies generally attempt to confer to affect's dynamism the constancy of a biological rootedness. In these visions, such an *a priori* body is seen to exist outside of the artificial processes of fiction and semiosis.

## Self-Consciousness and Meta-Representation: Against Arborescence and Homeostasis

What is the risk, however, of postulating a biological source for the emotionality of literary texts? In order to understand these dangers, we must first realise that, in a familiar lexical overlap, the attempt to postulate a natural, prior, corporally incarnated origin for artificial aesthetic feeling is deeply related to efforts to determine the 'reality' of fictional emotions more generally.[3] In perpetuating a binary between a natural corporality with real emotionality on the one hand, and an artificial textuality with fictional emotionality on the other, many naturalising theories develop highly hermetic distinctions between 'real' and 'fictional' affective modes. In the 2014 *Handbook of the Sociology of Emotions*, for instance, the emotional experiences of aesthetics are conceived 'as fictional emotions since, in contrast to "Real" emotions, they are produced by narrative, images and rhetoric devices; they arguably have no further consequences to one's social relationships; and they are excluded from one's experiences in the "real world"'.[4] Emotions felt in the 'real world', we may object, are also created, structured and influenced by narrative, rhetoric and image. They do not occur in a hermetic environment, just as the emotions felt in aesthetic contexts are in no way excluded from the continuity of our real-world apprehension.

Enclosing terms such as 'real' and 'real-world' in quotation marks, as is the case in the example above, is not sufficient to dispel the deleterious ramifications of these binaries. By implication, an impervious ontological enclosure is created around the body as natural origin of real feeling, into which diegesis does not penetrate. In such controversies, we find a range of new incarnations of older true/false emotional binaries, which here adopt the form of an ontological real/unreal, natural/artificial divide. In all these cases, what matters is the directional hierarchy of the hermeneutics, which recurrently moves from 'natural' body to 'artificial' texts. An important conviction of many cognitivist approaches is thus that the emotions expressed in aesthetic works may be understood with reference to systems of cognition previously established within the body to deal with 'real-life' affects. Reuven Tsur for instance argues that 'one major assumption of cognitive poetics is that poetry exploits, for aesthetic purposes, cognitive (including linguistic) processes that were initially evolved for non-aesthetic purposes'.[5] My contention is that such models often posit a deterministic, mechanicist view of pre-existing corporal systems, further deepening a rigid distinction between an aesthetic and a non-aesthetic realm. In an even more absolute version of the binary, Peter Stockwell proposes that 'the object of investigation [of cognitive poetics] is not the artifice of the literary text alone, or the reader alone, but the more natural process of reading when one is engaged with the other . . . Literary texts are artefacts, but "readings" are natural objects.'[6]

But what does it mean to claim that, because they take place in the body 'before' the subsequent operations of literary artifice, processes of reading somehow constitute 'natural objects'? In granting these processes the status of natural precursors to artificial emotions which would only subsequently emerge, these approaches imply a linear logic between corporal and textual emotion, with the former preceding the latter in a teleological arborescence. Moreover, the literary work constitutes here a mere perturbation or interruption of 'normal' cognitive and affective processes. Strongly linked to the concept of nature, pre-established cognitive and affective norms are at the heart of the controversy, in spite of both the practical difficulty of determining such baselines and the ethical risks of their application.

Reuven Tsur summarises the notion of perturbation in the following terms: 'in order to achieve art's end, these normal cognitive processes must be disturbed, deformed, slowed down.'[7] Poetry is an 'altered state of consciousness' because 'the reading of poetry involves the modification (or, sometimes, the deformation) of cognitive processes, and their adaptation for purposes for which they were not originally devised'.[8] In a rhetoric of purity and corruption, literature is conceived as a perturbation of a prior incarnated normality. And, in certain extreme cases, such disruption may even constitute 'organized violence against cognitive processes, to paraphrase the famous slogan of Russian Formalism'.[9]

This explicit reference to Russian Formalism is crucial. Indeed, the conception of literature as a perturbation of 'normal' cognitive and affective processes is a principle whose most famous formulation is the notion of *ostranenie* used by Viktor Shklovsky in his 1917 essay 'Art as Device'. What is ironic in the recuperation of Shklovskian *ostranenie* by cognitivist criticism is that, in Shklovsky as in Jakobson, *ostranenie* is not about disturbing the normal processes of perception in order to improve 'natural' cognition. Rather than breaking the norm, it is about creating in the reader or spectator of an aesthetic object an acute awareness of the artificiality inherent in this artefact. The processes of art are in this way made visible: technique is seen, with the reader of a text becoming conscious of the artificial – that is, constructed but not 'unreal' or 'fake' – character not only of the object being contemplated, but of all perception, aesthetic or otherwise.

Writing at the beginning of the twentieth century, following the impressionist criticism of a Pater or Sainte-Beuve, Shklovsky – like Brik, Tinianov or later Jakobson – attempts to prove that literary criticism may, like other specialities, claim the status of a science, and justify its prominence as an autonomous discipline distinct from literary history and philology.[10] At the dawn of modern literary criticism, the notions of 'norm' and 'nature' thus provided powerful arguments in favour of the autonomy and legitimacy of literary studies itself as a valid branch of the humanities. But in founding such legitimacy on pre-made systems of corporal inherency, naturalising tendencies – in retracing unruly emotions back to their ordered organic 'origins' – were also about controlling divergent and disruptive affective behaviours, and carried distinct overtones of sociopolitical control. Otniel E. Dror retraces the degree to which the disciplining of 'disorderly feelings' was central to nineteenth-century models of mechanised corporality:

> From the 1860s, the modern laboratory and its gentlemanly scientists became fascinated with disruptive emotions and disorderly feelings and attempted to discipline them ... Emotion was quantified, temporized, purified and preserved, and was gradually incorporated into the general schema of the body-as-machine.[11]

The question of the artifice and nature of both feelings and bodily systems was at the heart of these empirical experiments, testing the conviction that 'laboratory-produced emotions were not as authentic as emotions in real-life situations'.[12] In a clinical setting, controlled conditions are meant to guarantee a hypothetical neutrality, even if they remain unable to ensure an affective authenticity. Cerebral activity may be measured over a certain duration in order to determine a neural and chemical state representative of more or less dependable variation. In cognitive models, this stability is modulated by the introduction of perceptive and emotive stimuli in the form of imagistic or sonic catalysts. The literary text is viewed as one such stimulus. In comparing the brain's relative constancy to its stimulated variations, researchers attempt to determine the normal limits of cognition – in other words, the poles or parameters within which cerebral activity is considered part of a balanced homeostasis.[13]

Such an approach, and the vision of the body that it promotes, pose a variety of conceptual problems. Why should we think that the state of the brain 'at rest', without perceptive or affective stimuli, should constitute an emotional or cognitive norm? Even if we were to agree to this, who decides such a norm's qualitative and durational bounds? If a particular mental state seems, temporally and quantifiably, to dominate others conceived as abnormal outliers, why should such discrepancies be attributed more or less value with regard to a prior normality? To conceive of literature as an artificial disruption to such natural harmony is thus perilous. From the empirical observation that emotions emerge from and participate in the chemical and biological processes of the body is postulated that homeostasis may constitute a baseline against which affective experiences may be measured, including in their most self-reflexive states.

If a model based on the notions of norm, nature and equilibrium often efficiently describes the functioning of affect's most basic regulations – the hormonal levels of the endocrine system, for example – these parameters cannot simply be extrapolated to the subjective consciousness of affect in the mind, and within the individual as organic totality. The idea that a subject's conscious relationship to her own emotions would be a mere prolongation of homeostatic mechanisms is at best reductive, at worst a deterministic removal of the liberties of subjective life. Indeed, at this stage of representational complexity, homeostasis is no longer the desired end. It is difficult to imagine the naturalist argument that thought or reasoning seek to maintain a state of biological equilibrium, as they are perceived, in an Enlightenment heritage, as less determined by primary corporal structures. As Amélie O. Rorty observes, though the reliance on emotional determinism abounds, 'physicalists do not . . . claim to be able to identify the propositional content of a person's attitudes solely by reference to physically described brain states'.[14]

The problem is related to the fact that emotions are not merely representations of the body: they are meta-representations of the body, and by extension, of the perceiving subject. If the link between natural and artificial emotions poses a quandary for literary theory, it is in large part because this meta aspect of *biological* feeling, before even arriving at aesthetics, is neglected or at least underplayed. Modern philosophy of mind and neuroscience agree however on one point: to feel is to be conscious that one feels, and to be moved is to be conscious of being moved. Because consciousness and emotion are imbricated in a symbiotic interaction, 'natural' biological emotion rather presents us with a system as reflexive as the composite emotionalities of aesthetic works. In lieu of linear models, 'I feel that I feel' is the meta-consciousness required in any conception of affect, whether biological or literary.

## Naturalising Artificial Emotion, or Artificialising Natural Emotion?

Though cognitivist methodologies are the most recent in a long line of naturalising approaches to emotionality, an alternative tradition opposed to reifying essentialisms has roots which run just as deep. Such anti-naturalist frameworks are informed by currents that extend deep in Western philosophy, reaching back in particular to Gorgias and the Sophists, to Lucretius' *De rerum natura*, and, in modern contexts, to Nietzche's denunciation of the Stoics for the impossibility of living 'according to nature' and to the Heideggerian critique of conceptions of nature as achieved state rather than ongoing process.[15] Since the post-war era, numerous anti-naturalist currents, in various branches of the humanities, have crystallised around an opposition to Nature as a hierarchical principle. They are further informed by contemporary images of corporality as itself a representational conceit. Though pursued by its supposed biological rootedness, emotionality is part of this epistemological shift, of which the most well-known formulation is perhaps that of Maurice Merleau-Ponty:

> It is no more natural and no less conventional to shout in anger or to kiss in love than to call a table a 'table'. Feelings and passional conduct are invented like words. Even those which like paternity seem to be part and parcel of the human make-up are in reality institutions. It is impossible to superimpose on man a lower layer of behavior which one chooses to call 'natural' followed by a manufactured cultural or spiritual world. Everything is both manufactured and natural in man . . .[16]

In recognising emotion's participation in processes of active signification and nomination, such a perspective grants feeling entry to the realm of semiosis. Emotion is all too frequently excluded from this territory by naturalising determinisms, which frame it as a preformed object of organic systems. To think of feelings as 'invented like words' is to bestow upon them the same semiotic plasticity which we confer to language, and to recognise their involvement in questions of authority, for the reason that they too 'are in reality institutions'. Merleau-Ponty's insistence on the 'both/and' quality of emotional experience – 'both manufactured and natural' – is a way of thinking the body in terms which are all too often reserved for the aesthetic, whose 'genius for ambiguity' need not be proved.[17] Indeed, such incertitude may be seen as a *sine qua non* quality of biological existence, which never ceases to highlight the deviations from its own internal 'norms'.

Various other contemporary anti-naturalist approaches have emerged in the wake of such phenomenological critiques. Clément Rosset, for instance, attempts to forge an 'artificialist metaphysics' by arguing the anthropocentric character of nature as a concept: 'It is an anthopocentric referential – that which man is supposed to be able to accomplish, or not – which decides on the metaphysical difference between nature and artifice.'[18] Furthermore, Bruno Latour has sought to underline the detrimental effects of the transcendent status granted to nature with regard to the possibility of political engagement: 'After the death of God and the death of man, nature, too, had to give up the ghost. It was time: we were about to be unable to engage in politics any more at all.'[19] Similarly, commenting on Latour, Pierre Montebello observes that 'Nature is seen in the West as an index of what is true, as the source of unmistakable truth, the basis of all essentialism. By this transcendent position, the concept of nature blocks all political discussion.'[20] It is precisely for this quality that Timothy Morton advocates its exclusion from political thinking related to ecosystems: 'the very idea of "nature" which so many hold dear will have to wither away in an "ecological" state of human society.'[21]

These varied questionings of naturalising attitudes, so present in diverse disciplines of the humanities from philosophy to modern anthropology, are less so concerning the supposed biological rootedness of aesthetic feeling. For the vision of corporality that physicalist models of literary emotion express is often closer to classical Cartesian notions of a 'substantial' body than new paradigms of contemporary biochemistry, confronted with the extreme ambiguity of the definition of 'life' itself. With the limits of life becoming increasingly muddy, the questions 'what is an organism?' or 'what is it to be living?' pose central conceptual problems, for reasons that Georges Canguilhem has explored.[22] 'As a general rule', notes Canguilhem, underlining the difficulties of ever knowing organic life, 'analytically obtained knowledge can influence biological thought only when it is informed by reference to an organic existence grasped in its totality.'[23] Such a totality implies the recognition of the myriad aspects of corporal existence whose natural or artificial quality can never be resolved.

This ambiguity is today exacerbated for the reason that, as Rosset observes, 'molecular biology and biochemistry seem to make thinner by the day the already narrow margin that separates the notions of "living" and "natural" from those of "inert" and "fabricated"'.[24] The body itself thus begins to resemble an artificial structure, though only if we continue to recognise the validity of a natural/artificial binary. Recognising the body's artifice is part of an effort to restitute a degree of self-determination with regard to corporal processes otherwise deemed reductively autonomic. As Elaine Scarry contends: 'the presence of the body in the realm of artifice has as its counterpart the presence of artifice in the body, the recognition that in making the world, man remakes himself.'[25] Such self-determination is part of a wider recognition of the active role that the body plays as an agent, and not merely object, of various projects of internalised semiosis.

We find ourselves then in an ironic situation where an artificialist approach to affect may provide a more appropriate vision not only of aesthetic artefacts, but of the fabricated 'nature' of bodies themselves. It is not a question, as in Baudelairean or Wildean Decadence, of valuing artifice to the detriment of nature, but rather the dichotomy itself between a natural biological affect and an artificial aesthetic affect which begins to be undermined. Where various critics such as Jenefer Robinson have recourse to the notion of 'real-life emotions', this approach instead underlines the incoherence of divisions between real and fictional feeling, arguing that affective fictions constitute an integral quality of the emotional life of organisms, and not just works of art.[26]

'The artificial sign', affirms Merleau-Ponty, 'is not reducible to the natural sign because in man there is no natural sign.'[27] This means that, in an artificialising methodology, the so-called paradox of fiction does not appear as a paradox at all, for the reason that it privileges a biological emotion conceived of as natural and directive, and which maintains a teleological relationship to the 'subsequent' emotions of aesthetic works. While cognitivist procedures often search for the degree or modality of resemblance between aesthetic feeling and corporal processes, an artificialising philosophy considers that such a distinction poses an inherent problem, for it does not sufficiently interrogate the concept of bodily incarnation, neglecting the fictional qualities of emotion's formation (including those which seem the most biologically determined) at the level of the feeling self.

### True Emotion and Natural Emotion? The Circularity of Emotional Truth

Faced with such identifications of 'natural' emotional origins, we may be tempted to echo Nietzsche's refrain: 'Isn't the Stoic a *part* of nature?'[28] In other words, such a postulating of emotions' natural or organic foundations constitutes a perspective of manufactured exteriority, which transforms emotions into 'objects' of analysis, rather than active elements in a reflexive epistemological inquiry. We can thus summarise the controversy by a reversal. If naturalising approaches strive to naturalise the artificial emotion of literature, an artificialising approach attempts to artificialise the feelings of biological life. By artificialising natural emotion is meant: insisting on affect's modes of internal representation, on the consciousness of the self as other, and on the body's meta-consciousness, without which mediated affect cannot emerge. This meta-consciousness is a process which implies thought, language and a permanent semiosis; it may even appear as the condition of this operation, guaranteeing its quotient of rhetoricity.

Of course, it is not 'merely' rhetoricity. It is not about claiming that the body 'does not exist' or is simply 'text', but about redefining our understanding of the construction of affective embodiment in order to recognise its open, modifiable, fabricated status – in brief, its existence as artefact. This approach to literary affect contests neither the body's corporality nor its ontological state. It does not suppose that biological emotion would be – to caricature a post-structuralist heresy – a pure product of language or discourse. As Timothy Morton puts it in his critique of the notion of nature:

> Some will accuse me of being a postmodernist, by which they will mean that I believe that the world is made of text, that there is nothing real. Nothing could be further from the truth. The idea of nature is all too real, and it has an all too real effect upon all too real beliefs and practices, and decisions in the all too real world. True, I claim that there is no such 'thing' as nature, if by nature we mean something that is single, independent, and lasting.[29]

Biology would thus not be a foundation or substratum of literary emotion – as in a linear teleological model moving from 'body' to 'work' – but rather another active element in a vitalising continuum. By rejecting the hierarchisations and restrictive sequences of nature and its norms, can we hope to establish a more egalitarian reciprocity between textuality and corporality? What is at stake is the affirmation that, since our self-reflexive awareness of the body is incontrovertibly a part of affective experience, the body cannot be conceived as the natural root of an ulterior arborescence of artificial emotional productions. Such an approach is based on subjects' reflexive consciousness of inner emotional processes; on the evaluation and judgements they formulate; on the changes they create in their internal affective states; and on their profoundly reciprocal interactions with their own corporal stimuli. The body, and the self which is indissociable from embodied existence, are always already loci of fictional and aesthetic representations, and biological emotions necessarily states of a mediated subjective life.

## 'True lives belonged to others': Unknowable Artifice in Philip Roth

In line with these artificialist critiques, the novels of Philip Roth repeatedly stage acerbic examinations of the purportedly natural qualities of emotional experience. We frequently find in Roth an extreme affective circularity, pushed to a point of epistemological crisis within the infinitely reflexive minds of divided selves. Far from being the most reliable needle of an inner subjective compass, which indicates a unified individuality's infallible orientation, emotion becomes a mode of absolute ambiguity and internal discord which escapes all stable epistemic process. Such uncertainty often arises from the inability of Rothian anti-heroes to determine the natural or artificial character of their own emotional lives.[30]

This is strikingly the case in Roth's 1995 novel *Sabbath's Theater*, where we encounter recurrent scenes of the puppet master Mickey Sabbath's paradoxically self-conscious emotional intensity:

> Obeying the laws of disappointment, disobedient Sabbath began to cry, and not even he could tell whether the crying was an act or the measure of his misery . . . Sabbath (who liked to think that distrusting the sincerity of everyone armed him a little against betrayal by everything): I've even fooled a ghost. But while he thought this – his head a lumpish, sobbing sandbag on the table – he also thought, And yet how I crave to cry!
>
> Crave? Please. No, Sabbath didn't believe a word he said and hadn't for years; the closer he tried to get to describing how he arrived at becoming this failure rather than another, the further he seemed from the truth. True lives belonged to others, or so others believed.[31]

The competing levels of representation of a dialectical affect are manifold in this passage. The notions of obedience and disobedience are key, for what laws is Sabbath 'obeying'? To what laws is he being 'disobedient'? He is acting in apparent accordance with the laws of collective affective behaviour and majority-rule – those which associate 'disappointment' with tears – while at the same time disobeying such precepts, to the extent that he is not able to fully believe in the truth of his own emotional expressions. This epistemological problem is traceable to the impossibility of resorting to an absolute state of 'authentic' grief, since emotions are presented by Sabbath as the simple products of communal accord. He follows in fact the 'laws of disappointment', based on hypothetical agreements as to the visible signs of consensual feeling, inscribed within the social contract. This division between affective freedom and the strictures of society is captured in the ambivalence of the term 'laws', which can simultaneously refer to juridical contexts and to the abstracted 'laws of nature'. In both senses, what is emphasised is a breach between an individual's affective liberty and either the generalised concord of the social body or the transcendent structures of the natural world.

A negative democratisation is in this way outlined, according to which to cry 'the way anyone cries' is at once a liberation (due to its creation of communal feeling) and a confinement (in its deprivation of subjective unicity). Individual emotion demands to be compared to a universalised affect, conceived as a collective concord. In truth, this comparison remains impossible because of its activation of various modes – social, individual, transcendent – of incompatible truth. Sabbath therefore finds himself threatened by a quasi-nihilistic determinism; for the authenticity of his emotions, in the absence of natural groundings, is for him caused solely by shared social practices.

As for true feeling, within the theatricalised space of his own mind, the concept refers Sabbath to a question as crucial as it is impossible to resolve: namely, for whom is he performing? The very fact that he requires, for his spectacle of himself, not only exterior but also interior spectators explains in part the presence throughout the novel of his mother's persistent ghost. We thus understand Sabbath's pride when, pretending to experience emotions even when he is alone, he affirms: 'I've even fooled a ghost.'[32] Like Sabbath's feeling, the 'true' phenomenological quality of this phantom matters little: whether material substance or desired projection, the ghost's enduring spectre provides Sabbath's dramatic expression with an ethereal witness, whose imagined eyes remain riveted to this emotive stage.

In a further circularity, 'others' are also seen to ignore the constructed character of their own emotional lives, whose spontaneity and immediacy they take to be ultimate proofs of truth: 'True lives belonged to others, or so others believed.' This phrase immediately cancels the validity of the affirmative 'true lives', reducing such existences to mere products of personal belief. From an impossible truth of emotionality, Sabbath's epistemological crisis quickly spreads to the impossibility of knowing others: not because they do not tell the truth or manifest false signs, but because they too cannot know their own inner affective realities. For Sabbath, the ensuing crisis of affect is total: 'If there was ever anything to know, now he knew that he never had known it.'[33] This doubt extends not merely outwards, but inwards to a body whose organic manifestations are as artificial to him as the spectral bodies of other beings.

Sabbath contemplates such bodies, including his own, from the outside, and is in this sense always a spectator of the emotional performances of others and himself. He is at once actor and audience of his own affective theatre. Indeed, the theatrical metaphor for emotional processes is here essential. Because of Sabbath's theatricalised mechanisms of inner doubt – his constant oscillation between the poles of 'sincerity' and 'betrayal' – not only is Roth's narrator unable to fully represent such affects to us as readers, but Sabbath is unable to appropriately represent them to himself. In this profound interior conflict, Sabbath occupies an emotional space so ambiguous that any judgement regarding this struggle immediately gives way to a concomitant refusal of its truth.

A negative dialectic of doubt is established – 'The law of living: fluctuation. For every thought a counterthought, for every urge a counterurge' – by virtue of which all efforts to persuade oneself, by means of subtle rhetorical techniques, of the natural quality of a particular emotion remain internal efforts which the subject addresses to another aspect of himself.[34] To 'himself', or rather, to one of his many masks: Sabbath being, just like his first love, the actress Nikki, 'someone to whom the tangible and the immediate are repugnant, to whom only the illusion is fully real'.[35] This antinomical imposture is more explicitly an imposture of the self to itself, which takes place in a theatricalised consciousness unable, rather than unwilling, to distinguish between its various dramatic modes.

Emotional doubt always elicits, as Jane Thrailkill puts it, 'the problem of relativism, the stability and communicability of knowledge'.[36] For Sabbath, a distinct problem is created by the fact that no apparently neutral emotional state is possible: no degree zero from which one may measure or judge one's own feelings outside of their self-influencing loops. A reductive epistemology, which posits that the grief shown here is somehow more reliable (because it derives from the individual's 'interiority') than the external objects of sense perception, is thus excluded. In a mordant satire of such essentialism, Sabbath's desire for an authentic self is referred to in terms of culinary reduction: 'Sabbath was reduced the way a sauce is reduced, boiled down by his burners, the better to concentrate his essence and be *defiantly* himself.'[37] At odds with the romanticism of a supposedly heroic essence, Sabbath is diminished by this process, able to be more easily consumed by others like a mere aliment.

Feeling can no longer be considered separate then from its simultaneous internal reception. It follows that a distinction between artificial external presentation and natural internal representation is inconceivable, not only because all emotion is altered by the perspective of its presentation, but because everything here is reception, including what is occurring within the observing mind. Inside and outside are no longer distinct spaces but porous membranes of representational play. We are not dealing with an initially unified subject, whose emotions would subsequently be diffracted when received by others; instead, we are faced with a diffraction taking place within a pluralistic mind at the moment of such feelings' formation – a mind which maintains constant dialogues with itself regarding affective dynamisms which are themselves in ceaseless motion.

The division between external artifice and inner nature is profoundly questioned by this almost total porosity between the external presentation of emotional states to others and their interior representations to the self. In this condition, we can no longer conceive of a primary grief which, existing as a hermetic essence in an isolated corporeal interiority, would only later be modulated by the surrounding world. For this grief, internally and intrinsically, already resembles a presentation of oneself to another aspect of oneself.

It is moreover significant that almost all of the examples of extreme emotional scepticism in *Sabbath's Theater* concern the depiction of socially codified signs of inner emotional intensity. This is the case in the following scene devoted to the sufferings of Sabbath's student Kathy, who is devastated – following the intervention of a committee against sexual harassment – by the revelation of her and Sabbath's 'relationship':

> All the way down the eighteen hundred feet she wept with her whole body shaking, immersed in pain, as though he were lowering her alive into her grave. 'Oh, it's unbearable. Oh, it hurts. I'm so unhappy. I don't understand why this is happening to me.' She was a big girl whose production of secretions was considerable, and her tears were no exception. He'd never seen tears so large. Someone less of a connoisseur might have taken them for real.[38]

The term 'connoisseur' indicates the absorbed yet sardonically distant attitude that Sabbath adopts with respect to the emotions of others. If he is a connoisseur, it is not only because he practises emotional deception, but because he cultivates impressions of emotional truth in his own performances to himself. In the absence of any contextual signs about the event that gave rise to them, such tears, as famously biological signifiers – an organicity suggested by the medicalised 'secretions' – are rendered semiological. Organic manifestations are in this sense also plastic, modifiable – like the signs of language – according to various productive and receptive intentions.

Any idea of the universality of emotions, considered to be necessarily similar because shared by similar bodies, is jeopardised by Sabbath's conviction that no foundation, corporal or otherwise, can provide a stable substratum to such expressive signs. As emanations gifted with quasi-aesthetic qualities, Sabbath ironically notes that 'He'd never seen tears so large', as though the tears' sheer size could be proof of their natural source. In another instance of circular reasoning, Kathy's tears' excessive aspect is seen to overcompensate for a lack of legitimacy. Here, as throughout the text, such emotional intensity combined with artifice is misogynistically framed as typologically feminine comportment:

> 'Extremely immature behavior,' he said. 'The Sobbing Scene.'
> 'I want to suck you,' she managed to moan through her tears.
> 'The emotionality of young women. Why don't they ever come up with something new?'[39]

'Something new' implies both a hypothetically universal heritage of 'hysterical' feigning and its ahistorical communality. Sabbath places such suffering, framed as 'The Sobbing Scene', in a theatricalised *mise en scène*, which rather than increasing its power is meant to remove its aesthetic plausibility and ontological validity. Far from a suspicion that infects Sabbath alone, the narrator explicitly notes that 'she managed to moan through her tears', framing sexual desire within suffering in an equally ironic voice.

Sabbath's fundamental antinomy is thus not that of Diderot's paradox of the actor.[40] It is not simply a question of Sabbath or Kathy manipulatively showing the outward signs of an emotion that would be neither felt nor experienced in their inner selves. The artificiality of affect is instead much deeper: Sabbath feels 'truly', doubts his own truth of feeling, thereby altering its initial truth. Such artifice is not caused by a hermetic division between interior and exterior: between a dramatised, excessive expression and an inner world of harmonious emotional cohesion. It is instead based on a principle of permeability between emotion's internal and external representations, in a dynamic interpenetration which utterly undermines the spatial model of finite body and distinct world. Although alternately proud of, and disturbed by, his ability to create 'false' external signs, Sabbath remains internally divided, in search of a mythical emotional authenticity as much as a means of artificial control.

Mickey Sabbath was an artist before his arthritis, but he was not an artist like others: he was, crucially, a marionettist: a 'puppet master'. An ironic exemplar of feeling's artifice, the marionette displays a range of expressions which emanate not from within, but from the deft hands of a higher source. Like such puppets, is Sabbath a being deprived of all authority over his outward manifestations of anger, suffering or joy? Is he not the plaything of whoever holds his invisible strings?

Associations between the marionette and artificiality are, as Minsoo Kang explains, historically rooted in Romantic thought, which introduces a dualistic, often insurmountable tension between conceptions of the marionette as, on the one hand, subservient entity, and on the other, a possessed being infused with transfigured *animus*.[41] Both natural in its internalised energy of inner 'life' and unnatural in its constructed artifice, the marionette provides a powerful image of the feeling body as at once controlled and controlling, moved and self-moving, artificial and natural mechanism. Ultimately, it is even able to transcend such binaries into a realm where the distinction between various linear causalities is unclear. Such causal indeterminacy – strings or no strings – characterises not just the body's self-governing forces, but those of the feeling mind. Are we indeed both puppet deprived of emotional sovereignty and puppeteer who rules? Moreover, where does the search for the prime mover, at the supposedly natural origin of affective influence, cease? If, as beings at the beck and call of a higher master, puppets are not responsible for their emotional expression, is it possible that the puppet master has his own higher master, and a higher master still? Depriving himself of a position of mastery and thus moral responsibility, 'The puppet is *you*,' Sabbath says to himself – and perhaps, crucially, to the reader too.[42]

Sabbath's emotional affirmations are appropriately followed by their immediate negations: 'She did not begin to have Sabbath's skill at feigning what looked like genuine feeling . . . or did she?'[43] This mechanism does not merely indicate the self's servitude – like the puppet-self which leaps on strings – to internal processes that it does not control. It also implies that the self may be the constructed origin of its own affective states: that it too can decide to move, instead of being moved. If the decision to experience an emotion, however, can create it within the self, does such feeling have a necessarily artificial origin? With the self as puppet and puppet master, at precisely the same instant, a reductive equation between artifice and agency becomes untenable, and an alternate, non-linear vision of emotional causalities must be broached. Such an absence of clear hierarchies of affective ascendancy means, for example, that it is not only the tears of others which are questioned, but also Sabbath's own:

> He was crying now the way anyone cries who has had it. There was passion in his crying – terror, great sadness, and defeat.
> 
> Or was there? Despite the arthritis that disfigured his fingers, in his heart he was the puppeteer still, a lover and master of guile, artifice, and the unreal – this he hadn't yet torn out of himself. When that went, he would be dead.[44]

As yet another vanishing point in an infinite regression towards an always imaginary nature, Sabbath's feelings control and are controlled, are real and unreal at once. Emotional mastery, which (as in Diderot) overlaps with the question of affective knowledge, is confronted with an insurmountable epistemological barrier. All the while remaining master of the emotional expression of his puppets, Sabbath has no means of reaching a hypothetically inner state of being. We are again confronted with the problem of artifice as a defining quality of Sabbath's subjective coherency. When his artifice dies, he too 'would be dead', for the reason that artifice, in defining him utterly, is also his truth.

Faced with such a tenacious paradox, at recurrent points in the novel 'meaningfulness', as Patrick Hayes remarks, 'lies wholly in the affective intensity of the performance'.[45] In a paradigm whereby the intensity of emotional displays replaces other truth criteria, these acts of affective theatre become assimilated with an aesthetic ambition, potentially transforming depleted struggles for true feeling into a vitally creative show. The problem, however, is that Sabbath does not see himself as an accomplished artist: 'He'd paid the full price for art, only he hadn't made any. He'd suffered all the old-fashioned artistic sufferings . . . and nobody knew or cared. And though nobody knowing or caring was another form of artistic suffering, in his case it had no artistic meaning.'[46] No 'artistic meaning' implies that, although it takes place in a theatricalised emotional space, this stage is deprived of symbolic value: it represents merely a negative oscillation between emotions which appear now natural, now artificial. In turn, appearances which have the potential to be richly aesthetic are not full of possible significations but remain hermetically closed.

In spite of this, Sabbath justifies his perverse emotional manipulation of others by labelling it 'art' and coding himself not as a deviant but as a defiant iconoclast. This aesthetic metaphor is moreover couched in multiple references to a specific literary tradition, which both foregrounds 'authentic' emotional intensity and expresses scepticism as to its ultimate truth. At one point, Sabbath evokes *Lady Chatterley's Lover* ('Lawrence's gamekeeper') as a model of affective excess, and at another point exclaims: 'The robust road! I have a mistress! He felt as overcome and nonsensical as Emma

Bovary out riding with Rodolphe.'[47] To mention Emma Bovary is to simultaneously express a valuing of affective intensity, and to undermine this value because of the infamous origins of such excitement in what Flaubert deems a 'hysterical' female source. Affirmed only to be negated, emotion is undermined in the same breath as it is presented as the only possible access to transcendence.

Such fleeting moments of epiphany are quickly identified by Sabbath as equally theatrical, embodying an immanent performativity seen to characterise his deepest self, even – or especially – in the most intense moments of unmitigated feeling. Near-suicidal after his separation from his partner Roseanna, for instance, Sabbath cannot stop the flow of uninterpretable tears:

> Hospitalized. Until that word was spoken he had believed that all this crying could easily be spurious, and so it was a considerable disappointment to discover that it did not seem within his power to switch it off . . . If he was not coming apart but only simulating, then this was the greatest performance of his life. Even as his teeth chattered, even as he could feel his jowls tremble beneath his ridiculous beard Sabbath thought, So, something new. And more to come. And perhaps less of it to be chalked up to guile than to the fact that the inner reason for his being – whatever the hell that might be, perhaps guile itself – had ceased to exist.[48]

Sabbath is at first disturbed to find that his tears escape his control, a fact interpreted as proof that they may be authentic emotion made manifest. But the equating of uncontrollability and authenticity comes at a cost; for it is not the artificiality of Sabbath's feelings that disappoints him but, at least at the outset, their obviously natural character, which implies their transcendent hold over his will. All the while contemplating – as though from the outside, with the spectator's astonished gaze – the physical signs of his own distress, Sabbath observes his teeth chattering, his jowls trembling: corporal effects which we might think impossible to recreate by artifice's contriving tools. Sabbath's exteriority with regard to his own body, his lack of somatic absorption – coolly observing, 'So, something new' – implies that such signs are also new proofs of his acting's impressive range. Artifice thus touches even those bodily manifestations which may initially seem the most natural because ostensibly uncontrollable. Far from demonstrating emotion's naturalness, Sabbath's reactions are only an additional stratum of durable indecision: 'He was fairly sure that he was half faking the whole collapse.'[49] In this world of unworkable dualisms, 'half faking' is a crucial specification, suspending Sabbath forever above a void of true feeling's unknowable duality.[50]

Given such extreme situations of emotional indeterminacy, can we in fact imagine a projected end to emotional representation: a hypothetical point that would not immediately be endowed with performative intent? When Sabbath appears to leave the stage, he merely enters another receptive context, which can in no case represent a non-performative nature, distanced from theatricalised show. Trapped in a closed melodramatic world, Sabbath's emotions may seem to him to have no higher reason for being. He is confronted however with a central mystery: namely, they persist. 'Look at my emotions now,' Sabbath orders in the novel's final pages. 'I'm fifteen remembering this stuff. Emotions, when they're revved up, don't change, they're the same, fresh and raw. Everything passes? *Nothing* passes. The same emotions are here.'[51] Although involved in unceasing performance, affects remain permanently present and durably unknown. In the absence of emotional meaning, Sabbath goes on feeling – just as, in the absence of a 'meaning of his life', his existence still endures. Trying to explain, then, why he continues to feel though convinced that feeling is without meaning, Sabbath desperately seeks an exterior spectator for his ongoing affective display:

> Now, if what Sabbath felt pushing into him was indeed the tip of a knife milliseconds from impaling his liver, if Sabbath truly had the-desire-not-to-be-alive-any-longer, why did he bring the heel of his big boot so forcefully down on that beloved American's foot? If he no longer gave a shit, why did he give a shit? On the other hand, if this limitless despair was only so much simulation, if he was not so steeped in hopelessness as he pretended to be, whom was he deceiving other than himself?[52]

If Sabbath's own impression that he is feigning creates an abnegation of value, it follows that this position can itself be feigned. In a well-known paradox, nihilism is itself denied, and the impression of constantly pretending is itself no more than an extension of an ineluctable pretence.[53] Challenging his sense of 'limitless despair', Sabbath desires a spectator who can vouch that this emotion has value in his understanding of the world. But in his absolute isolation, for whom does he simulate? This question of exterior observation of Sabbath's emotional spectacle is implied in one of the novel's few metatextual moments, in a moment of direct readerly address: 'So little in life is knowable, Reader – don't be hard on Sabbath if he gets things wrong.'[54] Challenging the reader's pretensions to emotional or moral superiority, Sabbath's lack of knowledge is extrapolated to include our own.

Throughout *Sabbath's Theater*, such indeterminacy between feelings' nature and artifice sheds doubt more broadly on a widespread assumption that emotion is 'culturally conditioned in its expression but not in its biological substrate'.[55] For it may be quite possible to prove that Sabbath's distress is truly 'present' in his brain and body – that it empirically exists – without this observation diminishing to any extent the doubt that Sabbath casts on these feelings' natural character or their immanent truth. A closed hermeneutic circle is established; and in this image of a consciousness torn between self-falsifying propositions, the serpent of a naturally artificial, artificially natural emotion eternally eats its own tail. Such is Sabbath's paradox: artifice alone defines him, in the intimate depths of its being. The 'nature' of his emotional existence *is* its artifice. If Sabbath does not act at *not* being himself, then he is not himself. In this infinite circular logic, it is only when he wears his masks that we glimpse a true expression – even though, when they are momentarily removed, we see beneath them no natural face.

### Against a Rational Origin of Feeling: John Cheever's Geometry of Sentiment

John Cheever's 1966 short story 'The Geometry of Love' presents us with a further case of the impossible quest for affect's natural origins. The story centres on the everyman engineer Charlie Mallory who, faced with the difficulty of understanding emotional conflict, attempts to apply a rational grid of geometric equations to the varied challenges of his affective life. Mallory's project is to produce analytical solutions to emotional situations framed as 'problems' in the mathematical sense. In Cheever's story, the fantasy of a rational schema underlying affective interactions parodies similar aetiological searches, and especially those naturalising visions which aim at identifying feeling's corporal essence. For why should the search for geometrical laws for emotional fluidity be any less reductive than the claim that the body's biology constitutes a stable basis for affective processes? Both geometry and biology, after all, may be conceived as abstract systems that attempt to translate visceral dynamics. We may argue that the body's functions are in fact 'closer' to emotionality, organically and symbolically, than geometry's ideal laws. But the application of a geometric schema indicates the irony of imposing any model of spatialised 'clarification' on to emotional ambiguities, as though such schemas were automatically endowed with greater value because of their positivistic, but deceptive, clarity.

Charlie Mallory's decision to call on geometry to resolve the equivocacy of emotional suffering initially occurs because of what he considers to be the 'incomprehensible' behaviour of his wife Mathilda. It is important to note at the outset that 'The Geometry of Love' is rarely mentioned, let alone analysed, by Cheever's critics, in part due to the story's avowedly misogynistic portrait of feminine affective hypocrisy and 'hysteria'.[56] This judgement is in some ways overly dismissive, however, as this gendered chauvinism is complexified by the story's subsequent parody of masculine-coded recourses to rationality to explain women's supposedly 'irrational' comportment. In a recurrent echo of sexist tropes regarding feminine affective intensity – beset with 'paroxysms', 'panic' and 'sighs' – Mallory's wife Mathilda alternates between socially defined signifiers of intense emotional experience:

> In the afternoon, she went either to a matinee or a foreign movie. She preferred strenuous themes that would leave her emotionally exhausted – or, as she put it to herself, 'emptied'. Coming home on a late train, she would appear peaceful and sad. She often wept while she cooked the supper, and if Mallory asked what her trouble was, she would merely sigh.[57]

Mathilda's behaviour aims at a teleology of revelation: the hope that, with sufficient excitation, one may arrive at a point of emotional epiphany, a blinding light of love's truth. This dream is quasi-religious in nature, marked by the promise of inspiration and divination, followed by cathartic release. Her search for an epiphanic 'emptying' of emotion may be compared to Mallory's complementary choice of the rationalisations of science. For the story's larger project may be read as an attempt to undercut the presumption that a naturalising reason can ever be used to filter and clarify emotions' potent force. It is all the more revealing that, as in Mallory's binary vision of emotional logic – wherein affective 'problems' must be 'calculated' and 'resolved' – emotion is immediately presented as an enigma or conundrum: a 'bitter riddle' which, like the Sphinx for Thebes, would ideally lead to liberation from the terms of a terrible contract. In spite of their possible unreality, such rationalisations, as Mallory puts it, have a range of 'practical advantages':

> He knew that what he thought of as his discovery could be an illusion, but the practical advantages remained his. He felt much better. He felt that he had corrected the distance between his reality and those realities that pounded his spirit. He might not, had he possessed any philosophy or religion, have needed geometry, but the religious observances in his neighborhood seemed to him boring and threadbare, and he had no disposition for philosophy. Geometry served him beautifully for the metaphysics of understood pain.[58]

Without determining, as we may expect from such rationalisations, a definite ontology of the reality or 'illusion' of his technique, such a metaphysics renders up the goal of much religious searching: namely, a transcendent axiology less open to the fluidities of time and changing immanent circumstance. Geometry, as a science applied to the sensible world of practical pursuits – in Mallory's own profession of engineering, for instance – is revealed to be a metaphysical (rather than physical) solution to a metaphysical problem: one based on an ensemble of invisible principles. This is what makes such latent hierarchies tempting for an introvert such as Mallory, enclosed in his own emotional world: they provide an external Platonic ladder of values to which one may anchor affect's perpetual flux. Moreover, far from a mere pragmatic technics, geometry – since at least the Pythagoreans – has been framed as a spiritual art of transcendent scope. Faced with the impossibility of understanding his wife's 'irrational' affective reactions, Mallory appropriately describes his geometric methodology in distinctly metaphysical terms:

> It was not that he had lost his sense of reality but that the reality he observed had lost its fitness and symmetry. How could he apply reason . . . and yet how could he settle for unreason? . . . Dramatic misunderstandings with Mathilda were common, and he usually tackled them willingly, trying to decipher the chain of contingencies that had detonated the scene. This afternoon he was discouraged. The encounter seemed to resist diagnosis. What could he do? Should he consult a psychiatrist, a marriage counselor, a minister?[59]

In this attempt to 'apply reason' to a situation which escapes rational schemas, Mallory does not stop to question whether the categories of reason and unreason are themselves insufficient, and need to be replaced by more ductile concepts. His 'sense of reality' is crucially not lost, rather 'the reality he observed had lost its fitness and symmetry'. These latter terms reveal a desire to establish a formal equilibrium: a stable framework, characterised by adequation, beyond emotional instabilities. For do emotions indeed 'fit' their world? Are they somehow 'symmetrical' with regard to events? The irony of this demand is that feelings are not allowed to be dissonant or disruptive with regard to the real. As forces of cohesion, affects are meant to guarantee here one's subjective attachment to the world and involvement in events. The attempt is therefore to restore 'fitness and symmetry' to those aspects of felt experience which seem most inapt to rationalisation.

Mallory does not doubt reason's power, only the technical difficulty of harnessing and properly 'applying' it. He does not ask whether such criteria should be applied to affects. Rather, his solution is to push the utopian promise of rationality to the extreme. Here, as throughout the story, his inner dialogue reproduces a lexis of ersatz positivism, with terms culled from the fields of physics, medicine or psychiatry, with scattered references to the 'chain of contingencies', 'detonat[ion]', 'decipher[ing]', 'symmetry' or states which 'resist diagnosis'. The similar disciplinary list of 'psychiatrist', 'counselor' and 'minister' constitutes an ensemble of modern professionals each in possession of their own rationalising discourse. The relationship to emotionality which Mallory attempts to instigate is, we realise, a type of code-breaking, wherein the effort to 'decipher' takes pride of place. The code to affective experience, if ever one were possible, would of course be constantly changing, altered with each instant and eternally invented anew. For the greatest risk of any code is not that the code remains elusive, but that there is in fact no code to break.

Both reason and unreason are thus unsuitable solutions to emotional existence for the reason that they apply static chains of values to fluid situations, whose exterior and interior anchorages ceaselessly morph. Appropriately then, there is not in Cheever's story merely one solution to each affective 'riddle'. Mallory's project rather suggests that each emotional state, in its extreme particularity, requires a specific equation, meaning that the 'riddle of love', at each passing moment, will never be the same. This is why Mallory, attempting to mimic such temporal fluidity, must perform his geometric calculations without end. He is not striving after an ur-equation: a super solution which, in transcending all cases, would have the power to dissipate all affective 'problems' by the force of its unifying rationale. What Mallory elaborates are rather specific equations for specific emotions, with their own intimate structure, proper to them alone.

This means that, though his geometry of sentiment is meant to palliate the terrible ambiguities of emotional life, Mallory's process of resolution itself can never end. Indeed, he is required to work long into the night, futilely attempting to solve each day's array of new affective enigmas. For with each subtly new emotional state he must perform his calculations anew. After a disturbing evening at their neighbour's house, for instance, with talk of violence and suicide, Mallory must search for a universal but shifting concordance:

> He got out his slide rule and, working on the relation between the volume of a cone and that of its circumscribed prism, tried to put Mrs. McGowen's drunkenness and the destiny of the Mitchells' kitten into linear terms. Oh, Euclid, be with me now! What did Mallory want? He wanted radiance,

beauty, and order, no less; he wanted to rationalize the image of Mr. Mitchell, hanging by the neck . . . There was a vast number of imponderables in the picture, but he tried to hold his equation to the facts of the evening, and this occupied him until past midnight, when he went to sleep. He slept well.[60]

We see that it is not only emotions that Mallory attempts to rationalise but also the realities of the world, and more specifically the existence of pain. Though he ostensibly pretends to desire a geometry of sentiment, Mallory is necessarily engaged in a geometry of events: why things happen, and what order or chaos, justice or injustice their occurrence might reveal. Given the metaphysical extension of this questioning, the apostrophe 'Oh, Euclid, be with me now!' parodies a call to God, replacing the 'irrational' deity of theologies with Euclid as idol of rational process. Holding Mallory's 'equation to the facts' is a way of suggesting that the distressing event at the origin of this disturbance must not elicit competing reactions, but rather constitute a stable 'fact' on which to ground a fixed vision of a reliable world.

Where no feeling is present, or not the feelings one may expect, events themselves begin for Mallory to lack all reality. If all they produce is indifference, how may we even be sure that they occurred? In the passage above, Mr Mitchell's attempted suicide is presented by Mr McGowen in clinically unfeeling terms: 'her husband has this suicide thing.'[61] Part of what Mallory is unable to reconcile is the extreme intensity which 'should' be provoked by these events, but is replaced by the utter apathy of their social presentation. If the event is considered a logical origin of emotion – which, like the organic body in naturalising visions, is meant to provide a grounding for affective alterations – then one would expect that intense events should give rise to intense reactions, in a comprehensible spectrum of degrees. When this does not occur, the promise of Mallory's geometric model is to translate the world into terms which, because of their congruence, would allow empathy to emerge:

> The principal advantage was that he could regard, once he had put them into linear terms, Mathilda's moods and discontents with ardor and compassion. He was not a victor, but he was wonderfully safe from being

victimized. As he continued with his study and his practice, he discovered that the rudeness of headwaiters, the damp souls of clerks, and the scurrilities of traffic policemen could not touch his tranquility, and that these oppressors, in turn, sensing his strength, were less rude, damp, and scurrilous. He was able to carry the conviction of innocence, with which he woke each morning, well into the day. He thought of writing a book about his discovery: *Euclidean Emotion: The Geometry of Sentiment*.[62]

It is not by chance that Euclid's name here takes pride of place, for the 'genius' of canonical methods becomes a stable anchorage. Such accrued knowledge, not being open to the challenges of alteration, allows for a dogmatic mode of empathetic engagement: a 'conviction of innocence' which transforms all vital conflict into a decidedly suspect 'tranquility'.

In positing a darker irresolution at the heart of apparent emotional calm, this interpretation is somewhat opposed to critical visions which see Mallory arriving 'at soothing, calming solutions'.[63] Rationalisation is an attempt at emotional self-preservation, and as in his effort to 'rationalize the image of Mr. Mitchell', the aim is not to understand the event but to deaden its compelling impact. Though Mallory claims to be concerned with the 'facts' of the world, we soon realise that he is in reality haunted by the emotional impresses which these facts have left in their collision with his being. What Mallory desires is not a fluid affective spectrum, but a range of categorisable emotions able to be associated with finite values – the 'power of remorse, the beauty of shame' – thus providing the dependability of a fixed axiology.[64] For an equation is not formed by 'facts', much less by the curious anomaly represented by Mallory's 'facts of the evening'. In such expressions, various incompatible regimes of truth are combined as though they were comparable, and as though they maintained the same relationship to truth as either abstract concept or moral precept.

Rather than question whether a stable grounding to affect should ever be sought, Mallory merely replaces one badly functioning 'explanation' for feeling (the essentialised self) with another (his 'geometry of sentiment') which he hopes will prove more efficient. At no point does he question the value of such a model of adequation, which applies to affective experience the cut-and-dried 'solutions' of reductive formulas. Instead of a self-critical examination, each of Mallory's questions – 'Was he wrong to look for definitions of good and evil?' – remains rhetorical.[65] They need not be pursued for the reason that this rationalising search allows him to 'sleep well'. Mallory is not reassured because he has indeed 'resolved' an emotional problem (whatever that may mean). Rather, he reaches a place of superficial comfort with such thoughts by the very fact that he is engaged in a reductive analytic process.

The expected failure of Mallory's emotional geometry comes with his recognition that he can locate no source 'out there' in the world which would somehow be more stable than the maelstrom of his own affective life: 'Mallory examined the place – the flowers, the piles of fruit, the traffic in the square outside the window – and he could find in all of this no source for the sorrow and bitterness in her face.'[66] Recognising that there is, after all, 'no source' for his wife's pain is a way of renouncing a transcendent affective aetiology. Giving up the unrealisable prospect of a philosophy of affective causation, Mallory experiences a failure to identify emotional arborescences, which would situate feelings within the linear sequences of a casuistry:

> He worked out his problems with a slide rule on the back of a menu. When he returned to the hotel, she had gone out, but she came in at seven and began to cry as soon as she entered the room. The afternoon's geometry had proved to him that her happiness, as well as his and that of his children, suffered from some capricious, unfathomable, and submarine course of emotion that wound mysteriously through her nature, erupting with turbulence at intervals that had no regularity and no discernible cause. 'I'm sorry, my darling,' he said. 'What is the matter?'[67]

Ironically, rational operation has here 'proved' that at the basis of Mathilda's feelings is a fundamentally irrational force. Geometry proves to Mallory not that emotions can be reduced to the linear logics of a rationalised epistemology, but that many precisely cannot. If the origin of his wife's emotional distress is categorised as 'capricious, unfathomable, and submarine', the implication is that no further rational abstraction would do any good, for they have been classified *de facto* as beyond logic's scope.

It is for this reason that the lexis of essentialism employed throughout this passage is so revealing. For Mallory, such incomprehensible affective currents wind 'mysteriously through [Mathilda's] nature', with this final term indicating the extent to which we are again dealing with a conception of emotion not as a range of dynamic intentions, but as the constituted essence of a natural heart. This essentialist vision gives rise to a logic of surface and depth, wherein emotion 'erupt[s] with turbulence' at the periphery of the self. If one remains convinced of this view of emotional life, then discussion and mutual analysis of feeling is futile, for the reason that such forces are beyond subjective control.

If a regular and discerning science has concluded that, within the feeling body, there is 'no regularity and no discernible cause', then this non-solution can only lead to an impotent question: 'What is the matter?' Sadly, Mathilda can no more answer this than Mallory's abstracted technology. We may wonder if, faced with such failure, in spite of his declared aims, Mallory has ever sought to 'solve' emotional problems at all: 'If he could make a geometric analysis of his problems, mightn't he solve them, or at least create an atmosphere of solution?'[68] This final notion is crucial. The initial hope of a rational solution to emotional difficulties gives way to a lesser aim, namely to create an 'atmosphere' of solution – one which may not represent an objective truth, but may allow the troubled subject to exist within the feeling that truth has been found. This would, of course, be a subjective emotion rather than an objective verity. It may not be repeatable, nor provide others with a basis for the extrapolation of verifiable laws. But it may provide the individual with the reassurance that there perhaps exists an underlying coherency in our emotional encounters with the world.

A concern for emotions' unstable lack of reality is a recurrent obsession throughout Cheever's work. It is present in his journals, notably in his opinions of his own writing, where he is frequently disturbed at the temporal changeability of emotional perspectives:

> I read two stories of mine and find them too breezy. They were deeply felt at the time but there seems to be a lack of deep notes; no bass clef; a lack of fundamentals. Why should some of these lines, drawn from the deepest pain and pleasure I have known, seem to be glossy and so little else?[69]

Cheever's concern is directed at the evacuation of emotional power via temporality. Though his desire for 'deep notes' and 'fundamentals' is not as schematic as Mallory's geometric planes, it nevertheless establishes a hierarchical vision of affect structured according to verticality. What is harrowing for Cheever is not so much the existence of sadness and pain, but the extrapolated fear that this suffering may have no higher significance. 'It is not that these are stories of failure; that is not what is frightening,' Cheever writes of his first novel *The Wapshot Chronicle*.[70] 'It is that they are dull annals; that they are of no import; that Leander, walking in the garden at dusk in the throes of a violent passion, is of no importance to anyone. It does not matter. It does not matter.'[71] This fear of affective nihilism is at heart a metaphysical question: if emotions are not grounded in anything real outside of the self, because they seem utterly open to the modulations of subjective states, then is it possible to believe in such an outer world of objects and events? Do our doubts regarding emotions' ontological viability undermine the existence of an objective real, at least according to the terms of scientific method?

This search for a rational system of transcendent affective laws is the dream that emotionality could be grounded in higher principles, whether of Reason, the natural body or eternal metaphysical monuments such as the Good or the True. Whatever the point of anchorage may be, Cheever both idealises and parodies the fantasy of emotional concord, whereby one is able to navigate inner affective states by the light of a guiding star. All of which leads us to an essential point at the heart of Cheever's epistemological questioning: rather than being a basis of emotion, truth itself is formed of emotion, and indeed the concept itself can have no meaning if considered as a static reference point which somehow precedes affective force. 'The words "truth" and "reality" have no meaning at all', affirms Cheever in a 1976 interview in *The Paris Review*, 'unless they are fixed in a comprehensible frame of reference.'[72] This frame is, in the end, the entire contextual environment which qualifies an experience, and which integrates affective intensities as fundamental tenets of its make-up. Emotionality's disconnection from truth is a disturbing idea for the reason that it implies that feelings may have no inherent correspondence with events. For many of

Cheever's heroes, such scepticism concerning affect is instigated by an initial doubt, which in expanding risks encompassing the entire world in its nihilistic field.

Though it is not my intention to rehabilitate the story's more problematic elements, I would suggest that one reason 'The Geometry of Love' has posed particular problems for Cheever's critics, and for Cheever himself, is because of its highly ambiguous positioning with regard to questions of emotional truth. If the story has been read as improbable, more an allegory than a believable narrative, this is also due to the vision of emotionality that it portrays, as being neither real nor true in the sense of these terms established by a tradition of post-Enlightenment rationalism. That readers may question the story's verisimilitude is especially ironic in that the problem Cheever depicts is precisely that emotions cannot function according to a model of plausible correspondence. Or in Mallory's comically reductive formulation: 'The line formed by these elements, then, made an angle with the line representing his children, and the single fact here was that he loved them. He loved them!'[73] There is no possible geometry of love, no algebra of shame, no anatomy of desire, for the reason that there can be no abstract set of adequations wherein certain states equal others in a calculative logic.

The story may seem a simple illustration of this point if we do not realise that this is the very irony at play: that just as Mallory is unable to rationalise emotionality, both Cheever and his readers are unable to rationalise the rationaliser. 'The Geometry of Love' in this way becomes a strangely reflexive parable, with characters enacting increasingly implausible emotional states. Attempts to exclude the story from Cheever's canon are in this sense revealing, as they point to a discomfort with taking seriously a text which, though its project is to criticise essentialisms, is itself rife with essentialist logics (on affect, gender, sexuality or science). In attempting, by means of the geometric allegory, to criticise the notion that feeling may ever have a stable grounding, Cheever nevertheless fails to provide an alternative model of emotional systems. Appropriately, his characters betray an unusual flatness: they are types, masks or roles, rather than beings gifted with the contradictions of affective flux. Falling into the trap of categorisation which it seeks to critique, the story is itself a *mise en abîme* of the all-encompassing quality of rationalising temptations. These affect characters intra-diegetically, as well as at the level of narrative and form. This does not deprive the text of value, but complexifies the critical distance we may feel with regard to such positivistic projects.

'The Geometry of Love' thus indicates a range of dangers related to the search for emotion's origins within a hypothetical nature, namely that this quest is not only contestable when such reduction fails, but also when it succeeds. Neither the success nor the failure of such an endeavour is more beneficial to its object. In both cases, whether or not a geometry of sentiment 'resolves' an emotion, finding its base 'nature' and root cause, the result is that the quest for affective understanding has definitively ended. To live, on the contrary, in a world of affective half-tones at least has the advantage of engendering an endless self-reflection. But in naturalising projects such as Mallory's, the feeling in question is either resolved or unresolved – it either has, or does not have, a natural source. Once this binary has been established, there is no point continuing one's search. How then is one to relate to such feelings? After their resolution or irresolution, they nevertheless remain: curious affective objects which have been classified as either possessing, or not, a natural truth.

## Imaginary Nature: Towards Frames of Reference for the Real

A linear model which extends from biological emotion to the artifice of the decorporalised text is undermined in these various fictional contexts, in which we remark that the same artificial mechanisms are already at play in experiential situations without any apparent ties to either literature or aesthetics. In other words, the same often undecidable alternation between authenticity and inauthenticity, fiction and reality, nature and artifice, is already present at the stage of affect's biological experience. As Merleau-Ponty argues, 'there is no more [in emotion] than in the realm of instinct a human nature finally and immutably given'.[74] From this perspective, fictionality and semiosis are so characteristic of emotional negotiation in the body, outside of works of art, that their presence in aesthetics is a merely logical extrapolation. It is not a question of knowing how natural emotion 'becomes' fictional, by passing through the artificialising filters of language, but rather of determining the types of affective negotiations between body and text, which attempt to evaluate each other in a mutually formative process.

The rejection of naturalist visions of literary emotion has important consequences for the way we think about feeling in literature more generally. Liberated from the constraints of a reductive scientific or psychological positivism, literary emotionality may be read in the light of new aesthetic, semiotic and rhetorical criteria. The critique of the quest for natural emotion does not, however, amount to isolating literary pathos by separating it from the experience of events. By highlighting the paradoxes of naturalistic models, the fiction of writers such as Roth and Cheever insists that accepting affect's artifice may be the first stage in a new self-formation. Valuing the active fabrication of feeling means deviating from an approach based on a substantive body and a unified subject within, as well as on the anchoring of emotion in so-called 'real experience' or the production of appropriate comportment. It is an effort to wrest literary emotionality from a reductive mimeticism by showing the futility of the quest for an archetypal nature which is itself, necessarily, imaginary.

CHAPTER 3

# Inimitable Affect: On the Mimesis of Emotion

When viewed theoretically, affect appears curiously unsuited to mimetic reproduction. Even if we momentarily dismiss the problem of affect's mutability – meaning that its imitation can only ever be an arbitrary fixation on one of its fluid variations – we are confronted with the question: what indeed is the 'copy' of a feeling? Is it a mirroring of a hypothetical affective essence? Is it a reproduction of physiological causes or somatic effects? If, for the reasons outlined in the preceding chapter, we can no longer consider an *a priori* nature as the locus of stable feelings, to be subsequently and artificially reproduced, then what precisely, in representational contexts, are affect's imitated 'objects'? Are they the visible exterior signs of affective intensities which indicate projected emotions beneath? Are they a range of internal corporal states reproduced by characters and narrators within the diegetic confines of the literary work? Or are their objects in fact actions, in an Aristotelian sense, which by imitation of their powerful causalities may lead to compelling emotional effects?

All of these interrogations will prove crucial in this chapter's exploration of the work of Richard Yates, John Cheever, Kathleen Collins, James Baldwin and Richard Ford. For all of these supposed anchorings of an imitative affect encounter the same problem, namely the supposition that there exists an original emotionality that would serve as a model for subsequent copies. In such an equation – where imitation, as per a long tradition, is associated with the operations of artifice – the effort to locate true feeling becomes a quest to identify an 'uncopied' emotionality: one which would somehow not yet have been subject to a series of debasing reproductions, each one further distanced from an inner antecedent or source. In the context of post-war criticism, and especially in the wake of Barthesian and Foucauldian critiques of a transcendent authorial identity, the quintessential origin of textual emotion can no longer be seen to reside in the substantial body of a governing and regulating author. Even in everyday conceptions, 'imitated' emotionalities, as the product of mimetic procedures considered artificial and prior, are seen to degrade the power and purity of original affective essences. In such frameworks, imitation is coded as social and exterior, while the emotional objects being imitated are subjective and interior, with little recognition that such hypothetical ur-emotions inevitably contain multifarious imitated aspects of both self and world, all of which are integrated into their supposedly primordial quiddity.

In the fiction of Baldwin and Collins, such an impossible search is complicated by the fact that these supposed origins of affect, though universalised and de-racialised by the ambient culture, are most often coded in the terms of a normative White subjectivity, and thus frequently prove inapplicable to the specific interrogations of modern African American identity. Conversely, for Cheever and Yates, characters' inability to locate stable sources for their feelings becomes part of a profound sense of social and emotional isolation, further contributing to their conviction that a once privileged affective authenticity is now waning from the post-war world. Finally, in Richard Ford we encounter various contemporary extrapolations of this dilemma in characters who exist after the failure of such quests, where the struggle to locate feelings' absent origins is no longer even attempted, and has been replaced by a wayward errancy in an increasingly unclear emotional world.

## Truth Haunted by Mimesis: Affect's Absent Original and Infinite Reproductions

This modern predicament is of course part of a long tradition that Derrida calls 'Platonism' in the West, according to which an ontological superiority is intuitively granted to the original over the copy, the imitated (*imité*) over the imitator (*imitant*), instigating a metaphysical binarity wherein

> the being-present (the matrix-form of substance, of reality, of the oppositions between matter and form, essence and exterior, objectivity and subjectivity, etc.) is distinguished from the appearance, the image, the phenomenon, etc., that is, from anything that, presenting it *as* being-present, doubles it, re-presents it, and can therefore replace and de-present it.[1]

In the context of the dominant model of true feeling, 'reproduced' emotions, as *imitants*, would thus be artificially inferior to the natural *imités* of affective corporal quintessences. Plato famously – in the 'twice-removed' status of poetry as mimesis – distrusts both copies without originals and those copies which take other copies as their dependent source.[2] At the same time, the central ambivalence between literature as an unveiling of the real and as a counterfeit 'copy of a copy' is ever-present in the Platonic bivalency regarding mimetic truth. Significant problems with such a heritage arise when subjects begin to feel that the 'unimitated' corporalities they depend on as ontological guarantors are in fact already sites of active reproduction. Joy, anger, grief, as well as their aesthetic incarnations, may then seem less a 'spontaneous overflow of powerful feeling' than mediated copies of the feelings of others and of oneself.[3]

To interpret such processes of affective imitation merely as a degradation of prior emotional originals is to enter into a new aspect of true feeling as hegemonic regime. For whether condemned by Plato as in itself inherently deceptive, or simply for its choice of inappropriate objects, '*mimēsis* is lined up alongside truth: either it hinders the unveiling of the thing itself by substituting a copy or double for what is; or else it works in the service of truth through the double's resemblance (*homoiōsis*)'.[4] Whether in the service of truth or against it, mimesis 'has to follow the process of truth. The presence of the present is its norm, its order, its law. It is in the name of truth, its only reference – *reference* itself – that mimesis is judged, proscribed or prescribed according to a regular alternation.'[5]

In the same way as for efforts to anchor affect in a binary falsity or truth, such alternation turns out to be part of mimesis's performative play. For in case it appears that mimesis adopts a position of docile submission with regard to truth's hierarchical dominance, we must note that the initial 'truth' which mimesis refers to is already a site of representational doubling. Thomas Dutoit's analysis of the fictionality of mimetic truth is here highly applicable:

> Mimetic 'truth' is 'pre-originary' because its 'originality' is that of the *copy*, of representation ... 'Truth' is therefore haunted by mimesis (the irreducibility and pre-originarity of the ghost, of representation). Hence, 'truth' is an actor, a performance of a role and not a stable fixed position outside representation.[6]

Within all mimesis then, there is never a hypothetical 'original' outside of all depiction. It follows that no singular act of mimesis can occur without the promise of its future doubling. There is no unique point, no hermetic space at which mimesis may be seen to end, to stop taking itself as its own future model, thereby containing and expressing both its own original and its eternally projected copies. In the same sense, the cells of the body through which affect dynamically passes are 'originals' and 'copies' of their organic ancestors and progeny, at once incomparable structures of sovereign newness and branching derivatives of existing forms. For like affective intensities, so too does mimesis constantly double itself:

> What announces itself here is an internal division within *mimesis*, a self-duplication of repetition itself; *ad infinitum*, since this movement feeds its own proliferation. Perhaps, then, there is always more than one kind of *mimesis*; and perhaps it is in the strange mirror that reflects but also displaces and distorts *one mimesis* into the other, as though it were itself destined to mime or mask *itself*, that history – the history of literature – is lodged, along with the whole of its interpretation.[7]

In this 'self-duplication of repetition', mimesis, like affect, becomes an unlimited refraction. This model is one of overlapping imitations, which moreover exist in constant transformation, underlining the shifting status of original to copy which holds true for processes of affective repetition that, in the end, are acts of re-creation.

Traversed by incalculable emotional 'copies' having their original objects both outside and inside the self, emotionality begins to resemble an ongoing mimetic negotiation with an endless variety of branchings, rather than the one-time division of an ontological exemplar and replica. It follows that attempts to distinguish between imitated and non-imitated emotion will reflexively implicate the feeling self in its own internal arbitrations, creating a subject who, in attempting to verify the anti-mimetic quality of affective states, is engaged in an eternal search for non-resemblance. Given that all emotion, by nature of its fluidity and porosity, resembles, this quest for a non-imitative affect can only ever be frustrated by emotions' incessant bleeding into one another in an unrelenting transgression of categorical fields.

Distinguishing, even before the stage of aesthetic incarnation, between imitation and copy in an affective world where all is at once resembling and re-assembling is to embark on an impossible hermeneutic quest. Though the intensity of reflexivity is enhanced in the case of literary emotionality, this interminable self-verification concerns all instances of mimesis, including those that occur at the level of the body's affective semiosis. And because mimesis necessarily involves remembering – it is after all 'hard to separate mnēmē from mimesis' – the prior original to which an imitation is compared will always be interiorised within the self's temporal layers, in a doubling and re-doubling with regard to that self's ongoing subjective life.[8]

## Does Realism Impose on Emotion a Reductive Mimesis?

If affect appears resistant to binary models of imitative reproduction – for the reason, among others, that original emotionality seems inconceivable – does this mean that realist texts, with their frequent reliance on mimetic principles of resemblance, fail to account for emotionality's true representational complexity? Is mimesis best seen as a constraining principle from which literary emotion must break free? Or does a further multiplication of affect's many layers in fact occur within mimetic systems, which have always, after all, incorporated a self-reflexive awareness of their own limits into their solipsistic processes?

How, in other words, can realist mimesis deal with those aspects of literature, such as affect, which seem most resistant to reproduction? The dynamism of affective states, combined with their refusal of nomenclature and categorisation, make them particularly slippery as the objects of any representative impulse. In spite of this, much of what Auerbach calls 'modern realism' – with Balzac, Flaubert and Zola as *chefs de file* – forged and sustained a myth of literature's power as an art at once founded on the faithful representation of 'nature', and unique in its ability to display interior emotional states.[9] According to this myth – itself dependent on the arsenal of narrative techniques forged by nineteenth-century realist forms – only literature, in opposition to the other arts, can seek to imitate the full play of the feeling subject's inner emotional life.

As the foundational paradigm of a particular vision of literature, this myth not only does disservice to the expressive powers of the other arts, but insinuates that subjective insight into characters' thoughts is somehow representationally transparent. This myth of the realist novel being imbued, with regard to affect, with unique mimetic powers has a variety of negative consequences. Most importantly, it presumes that there exists an original affective stasis upon which the emotions of literature may be grounded. In the scientific positivism of Zola, the feeling organism is seen as a phenomenal anchorage: the stable trunk of which complex emotions would be the moving leaves. This position is well represented by Zola's well-known affirmation regarding Naturalism: 'If we will never give you the entirety of nature, we will at least give you true nature.'[10] Because the body, and much less the corporalised subject, is anything but transparent or stable, the notion that there exists a 'true nature' from which aesthetic emotions would divide and multiply mimetically comes to seem particularly ill-founded. And indeed, in the novels analysed in this chapter, the very existence of an original emotionality is presented as a deleterious myth. This fiction most often does not seek to give primacy to the imitator, but rather suggests that this division between emotional precedents and reproductions is inoperative, in that it fails to account for the semiotic intermingling of affective processes which are always, simultaneously, both archetypes and duplicates, and as such deprived of primordial origins.

## 'Embellishing your own sobs': The Search for Non-Imitative Affect in Richard Yates, John Cheever and Kathleen Collins

In much post-war realist fiction, the search for the original precursors of ulterior emotional copies remains fundamentally elusive. In the place of this quest for origins we encounter a rhetorical interplay of affective suppositions in which neither author, character nor reader is able to determine the primary or derivative quality of the emotions being explored. In the presence of such indetermination, the category of original affect begins to break down, though its disintegration – the realisation that an emotion may perhaps have no ontological ancestor – is usually more an experience of anguish than a liberation from mimetic ties.

We may initially wonder why this is so disturbing if, in Platonic terms, all mimesis is the copy of a copy. Why then should the awareness of affect's iterability be any different? This discovery is perhaps more impactful because of the post-Enlightenment construction of emotion as a sovereign inner truth, and therefore as a subjective experience particularly resistant to epistemological doubt.[11] According to this model, affect, being more intimately woven with the systemic operations of the body than thoughts, convictions or beliefs, seems less open to the Cartesian or Empiricist scepticism which may undermine the representation of phenomena. Indeed, many Romantic epistemologies – as we know from the vogue of Wertherism and the pan-European evolution of a notion such as sentiment – inherited a philosophical conception of affect as more rooted in biological processes than the rationality of thought.[12] The advantage of this inability of the Romantic subject to fully control his or her affective effusions was the ironic conviction as to their reality: in other words, the very fact such expressions could not be controlled meant they were truly related to something in the palpable world. After all, if one cannot stop crying, then even in the absence of an event or object that 'makes' one cry, one cannot deny that the body is manifesting real physiological effects. Errors arise, however, in thinking that these are phenomenal proofs of a reliable truth. If one looks inward, and finds only feelings which infinitely mirror others, what does this interplay of reflection imply? Is there in the end no unimitated interiority within the reflexive self?

The affective phenomenon of tears in Richard Yates's 1961 novel *Revolutionary Road* provides us with an intricate example of these dilemmas. Crying is a revealing case of the myth of the mimetic basis of literary emotionality in that tears, according to a deterministic expressivity, seem to promise a direct concordance between original emotion and its uncontrollable corporal expression. As confirmatory signs, it is as though tears allowed affect's inceptive authenticity to be traced upon the body. Conversely, and as previously observed regarding Philip Roth, it is precisely tears' reputation as privileged signs of affective immediacy that make them ideal tools for imitative feigning.[13] The logic of tears is implacable. They indicate a crucial rule, namely that the more an external sign may be a convincing proof of true feeling, the more it is subject to the accusation of feigning. If, after all, one is to fake emotion, then why fabricate meagre proofs of inner affective intensities when one may aim for the most powerful exterior sign, supposed to demonstrate the strongest concord between body and mind?

It is no doubt for these reasons that inauthentic tears are a veritable *leitmotif* of emotional deception and self-deception throughout American realist fiction. *Revolutionary Road* centres on Frank and April Wheeler, a young suburban couple who move with their two small children to the middle-class suburbs of post-war Western Connecticut. Though Frank fancies himself an intellectual, having graduated from Columbia on the G.I. Bill after his return from the war, he commutes to the city each day to a job he hates at Knox Business Machines, which used to employ his father. April, despite past dreams of becoming an actress, remains at home, caring for the family's children and playing the defined domestic role of 1950s housewife. For the Wheelers, however, this stereotypical post-war environment is in no way a site of fulfilment. Rather, they spend long evenings with their only close friends, their neighbours Shep and Milly Campbell, railing against what they see as the insufferable conformity and moral hypocrisy of their suburban middle-class fate. Denouncing 'all the idiots I ride with on the train every day', in a typical dramatic tirade rich in rhetoricised entreaties, Frank fails to recognise his own implication in this collectivity, thereby isolating the Wheelers even further from the perceived conventionality of their fellow suburbanites. 'It's a disease,' he exclaims, pathologising such ideology as an internalised bodily state. 'Nobody thinks or feels or cares any more; nobody gets excited or believes in anything except their own comfortable little God damn mediocrity.'[14]

The novel is marked by constant interrogations concerning emotional performativity, which are combined with the Wheelers' and Campbells' search for true selves supposed to lie beneath the play of social masks.[15] As we read at the book's opening, in the free indirect speech representative of a dominant discourse: 'Economic circumstances might force you to live in this environment, but the important thing was to keep from being contaminated. The important thing, always, was to remember who you were.'[16] Frank and April's rebellion, however, against an ambient ideology, is maintained even while they steadfastly remain in this environment, and begins to seem not merely a result of social circumstance but a paradoxical need to occupy a passively iconoclastic role. April dreams of leaving for Paris and establishing a brave new existence. Though Frank appears to agree, it soon becomes clear that he is in fact paralysed with fear before this possibility, which threatens both his masculine dominance and the material comforts he elsewhere decries. When April subsequently learns of her unplanned third pregnancy, Frank seizes this news as a chance to avoid, or at least eternally delay, the long-planned European escape. Against April's desire to have an abortion, Frank pressures her to pursue the pregnancy, thus forcing the couple – in a utilitarian logic of socioeconomic 'responsibility' – to remain in the place they nominally detest. In the ensuing spiralling descent of their relationship, Frank, in the throes of a threatened virility, has an affair with his secretary Maureen, and April a drunken fling with Shep, who has fomented an idealised love for her for years. At the novel's close, with little other possibility for a desired but unattainable change, April attempts to abort her pregnancy herself, resulting in her death.

In a despairing scene that occurs in the wake of April's passing, Shep Campbell retires alone to the suburban backyard of what used to be, not very long ago, the Wheelers' home. Stranded between the suffocating comfort of a lit domestic space and the metaphysical potency of the night sky's distant absolute, Shep recalls April, who was alive at the same time just last year, and finds himself overwhelmed by grief:

> He took a gulp of whiskey, seeing a quick blur of stars and moon through the wet dome of his glass. Then he started back for the house, but he didn't make it; he had to turn around again and head out to the far border of the lawn and walk around out there in little circles; he was crying.
>
> It was the smell of spring in the air that did it – earth and flowers – because it was almost exactly a year now since the time of the Laurel Players, and to remember the Laurel Players was to remember April Wheeler's way of walking across the stage, and her smile, and the sound of her voice ('Wouldn't you like to be loved by me?'), and in remembering all this there was nothing for Shep Campbell to do but walk around on the grass and cry, a big wretched baby with his fist in his mouth and the warm tears spilling down his knuckles.[17]

The 'little circles' of Shep's physical movement mirror the cyclicity of inner emotional revolutions, in a gyre-like descent uncoiling a tragic past. Crucially, he recalls April not in the light of her everyday existence, but beneath the spotlight of theatricality. He sees her, as at the novel's incipit, playing the role of Gabrielle in the local community theatre production of Robert Sherwood's *The Petrified Forest*.[18] On this 'stage' of remembered and present feeling, which ceaselessly and imitatively overlap, the words April speaks, and which Shep imagines applied to him, are not transparently her own, but those of her incarnated character.

Not only were these words, and this love by extension, not expressed for Shep, but the 'smile', 'voice' and emotions April represented on stage were those of theatricalised drama. Layers of imitated fictionality are already implicated in what otherwise appears to be Shep's spontaneous affective expression. Moreover, Shep and the reader are thrown *in medias res*, for the initial emergence of the act of crying is obfuscated, as though the original moment to be imitated could be neither represented nor cognitively captured. The focalisation turns away from Shep, so that we do not witness – and nor, it seems, does he – the instant of affective transition. It is as though he has caught himself in the middle of the action, and feels self-reflexive surprise at his own emotional state. Both the semi-colon and the unusual use of the past continuous insist on this, and effectively distance this feeling from any apparent cause. Shep or the narrative voice is able only to subsequently reconstruct the hypothetical origin of this shift: 'It was the smell of spring in the air that did it.' This stimulus instigates a chain of causality – 'smell of spring', Laurel Players, April Wheeler – in which Shep has no subjective control.

If Yates's passage ended here, however, we may think that such a thing as an original emotionality indeed exists, and that the body may in fact be an unambiguous vehicle of non-mimetic affective states. But the scene goes on:

> He found it so easy and pleasant to cry that he didn't try to stop for a while, until he realized he was forcing his sobs a little, exaggerating their depth with unnecessary shudders. Then, ashamed of himself, he bent over and carefully set his drink on the grass, got out his handkerchief and blew his nose.
>
> The whole point of crying was to quit before you cornied it up. The whole point of grief itself was to cut it out while it was still honest, while it still meant something. Because the thing was so easily corrupted: you let yourself go and you started embellishing your own sobs, or you started telling about the Wheelers with a sad, sentimental smile and saying Frank was courageous, and then what the hell did you have?[19]

Yates's narrative voice identifies here a teleology of affect, a spectrum which moves from the spontaneous to the imitated, revealed by the temporal qualifiers. The problem is that if grief progresses on a scale from non-imitative original towards increasing layers of representation, then any original grief is eternally pushed back into the past. Just as for Shep Campbell's inability to pinpoint the instant when emotion emerges, we are unable to identify an uncopied affect, uncorrupted by both self-awareness and the artifice of subjective reproductions.

Appropriately then, the lexis used is one of essentialism and materialism, wherein are posited an initial unimitated emotion and an original semiotics of affect which is subsequently 'embellished' in reproduced copies. In an increasingly hyperbolic rhetoric of sentiment, 'the whole point of grief itself was to cut it out while it was still honest' is perhaps the passage's most revealing phrase. Upon reflection, the notion is unsettling: if grief, according to a utilitarian ideal, does indeed have 'a point', it is disturbing to think that it may consist only in the preservation of its own truth.

We thus witness an instance of unidentifiable affective origin, where the mythologised moment of feeling's beginning is eluded inwardly by Shep, and by the focalisation of the realist narrator. Both turn away from this unknowable point. And in case we were to interpret this as an isolated occurrence among the authors of this era, a highly similar scene occurs in John Cheever's well-known 1964 short story 'The Swimmer', about a man who resolves one afternoon to swim across all of the pools of his affluent suburban neighbourhood. At the story's end, with his final swim completed, Ned Merrill is finally confronted with the emotional realities he has been trying so long to suppress:

> Going out onto the dark lawn he smelled chrysanthemums or marigolds – some stubborn autumnal fragrance – on the night air, strong as gas. Looking overhead he saw that the stars had come out, but why should he seem to see Andromeda, Cepheus, and Cassiopeia? What had become of the constellations of midsummer? He began to cry.[20]

Like the 'blur of stars and moon' and the 'smell of spring in the air' in Yates, Cheever's passage is marked by indicators of temporal impermanency and the inability to situate oneself in a state of affective disarray. Both passages take place beneath the stars as symbols of navigational stability, in contrast to feeling's mutability. And just as in Yates, Cheever's 'He began to cry' constitutes an abrupt limit, which specifies no interior causality. The perspective precipitously shifts from the constellations' transcendence – a higher original order – to an unilluminated interiority. Time cannot fix feeling's origins, for we have no clarity on the moment of such tears' emergence, nor what has happened in the preceding months that Ned has now forgotten. In fact, the stars' position has informed him of the breakdown of his life and the true situation of his fractured world: that his marriage is over, his family has disintegrated and the heavens above are in misalignment.

These indicators seem to return Ned to the real: but in doing so, they are also strangely intoxicating, as 'strong as gas', altering his perception as much as they transport him back to a noumenal base. And while the constellations show the reality of time's passage, they trace in the end a macroscopic time, far distanced from the particularity of his experience. It may 'in truth' – for others and the outside world – be autumn now, and summer no longer: but this disjunction between inner truth and outer real does not mean that one can so quickly accord primacy to the latter. Indeed, Ned's situation translates the extent to which such tears are not epiphanic, for his incomprehension is still just as intense:

> It was probably the first time in his adult life that he had ever cried, certainly the first time in his life that he had ever felt so miserable, cold, tired, and bewildered. He could not understand the rudeness of the caterer's barkeep or the rudeness of a mistress who had come to him on her knees and showered his trousers with tears.[21]

As though tears belonged only to the child within him – to some lost self from which he is forever excluded – crying is equated not with revelation but with mere discomfort. Here as throughout the story, the motif of immersion is dominant. It is a suspension in the unreality of the pools' glistening simulacra which becomes, in turn, an absorption in an overwhelmingly emotional world. This dynamism of liquid feeling, ignored by Ned for so many years in the desiccation of pragmatic life, surges forth to engulf his submerged body, inundated by affective fluidity. Against a background of emotional repression, the shift in seasonal time is a resurgence of the factual real, and an attendant restoration of the reality of affective woe.

Like the relationship between imitation and copy, neither Shep nor Ned can situate himself between the microcosmic and macrocosmic, the flowers and constellations, interior singularity and exterior representativity. Both Cheever's and Yates's fiction has been read by critics as a condemnation of the inability of 'damaged selves' to attain a longed-for true feeling.[22] Here as elsewhere, however, it is less a question of making emotional desires into reality than of recognising such desires' terrible weight. The real itself proves elusive in a context in which imitation applies as much to the inner representation of feeling as to its exterior social masks. Attributing such thwarted aspirations to a personal failing on the part of characters risks missing a crucial point. For the problem lies not only in an inability to bring passions to fruition, but in the crushing weight borne by those who attempt to make such passions feel legitimate, even at the stage of their initiation.

In a further extension of the paradigm, Kathleen Collins's 'The Uncle', from her posthumous short-story collection *Whatever Happened to Interracial Love?*, focuses on tears as complex emblems of affective iteration and on the myth of their expression of a universal human grief.[23] Such universality is in part constructed by the fact that 'The Uncle' portrays a nameless Black man whose specificity, like that of Ralph Ellison's famed protagonist, remains forever shrouded behind his emotional displays. In stark contrast however to *Invisible Man*'s echoes of an ironic *Bildungsroman*, Collins's character – who is described moreover by an unnamed woman narrator – spends the entirety of the story engulfed not in failed enterprises of social change and self-betterment, but in endless emphatic tears.

Designated only through the status of his familial ties, the Uncle is known and unknown, denied the particularity of a named identity yet inserted in a relational web of interdependent pain. As though each generation's new suffering were a repetition, like the recurrence of tears each day, Collins's anti-hero is in this sense an inverse of post-war masculine reserve, and specifically the trope – with regard to African American masculinity – of affect unexpressed. 'My mind was empty,' the narrator David states for instance in James Baldwin's *Giovanni's Room*, when faced with his once lover Giovanni's death, ' – or it was as though my mind had become one enormous, anaesthetized wound. I thought only, *One day I'll weep for this. One of these days I'll start to cry.*'[24]

From its opening sentence, on the contrary, Collins's story is invested in interrogating the value of a harrowing affect pushed to its iterative extreme: 'I had an uncle who cried himself to sleep. Yes, it's quite a true story and it ended badly. That is to say, one night he cried himself to death.'[25] The rhetorical understatement of this qualifying turn – 'That is to say . . .' – is typical of Collins's uncertain tones, with apparently neutral affirmations concealing deeper currents of distress. Such moments are moreover difficult to critically judge as either comic or tragic, ironic or sincere, as is the case with the eponymous character's initial description:

> A former athlete of Olympic stature . . . He was quite handsome. Negro. But a real double for Marlon Brando. A story runs through my family that one day, on a street in Philadelphia, my uncle and Marlon Brando passed each other and stopped, each stunned by the resemblance.[26]

This cinematic avatar and mirage of Olympus situates the Uncle as a figure torn between two reflections: one Black and one White, one racialised within prejudicial constraints and one free from denigrative ideologies in an idealised realm of transcendence. In this metaphor, the Uncle is presented as a literal copy: a mirror of the heroic version of cinematic masculinity, coded as White by a normative White majority. The Uncle's subsequent downfall – his decline into an isolated emotive figure wracked with affective agony – is framed by the narrator in surprising terms; for rather than seeing such tears, as we may expect in the protest fiction of a Richard Wright, as merely the result of systemic racism's societal and generational effects, she views them with an emergent admiration:[27]

> Then a strange thing happened. In the middle of the night he woke me up, shook me awake with his violent crying and sobbing and begged me to come downstairs and talk with him.
> I did.
> We sat up the rest of the night, and he cried with only slight coherent moments in between . . . How he could cry! Give in to his crying, allow it full possession of his being as if life were a vast well of tears and one must cry to be at the center of it![28]

It is crying as intense and reiterated affect which here takes 'full possession' of the Uncle's self, granting him a position of terrible 'centrality' in a life otherwise plagued by periphery and exile. Such possession may also be understood in explicitly ritualistic terms: as the spirit or demon of powerful feeling which inhabits the body, holding dominion over the suffering self, but with no desired exorcism. In the light of the problem of affective restraint imposed upon Black affect, at constant risk of social opprobrium and violence, the Uncle's tears become a quasi-sacred rebellion: a dissident refusal to accept restrictive norms of comportment in the wake of personal and collective pain.

But is it indeed possible to view the act of crying oneself to death in a positive light, as an act of iconoclastic defiance? To what extent should we take seriously the narrator's growing reverence for this grief? Importantly, the Uncle's limitless sorrow is presented in Collins's story in such eerily mundane tones that it links both literally and symbolically with the societal banalisation of Black suffering analysed by theorists such as Christina Sharpe.[29] Given this tradition, the narrator's refusal to pathologise such expressivity is ambivalent: on the one hand it seems an insurgent gesture against the normalisation of Black pain, while on the other it remains a simple confirmation of the terrible cultural ordinariness of this state.

Nevertheless, and in spite of the myriad precedents of nineteenth-century somatic ailments, to die from sadness is rarely a recognised autopsy finding or clinical diagnosis. On the contrary, it is affect beyond 'reason', locating the sense of anguish without origin in an apotheosis which escapes sense itself – for there is nothing in the Uncle's life powerful enough to explain it. For the narrator, the value of such tears comes to lie in the extent to which they reconnect with an 'ancient ritual', a myth of origins which provides such suffering with a spiritual dimension beyond its racialisation:

> I was having dinner with my parents when the phone call came that told of his death . . . I offered to drive down with my father to his house. On the way my father filled me in on the last years of his life . . . How night after night he kept everyone awake . . . with his laments, his great heartrending sobbing that went on hour after relentless hour until the morning, when he would fall asleep and sleep the day away only to awaken again at night and begin this vigilant lamentation. His children had grown up inside his sorrow. His brothers and sisters would come time and time again and try to coax him back into life . . . But he kept to his bed, his mournful inverted existence; cried in his pillow until death took him away.[30]

From the underground narrator of Ellison's *Invisible Man* to Toni Morrison's spectral identities, such an 'inverted existence' recalls the trope of modern African American experience as a reflected reality: an implied opposite to a homogenised White archetype. It in turn carries echoes of W. E. B. Du Bois's concept of 'double-consciousness': the 'peculiar sensation' for Black Americans of 'always looking at one's self through the eyes of others'.[31] In this perspective, the mythologised meeting between the Uncle and a mirrored Marlon Brando seems less a comical escapade than a troubling incarnation of Du Bois's description of the impossibility to independently self-define. 'One ever feels his two-ness,' as Du Bois puts it:

> – an American, a Negro; two souls, two thoughts, two unreconciled strivings . . . The history of the American Negro is the history of this strife, – this longing to attain self-conscious manhood, to merge his double self into a better and truer self. In this merging he wishes neither of the older selves to be lost.[32]

By the end of Collins's story, there is appropriately no resolution to this division. Simply, the act of crying oneself to death becomes ambiguously coded as a valiant provocation, at once heroic and 'perverse':

> The wide old-fashioned bed where he'd lived dominated the room, stood there like a monument to his perverse pursuit of humiliation and sorrow. It was surely perverse, surely bound to the color of his skin and its bastard possibilities. But his weeping, wailing, and gnashing of teeth brimmed potent to overflowing in the room, and I began to weep for him, weep tears of pride and joy that he should have so soaked his life in sorrow and gone back to some ancient ritual beyond the blunt humiliation of his skin, with its bound-and-sealed possibilities; so refused to overcome his sorrow as some affliction to be transcended . . . He utterly honored his sorrow, gave in to it with such deep and boundless weeping that it seemed as I stood there he was the bravest man I had ever known.[33]

The story's apparently affirmative end is beguiling.[34] Crying, in its contagious spreading to the narrator and expansion into a powerful universal, is at once an obdurate victory over prejudicial limitations and a denial of this situation's specificities. In its collapsing of, or refusal to bear witness to, such pain's particularity, this generalised despair – 'beyond the blunt humiliation of his skin' – risks denying distinct racial and historical realities. For the narrator's uncle is not presented as victorious because he cries for the injustices proper to Black experience, from transatlantic chattel slavery on; rather, he is victorious because his suffering is 'beyond' race and racialisation, because it supposedly transports him to a realm of affective apotheosis, in a dubious liberation – via the universal – from the sorrows of sociopolitical inequity.

As in the passages from Yates and Cheever analysed above, the Uncle of Collins's story is always already crying: there is no beginning and no end, no recognisable telos in the continuity of his grief. Far from a vain repetition, the Uncle would supposedly, in tears and death, become free. The unanswered question however is whether such a universalising movement amounts to a denial of the historical realities at the origin of this torment. Such realities, rather than glossed into a ubiquitous affect of purely 'human' pain, are defined by the inescapable lineage of America's colonial past and postcolonial present. The dream of transcendent healing is moreover omnipresent in what Aida Levy-Hussen has called the 'fantasies of historical repair' that pervade many aspects of post-war African American fiction's 'historical turn'.[35]

Importantly, Kathleen Collins frequently parodies, or at least ambiguously renders, such supposed overcoming of sociopolitical facts. In a story like the titular 'Whatever Happened to Interracial Love?', idealistic characters experience an emotional transcendence over racialised values, as when a young Black woman is confronted with her father's more cynical scepticism:

> He does not seem to understand that this young colored woman he has spawned does not, herself, believe in color: that to her the young freedom rider of her dreams is colorless (as indeed he is), that their feelings begin where color ends (as indeed they must), that if only he could understand that race as an issue, race as a social factor, race as a political or economic stumbling block – race is part of the past. Can't he see that love is color-free? She is close to tears.[36]

In Collins's fiction, such universalising affirmations appear both as valuable truths and as dangerous idealisations. The Uncle's tears, in their daily repetition, may seem similarly irrational and rational (according to dominant emotional standards), legitimate and illegitimate (in an intransigent legacy of oppression). This aura of abnormality is moreover due to the fact that, as Beth Hinderliter and Steve Peraza have observed, the 'specific affects and emotions that pervade white supremacy' are presented as simply 'rational and neutral'.[37] For the supreme irony is that the moment when the Uncle attains a supposedly universal affect is also the moment of his death. In 'proving' his humanity (which should always be evident) he simultaneously ceases to be. Of course, to achieve true feeling at the moment of one's corporal dissolution is a highly equivocal fate. It is an ambivalent response, moreover, to the claim of being 'more than our pain' which forms the basis of this recent recontextualisation of African American affect.[38] The challenge in Collins's story is that, though the Uncle may appear to enact a bold emotional insurrection, he is also in some sense 'reduced' to his totalising grief: deprived of all other particulars, he remains a character defined by one agonising expression. The apparent victory of the story's coda therefore appears deeply pyrrhic. For in spite of its deceptively positive tone, to have cried oneself to death in order to reach an inclusive human feeling is hardly an ideal resolution to the realities of overwhelming personal and historical ordeals.

## 'We're all in this together': The Critique of Emotional Communion in James Baldwin

As in many of Collins's stories, we encounter in almost all of James Baldwin's essays and fiction an explicit distrust of the notion of emotional communion, framed however in far less ironic tones. For Baldwin's work often expresses far more directly both a suspicion regarding emotional authenticity as a value, and an apparently inverse warning against the false clichés of sentimentalism. Given that anti-sentimentalist discourses are so often part of the rhetoric of those who cherish emotional truth, it is crucial that we find in Baldwin a figure as sceptical of declarations of true feeling as of accusations of sentimentalist manipulation. Seeing them as part of the same spectrum, Baldwin is thus able to assert both that 'sentimentality, the ostentatious parading of excessive and spurious emotion, is the mark of dishonesty', and that 'no one is more dangerous than he who imagines himself pure in heart'.[39]

The praise of true feeling and attacks against false feeling alternately appear in Baldwin as aspects of the same struggle, namely the attempt to escape from a derivative emotional life, formed only of imitated affects imposed by regimes of social subordination. To prove the iconoclastic power of affects which do not cohere to a mimetic model, itself necessarily devised along racial, gendered and class lines, is in this way central to Baldwin's broader literary and philosophical project.

Like much of his fiction, the 1948 short story 'Previous Condition' delves into the recurrent problem of the pathologisation of Black affect.[40] The story follows the barely suppressed anger of its protagonist, Peter, at the proscription of a range of feelings deemed socially impermissible for a Black man. This problem reaches its crisis when Peter is evicted from an apartment that his friend Jules – who is Jewish but passes as White for the racist landlady – was able to rent in his own name. As the story progresses, Peter's struggle against alienation leads to his refusal of affective truth as a concept, but also a concomitant denial of his own worth. As Peter himself puts it, in a powerful revision of affirmative versions of the fight for civil rights: 'I've been fighting so goddamn long I'm not a person anymore.'[41]

As an aspiring actor, Peter's identity is defined by his skills in affective plasticity. Such theatrical role-playing is reflected at various points by his need to adopt changing masks in a context of relentless racism. In this sense, the positive artifice of acting is ceaselessly mirrored by the negative artifice of an alternate performativity, one which Peter must employ throughout his daily life to ward off the omnipresent threat of violence. As we read regarding his *modus operandi* when confronted with White authority figures:

> When I faced a policeman I acted like I didn't know a thing. I let my jaw drop and I let my eyes get big. I didn't give him any smart answers, none of the crap about my rights. I figured out what answers he wanted and I gave them to him. I never let him think he wasn't king. If it was more than routine, if I was picked up on suspicion of robbery or murder in the

neighborhood, I looked as humble as I could and kept my mouth shut and prayed.[42]

The structure 'I acted like' takes on an ambiguous valency, linked to diverse meanings of performativity in both its theatrical and social sense. For such exaggerated emotional expressivity plays on a long history of racist tropes of African American affect, particularly redolent of the buffoonish stock characters of nineteenth-century minstrelsy. Such burlesque is deployed, however, as a paradoxical mode of affective protection. In terms of the imitative paradigms that are this chapter's focus, Peter enacts inherited emotional expressions which, to minimise the risk to his own safety, he is beholden to reproduce. Such defensive techniques nevertheless engender a feeling of deep interior division:

> There are times and places when a Negro can use his color like a shield. He can trade on the subterranean Anglo-Saxon guilt and get what he wants that way . . . I knew these things long before I realized that I knew them and in the beginning I used them, not knowing what I was doing. Then when I began to see it, I felt betrayed. I felt beaten as a person. I had no honest place to stand.[43]

The subject committing such a 'betrayal' is left undefined. We are of course dealing with Peter's betrayal by others who, in an oppressive cultural environment, have reduced his affective options to mere simulacra. But in adopting such survival strategies, he also betrays his own self in an imposed reproduction of racist tropes. His final affirmation is testament to the damage caused by a historical legacy that has made the notion of affective authenticity seem absurd.

As an actor deeply involved in the emotionality of others, the lines for Peter between truth and reality, as well as between an original affect and its subsequent iterations, become increasingly blurred, to the extent that he no longer believes in human feeling's most basic expressions:

> I'd been acting in stock companies and little theaters; sometimes fairly good parts. People were nice to me. They told me I had talent. They said it sadly, as though they were thinking, What a pity, he'll never get anywhere.

I had got to the point where I resented praise and I resented pity and I wondered what people were thinking when they shook my hand. In New York I met some pretty fine people; easygoing, hard-drinking, flotsam and jetsam; and they liked me; and I wondered if I trusted them; if I was able any longer to trust anybody. Not on top, where all the world could see, but underneath where everybody lives.[44]

This distinction between a surface world of accessible feigning and a 'real world' of inaccessible depths is precisely the myth of true feeling as an exclusive realm, into which only privileged initiates may penetrate. The overlap between theatrical play and social performance does not lead to a positive artifice, in which the self is freed to move among varied registers, but one in which it is drastically constricted. In what amounts to a paradigm of affective segregation, Peter's exclusion from a concealed emotional fellowship – as much as his eviction from his apartment because of his race – is the result of systemic operations far beyond his conscious control.

Although, during this traumatic episode, Peter is not permitted to show his anger – despite his landlady declaring: 'This is a white neighborhood, I don't rent to colored people' – his body assumes the task of processing intense affect, though it occurs at a somatic level below that of consciousness:

'Get out of the door,' I said. 'I want to get dressed.'
But I knew that she had won, that I was already on my way. We stared at each other. Neither of us moved. From her came an emanation of fear and fury and something else. You maggot-eaten bitch, I thought. I said evilly, 'You wanna come in and watch me?' Her face didn't change, she didn't take her foot away. My skin prickled, tiny hot needles punctured my flesh. I was aware of my body under the bathrobe; and it was as though I had done something wrong, something monstrous, years ago, which no one had forgotten and for which I would be killed.
'If you don't get out,' she said, 'I'll get a policeman to put you out.'[45]

It is at this point, faced with promised violence, that a scission between embodiment and consciousness occurs. For phrases such as 'I was aware of my body', in establishing an alienated distance, indicate a slippage into dualism in which one's skin may prickle of its own accord. Inherent affect thus asserts itself, its sensations demanding to be taken into account in spite of the impossibility of social expression.

If such dissociation is logical in contexts of discrimination and aggression, it also crucially emerges from attempts at emotional complicity. Indeed, the pain caused by failed efforts at concord is one of the story's central themes, for it is when others claim to fully understand and share Peter's feelings that the strongest symptoms of alienation occur. Following his unjust eviction, for example, Jules repeatedly attempts to assuage his anger:

> 'Cheer up, baby. The world's wide and life – life, she is very long.'
> 'Shut up. I don't want to hear any of your bad philosophy.'
> 'Sorry.'
> 'I mean, let's not talk about the good, the true, and the beautiful.'
> 'All right. But don't sit there holding onto your table manners. Scream if you want to.'
> 'Screaming won't do any good. Besides I'm a big boy now.'[46]

In spite of Jules's invitation to emotional expression, Peter's ultimate reply carries a melancholy resonance. For he is well aware that to scream – as occurs later when he is faced with the optimistic minimisations of his White lover, Ida – would not just be useless, but would further expose him to the panicked reactions of White citizens anxious to dull or suppress his 'excessive' response. Language breaks down in the face of abstracting commonplaces – the 'bad philosophy' of empty Platonic quintessences – whose idealism cannot stand firm in the face of injustice. Peter cannot give in to the self-help cliché of 'scream if you want to' for the reason that such anger is both pragmatically futile and personally exhausting. As he puts it:

> 'I'm not Booker T. Washington. I've got no vision of emancipating anybody. I want to emancipate myself. If this goes on much longer, they'll send me to Bellevue, I'll blow my top, I'll break somebody's head. I'm not worried about that miserable little room. I'm worried about what's happening to me, to me, inside. I don't walk the streets, I crawl. I've never been like this before. Now when I go to a strange place I wonder what will

happen, will I be accepted, if I'm accepted, can I accept? –'
'Take it easy,' Jules said.
'Jules, I'm beaten.'
'I don't think you are. Drink your coffee.'[47]

From prior encouragements, Jules has now slipped into a mode of affective depreciation of both the intensity and legitimacy of Peter's torment. For 'take it easy' is the same reproof used by an oppressive White privilege to dampen Black affects' legitimate force. Whatever the intention then – to preserve Peter's endangered sense of self or to keep him in a state of sociopolitical incapacity – the result is the same, namely the maintenance of an emotional dynamic in which the passionate cry 'I want to emancipate myself' is too threatening to be heard.

And indeed, this constant struggle for affective legitimacy is the cause of Peter's descent into uncertainty regarding the truth of his own emotional states: '"Oh," I cried. "I know you think I'm making it dramatic, that I'm paranoiac and just inventing trouble! Maybe I think so sometimes, how can I tell?"'[48] Such doubt precludes the possibility of empathy or emotional communication, as the demands for mutual understanding are themselves corrupted by a systemic prejudice. 'How can I say what it feels like?' Peter desperately asks:

> 'I don't know. I know everybody's in trouble and nothing is easy, but how can I explain to you what it feels like to be black when I don't understand it and don't want to and spend all my time trying to forget it? I don't want to hate anybody – but now maybe, I can't love anybody either – are we friends? Can we be really friends?'[49]

The unfeasibility of emotional explanation is predicated on the related impossibility of self-understanding. Forced to understand and then express the affective realities of racial oppression, Peter is subject to the pressures of true feeling as hegemonic imperative. For it is implicitly his task to communicate his own internal state: the onus is his both to contemplate his condition and to articulate it to sympathetic non-Black friends, granting them entry into the inner enclave of his pain.

In short, the task is immense and the burden heavy: for this means that even if emotional communion seems on occasion possible, it is frequently based on a toxic optimism which highlights the superficiality of such a connection. As, for Peter, to spend one's life striving to express what it 'feels like to be black' is not a liberation, but an imposed subservience. 'Can we be really friends?' is thus necessarily an unanswered question, leading to either the particularity of disappointed division or the universality of naïve togetherness. This is why Jules's insistence on similitude as the foundation of their friendship is so difficult for Peter to accept:

> 'We're friends,' Jules said, 'don't worry about it.' He scowled. 'If I wasn't Jewish I'd ask you why you don't live in Harlem.' I looked at him. He raised his hand and smiled – 'But I'm Jewish, so I didn't ask you. Ah Peter,' he said, 'I can't help you – take a walk, get drunk, we're all in this together.'[50]

This final affirmation can be nothing more than an ingenuous platitude, which fails to recognise the validity of Peter's outrage and its sociohistorical weft. Jules's attempted expressions of support prove powerless in the face of broader architectures of prejudice, with 'I can't help you' showing his symbolic championing to be of little practical use.

Faced with such tendencies to gloss over the seriousness of his trauma, it is hardly surprising that Peter, when he recounts the tale to his lover Ida over dinner in a restaurant, is unable to present it as a problem worth discussing, but merely as a passing 'mood':

> 'What happened to you today?'
> I resented her concern; I resented my need. 'Nothing worth talking about,' I muttered, 'just a mood.'
> And I tried to smile at her, to wipe away the bitterness.[51]

'Nothing worth talking about' is, in Baldwin, a recurrent motif of the modern neglect of Black affect, even (or especially) among progressive social movements. For Peter's suffering seems unworthy of attention – even to himself – not because it is an anomaly, but on the contrary because it is all too habitual: excessively ordinary in a society where such discrimination is at once a practical and an emotional norm. The transformation of such anguish into a mere 'mood' equates both affect and racial prejudice with inconsequential lived experiences. Moreover, it places the responsibility for Peter's anger squarely on him, as though it were deprived of a valid external cause.

It is no surprise then that just as Jules attempted to insist on friendship as an antidote to affective distress, so too does Ida adopt a reductive rhetoric of harmony in an effort to soothe disruptive pain. In doing so, she unwittingly collapses the specificities of racist prejudice into the common struggles of a universalised humanity:

> 'Peter,' she said, 'try not to feel so badly. We're all in this together the whole world. Don't let it throw you. What can't be helped you have to learn to live with.'
> 'That's easy for you to say,' I told her.
> She looked at me quickly and looked away. 'I'm not pretending that it's easy to do,' she said.
> I didn't believe that she could really understand it; and there was nothing I could say. I sat like a child being scolded, looking down at my plate, not eating, not saying anything. I wanted her to stop talking, to stop being intelligent about it, to stop being calm and grown-up about it . . .[52]

The emptiness of these truisms hides the fact that to be 'intelligent about it', to be 'calm and grown-up', are euphemisms for a darker call to social and emotional subservience, which never questions the affective regime of White supremacy. Faced with such oppression, to be pushed to one's limit is not considered an appropriate reaction even by those who purport to be on Peter's side. Though they may claim pragmatic support, and may be thinking of Peter's welfare – what may happen were he to let his justified rage surge forth – their banal bromides lead us to suspect that both Jules and Ida are themselves unable to escape the imitative patterns of emotional delegitimisation which they too claim to abhor.

Whether their allies are nominally for or against racist emotional superstructures, many Black protagonists' affective expression remains curbed by inherited clichés of Black affect, framed by the dual polarity of 'too much' or 'not enough'. The flattening effect of Ida's insistence on universality, with its stockpile of commonplaces, can therefore be emotionally countered only by artifice's 'painted grin' (please be warned that the n-word is present in the following direct quotation):

> 'It's no better anywhere else,' she was saying. 'In all of Europe there's famine and disease, in France and England they hate the Jews – nothing's going to change, baby, people are too empty-headed, too empty-hearted – it's always been like that, people always try to destroy what they don't understand – and they hate almost everything because they understand so little –'
> I began to sweat in my side of the booth. I wanted to stop her voice. I wanted her to eat and be quiet and leave me alone . . .
> 'Peter,' Ida said, 'Peter please don't look like that.'
> I grinned: the painted grin of the professional clown. 'Don't worry, baby, I'm all right. I know what I'm going to do. I'm gonna go back to my people where I belong and find me a nice, black nigger wench and raise me a flock of babies.'[53]

Again faced with the collapsing of all suffering into a meaningless universal, Peter's response is to practise emotional feigning as a mode of social defence. It is affect deployed as a barrier against true feeling's force of coercion, which glazes historical specificities into a narrative of undifferentiated 'hate'. Empty stereotypes dismiss the specific anger that Peter feels with regard to a specific event: his literal eviction, set here on the irrelevant macro scale of world events.

At the story's close, upon Peter's return to Harlem, Baldwin takes pains to underline that it is not when Peter finds himself in a predominantly Black community that affective intimacy suddenly or organically occurs. On the contrary, Peter is struck by the superficiality of his surface resemblance to other African American citizens. Sitting in a bar in Harlem, he observes:

> I longed for some opening, some sign, something to make me part of the life around me. But there was nothing except my color. A white outsider coming in would have seen a young Negro drinking in a Negro bar,

perfectly in his element, in his place, as the saying goes. But the people here knew differently, as I did. I didn't seem to have a place.[54]

Such kinship is not just superficial, but is projected by an imagined White gaze which prioritises colour in a simplistic schema of racial belonging. If the hypothetical White spectator could not imagine Peter feeling alienated 'in his place', it is because race homogenises affect, erasing individual particularity to such an extent that one cannot be alienated in one's 'element'. For to feel emotionally isolated, as is Peter's case, from both White and Black people is an admissible affect only if we fundamentally question the concept of true feeling itself as a myth of imposed concordance. And indeed, the final interaction at the story's close picks up again on the 'unimportance' of all that has befallen Peter, in a world unable to accord his feelings any worth:

'Baby,' said the old one, 'what's your story?'
The man put three beers on the counter.
'I got no story, Ma,' I said.[55]

Existing in a world of imitative affect, in the nightmare of the actor unable to escape his socially imposed roles, Peter as protagonist metatextually renounces the very story he has just told. Deprived of the possibility not only of feeling but of language too, he is not even able to proffer original signifiers about an experience whose value has been sapped by constant minimisations. In such an environment, mimesis fails and imitation ends. 'What's your story?' is a question with no answer in a world where both feeling and language have been emptied of their validity, in which all of Peter's attempts to express rage or even regret are met with counter-claims to a merely superficial union.

## Truth on Trial: Mimesis and the Exceptional Status of True Feeling in Richard Ford

What is rejected in all of these texts is the utopian premise of the nineteenth-century realist novel according to which, as Auerbach puts it, the mind would seek to attain 'a self-forgetful absorption in the subjects of reality'.⁵⁶ Transcending the need for mimesis, such absorption promises a non-imitative realm of pure experience. In a paradox similar to that which Derrida outlines, realism in this way stakes claims to truth both because of its mimetic reproduction of the real (mimesis as imitation), and because of its power for world-creating immersion (mimesis as the autarchic unfolding of *physis*).⁵⁷

As argued previously, whereas for experimental modernist and postmodernist fictions the questioning of mimetic models of art is foregrounded by fractious formal processes – collage, polyvocality, intertextuality – these are often absent from realist modes for reasons which go beyond questions of mere receptive accessibility. Such dissimulation does not mean, however, that explicit critiques of affective mimeticism are not present in realist procedures. This fact is constantly evident in Richard Ford's 1986 novel *The Sportswriter*, in which the absence of diegetic disjunction mirrors the detachment from emotional intensities of Ford's withdrawn protagonist. In the decades since the fiction of Baldwin and Yates, we realise that though the dual trope of emotional detachment and repression endures, it has now become a pseudo-philosophical position, erected to the status of ersatz moral doctrine and metaphysics, moreover justified by its running counter to an ambient culture of materialism and the cult of success.

Nearing forty, the sportswriter Frank Bascombe lives in a state of affective reverie and uprootedness after the death of his youngest son, nine-year-old Ralph. In the wake of Ralph's death, Frank has various affairs, leading to the break-up of his marriage to a woman referred to only as 'X'. What value could any feeling have after such events? As Frank's ex-wife observes during the novel's first scene, when they meet again at Ralph's grave as they do every year upon his birthday: 'Sometimes I don't think anyone can be happy anymore.'⁵⁸ The extrapolation of such loss to the whole of humanity is a sentiment to which Frank responds with typical forward-looking stoicism: 'I think we're all released to the rest of our lives.'⁵⁹

Frank will later embark, in the second novel of the series, *Independence Day*, on an era he refers to as 'the Existence period': a time of simple continuation, an anti-climactic moving through life, or what he calls 'the part that comes after the big struggle which led to the big blow-up'.[60] This period is one of post: post-event, post-action, but also post-reflection and post-understanding. In contrast to the previous generation's heroic narratives of tragic intensity in Fitzgerald or Hemingway, Ford's narrator is divested of the invigorating energies of action, yet is unsure – as are we as readers – whether this detachment is a form of psychological protection or a state of spiritual acceptance.

The two possibilities are not, of course, mutually exclusive, for Frank's usual frame of mind seems equal parts distraction and acknowledgement, unfeeling dissociation and composed abandonment. We are witness to a broader interrogation of the notion of original feeling which, as in the following passage, implies the question of individual control:

> For the last year I was married to X, I was always able to 'see around the sides' of whatever I was feeling. If I was mad or ecstatic, I always realized I could just as easily feel or act another way if I wanted to – somber or resentful, ironic or generous – even though I might've been convinced that the way I was acting probably represented the way I really felt even if I hadn't seen the other ways open.[61]

Those attitudes seen to be most determined by spontaneous originality – to be 'mad or ecstatic', as in Platonic inspiration – are framed as preferences which can be altered by conscious choice.[62] For Frank, in an image of physical presence and immovability, seeing 'around the sides' of feeling deprives it of unicity. If what one is feeling is not absolutely original, plasticity becomes conceivable even in terms of its most essential qualities. This mutability is not merely a positive taking charge, as the risk of relativism and even nihilism is ever-present.

Regaining subjective agency with regard to affect can never, in any case, consist in denying the existence of imitation and representation, but only in harnessing self-replication as an active formation of the self. In other words, for one's own affective states, one must strive to become (as Frank does in his writing) a veritable artist, employing both mimetic and non-mimetic means:

'Seeing around' is exactly what I did in my stories (though I didn't know it), and in the novel I abandoned, and one reason why I had to quit. I could always think of other ways I might be feeling about what I was writing, or other voices I might be speaking in. In fact, I would usually think of quite a number of things I might be doing at any moment! And what real writing requires, of course, is that you merge in *the oneness of the writer's vision* – something I could never quite get the hang of, though I tried like hell and eventually sunk myself.[63]

We must be careful not to take these claims literally, as Frank's vision of writing – moreover presented in italics, echoing reported speech – smacks of popular perceptions of the writerly *métier* filtered through the lens of an expressive European Romanticism.[64] For there is nothing further from the internal paradoxes of Ford's own protagonist than this image of literature as an immersion in the feelings of a unified self. As though to reflect this posturing, the subsequent description of X as being 'as clear as spring water' is immediately undermined, with her famed reliability degraded, in the same sentence, to a divided affective uncertainty: 'I'm not certain she's so sure about things now.'[65]

Because of this association of art with an inherited myth of unified absorption, it is self-awareness that prevents Ford's narrator from pursuing a career as a novelist, and leads him to reject the value of all affective insight:

> I do not think, in any event, it's a good idea to want to know what people are thinking (that would disqualify you as a writer right there, since what else is literature but somebody telling us what somebody else is thinking). For my money there are at least a hundred good reasons not to want to know such things. People never tell the truth anyway.[66]

We see the problem when a mimetic principle is applied not to actions in the Aristotelian sense, but to emotions and mental processes, as by the end of this passage Ford's narrator has himself become contaminated by this very injunction regarding literature and emotional truth. Though this passage adopts the codes of realist narrative – with an absence of semantic interruption, formal disruption or stylistic play – the irony of the opening sentence is evident. Our narrator reveals to us his inner emotional states, all the while informing us that such revelations are necessarily misleading. In the first of many incarnations throughout the text of Epimenides' liar paradox, if 'people never tell the truth' then Frank too is not immune from this admonition; and if, as he goes on to say, 'most people's minds, like mine, never contain much worth reporting', then the act of reporting this is itself null and void.[67]

An infinite play of mimetic mirrors leads such condemnations to cancel out their own affirmative qualities. What else is literature but somebody telling us what somebody else is thinking? Far more, one would hope. The limits of presuming an affective transparency as literature's ultimate goal become plain. They are expressed by Frank in a complex passage, after he discusses the possibility of marriage with his new girlfriend Vicki:

> And I feel what at this debarking moment?
> At least a hundred things at once, all competing to take the moment and make it their own, reduce undramatic life to a gritty, knowable kernel.
> This, of course, is a minor but pernicious lie of literature, that at times like these, after significant or disappointing divulgences, at arrivals or departures of obvious importance, when touchdowns are scored, knockouts recorded, loved ones buried, orgasms notched, that at such times we are any of us altogether in an emotion, that we are within ourselves and not able to detect other emotions we might also be feeling, or be about to feel, or prefer to feel.[68]

The mimetic model – replete with the realist conviction that literature provides privileged insight into unique emotional states – is simultaneously presented and represented, in an apparently forthright speech on the falsity of this same discourse. The emotion in question is mimetically produced and debunked by a narrator who is not merely unreliable but who, in involving himself in his own critique, effectively cancels himself out as a source of emotional discernment:

> If it's literature's job to tell the truth about these moments, it usually fails, in my opinion, and it's the writer's fault for falling into such conventions. (I tried to explain all of this to my students at Berkshire College, using

Joyce's epiphanies as a good example of falsehood. But none of them understood the first thing I was talking about.[69]

The irony of the reference to the Joyce of *Dubliners* is clear: the rejection of an epiphanic model of emotion is itself an epiphany, and the realist model followed precisely to show its limitations: to push its presumptions regarding affective revelation to their event-horizon where they no longer resist the tension of competing paradoxes. In spite of what Frank claims, the notion that emotional plurality and equivocacy can be concentrated to a 'knowable kernel' is in no way a 'minor' lie of literature, but a prevailing hegemony of the myth of true feeling, which moreover translates into a particularly reductive vision of literary mimesis.

'We do not, after all, deal in truths, only potentialities,' Frank affirms. 'Too much truth can be worse than death, and last longer.'[70] In seeking, albeit antinomically, to liberate the subject from the strictures of institutionalised feeling, Frank promotes an ambiguous vision of a purely experiential truth: 'The only truth that can never be a lie, let me tell you, is life itself – the thing that happens.'[71] This type of formula posits the existence of an empirical reality, 'life', whose truth – if such a property can be attributed to a continuity of being – is not open to debate, for the reason that its axiology is based on its ontology: on the simple fact that it is there. Faced with this primacy of experience over reflection, Frank's more humble goal becomes to 'maintain a supportable existence that resembles actual life'.[72] An existence like life, but which is not life 'itself' – life being, for him, a purely hypothetical concept beyond the scope of subjective resolution.

'Explaining is where we all get into trouble,' Frank affirms in *The Sportswriter* after a vast amount of self-explaining.[73] In a continuation of Epimenides' paradox, Bascombe spends a great deal of the novel explaining why explanation must be avoided, and producing pages of interpretable text to prove why life must not be interpreted, but rather lived. No longer able, like prior heroic American avatars, to accord a value of unicity to affective intensities, his reticence towards emotional interpretation – all the while interpreting *ad infinitum* this reticence itself – is in accordance with his conviction that life depletes as it progresses. For Frank is certain of a steady loss of valency, throughout existence, caused by the constant effort to process experience and understand it. This effort leaves one, in his eyes, anaesthetised with regard to the very experiences which initially commanded understanding.

Such disengagement is buttressed by what Lene M. Johannessen calls 'a narrative mode of hazy monotony and semi-apathy' which, perpetuating a mask of neutrality, means that 'the reader, as well as the narrator, is far too immersed in the monotonous and levelled narrative to be able to conceptualize this choice as an ideational position, a deliberate act on the part of the protagonist'.[74] Appropriately, Frank Bascombe's ideal of emotional life – the individual who most incarnates the being-present of what he calls 'literalness' – is a highly anti-mimetic figure, namely the athlete. For Frank, the athlete is gifted with

> a rare selfishness that means he isn't looking around the sides of his emotions to wonder about alternatives for what he's saying or thinking about. In fact, athletes at the height of their powers make literalness into a mystery all its own simply by becoming absorbed in what they're doing.[75]

Like the adolescent Swede before his downfall in Roth's *American Pastoral* or tennis players in Foster Wallace's *Infinite Jest*, the athlete becomes for Bascombe an incarnation of a specific American ideal, namely the individual who, though he has not forsaken feeling, has mastered the ability to transfer emotional turmoil into original action – even if this action may appear, to an outside observer, vain or solipsistic.[76] It is the athlete's absorption that provides a possible solution to the suffering produced by the problem of absent emotional originals. As an antithesis to Ford's narrator, but one to which he aspires, the athlete is an image of affective control. This absorptive capacity requires a certain egotism: the price to pay, for Frank, in order to avoid the endless imitation that over-thinking and over-feeling for him necessarily imply.

Again, the self-reflexive quality of Bascombe's reflections is salient. He respects in athletes the capacity for action which he not only lacks, but discourses at length about. He makes us witness a verbose attack against verbosity, esteeming original action in an imitative manner, devoid of the very immediacy that it sets out to praise. Regarding questions then of feeling's representation, it is not just that Frank as narrator finds himself in an antinomical position of which he seems unaware, but that his narrative supports the contention it is arguing against. Mimesis is ironically undone, for if actions cannot be directly imitated, and are instead replaced by the representations which are feelings and thoughts, the latter can only with great difficulty contend that action is indeed superior. For how is literature able to imitate the 'unemotional' action of the athlete if literature itself – as soon as it sets about representing or describing such action – necessarily transforms it into the less immediate material of a subsidiary *imitant*? Frank's admiration is projected on to what he perceives as both less emotional and more resistant to being captured in literary form. Literature may well be able to depict the tergiversations of the undecided mind, but the pure state of presence represented by athletic being-in-the-world proves, for Bascombe at least, impossible to recount.

An athlete thus 'knows what makes him happy, what makes him mad, and what to do about each'.[77] Such univocity hardly makes such an individual, as Frank claims in a *non sequitur* conclusion, 'a true adult', implying that adulthood is defined merely by knowing the origin of one's emotions in order to cathartically expurgate them. Being an adult, on the contrary, may precisely lie in the extent to which one recognises that emotional disturbances are not simply to be banished from the body by mechanistic exertions. Emotionality in general is better understood as an elaborate fluctuating system in which one can never entirely know what 'makes' one happy or mad. For Frank, a true adult is made of true feelings, whose elemental origins have been recognised then actively expelled. Rather than emotional maturity, this ideation represents a naïve desire for resolution of affective derangement via expurgation, in order to create a doubtful calm. 'It's all but impossible', Frank concludes, for such an idealised athlete 'to be your friend': able to ascend above feeling's imitative processes, such a figure becomes an isolated subject, unable to interact with other beings traversed by the dynamism of emotional imitation.

These circumlocutions, energised by reductive conceptions of emotional truth, are typical of Frank's reasoning. As he puts it in a moment of apparent sincerity:

> I even had, in fact, a number of different voices, a voice that wanted to be persuasive, to promote good effects, to express love and be sincere, and make other people happy – even if what I was saying was a total lie and as distant from the truth as Athens is from Rome. It was a voice that totally lacked commitment, though it may well be this is as close as you can ever come to yourself, your own voice, especially with someone you love: mutual agreement with no significant irony. This is what people mean when they say that so-and-so is 'distanced from his feelings'. Only it's my belief that when you reach adulthood that distance has to close until you no longer see those choices, but simply do what you do and feel what you feel.[78]

This passage begins with the recognition of a multiplicity of voices within the self, only to conclude with the reduction of this abundance to 'your own voice', postulated as a singular ideal. Framed as an unattainable unicity, such unified subjectivity is moreover defined by its positive intentions rather than by the truth of what it says. In this pragmatic rhetoric, Frank adopts a range of imitated emotional positions, though in the end he still aspires to a final unity. In spite of his Socratic tonalities, his definition of love reveals a disturbing superficiality. 'Do what you do and feel what you feel' becomes the deterministic rule of a life lived in supposed immediacy, but which is in fact a closure of all other emotional perspectives. For what is interpreted by others as emotional distance is seen as a beneficial unity, where one no longer sees the choices – the imitated emotional replicas – of other ways of being.

'You can never successfully argue the case for your own passions,' Frank affirms, further implying that passions are above and beyond not only language and a rational *logos*, but the epistemological searchings of the self.[79] This lexical choice is moreover crucial, for 'passions' refers to a specific historicised conception of emotional intensities, one emerging out of Hippocratic models of the balance of the humours, and particularly from Galen's sixteenth-century identification of 'non-naturals', which included 'the passions or perturbations of the soul'.[80] Accordingly, in spite of his insistence that life must not be reproduced, but rather lived, Frank constantly foregrounds his own efforts to describe and reproduce, often in extreme detail, his own emotional states. 'What I feel, in truth' is a phrase which seeks to convince us of the sincerity of its expression, and to persist in a self-described 'uncomplicated' state.[81] Indeed, the anaphora of 'I feel' throughout at first seems to support the valuing of feeling's immediacy; but in reality, such repetition demonstrates how processed such feeling is, by the thought that reconstructs it and the language which gives it form.

Towards the beginning of *The Sportswriter*, Frank affirms: 'That is the truth of what I feel and think. To expect anything less or different is idiotic.'[82] Simultaneous to this statement, the narrative's tangled diegesis – replete with self-cancelling rhetorics – demonstrates that to affirm this is only partially and temporarily meaningful. As the novel advances, and having criticised the notion of emotional absorption as a 'pernicious lie of literature', Frank consistently claims that he has progressed in his ability to not be self-reflexive about feeling, and thus to live 'in the moment': 'When you are fully in your emotions, when they are simple and appealing enough to be in, and the distance is closed between what you feel and what you might *also* feel, then your instincts can be trusted.'[83] We see that his entire ideology of emotional directness, undercut by the tensions of his own telling, is founded on essentialist 'instincts', which ground true feeling in a dream of bodily primacy. Frank moreover insists on the uniformity of affective life, proclaiming 'there's no way that I could feel what hundreds of millions of other citizens haven't'.[84] At no point does he question, however, whether what one 'truly feels' may be ever-changing, or open to interpretation – whether it is in fact impossible to declare yourself 'fully in your emotions' for the reason that, once 'inside' them, both such emotions and one's perspective on them have inevitably changed.

Appropriately, love becomes within this framework another essentialised value, precluding the possibility of reflection:

> And finally, when I say to Vicki Arcenault, 'I love you,' I'm not saying anything but the obvious. Who cares if I don't love her forever? Or she me? Nothing persists. I love her now, and I'm not deluding myself or her. What else does truth have to hold?[85]

Again we encounter the longing for an original affect that would exist beyond representation, even when the signs of representation are present at every turn. Moreover, we realise here the cynical potential of Frank's pseudo-philosophy of emotional literalness. In a language of *laissez-faire* immediacy, emotional truth is portrayed as a momentary quality, re-evaluated at every instant. Though we may be tempted to approve of this vision as anti-essentialistic, Frank's conclusion is in fact disturbing: because of emotions' transitory nature, no promise of stability is possible, thereby delivering him from all need to project into an ongoing affective future. What is proposed as an enlightened conviction of the transitory nature of the self's desires is better viewed as a shirking of all emotional engagement. In demanding that the phrase 'I love you' refer only to the instant of its enunciation, Frank strips love of the future projection that, for Vicki, must define the concept. In this specious reasoning, he produces the ideal moral philosophy to justify the behaviour of the narcissist: 'I could forget about being *in* my emotions and not be bothered by such things.'[86] Not being in one's emotions is also not to be troubled by the difficult communication required in the interpersonal negotiations of affective exchange.

At the end of this process is the temptation, but ultimate impossibility, of accepting a Socratic condition of affective ignorance. This dilemma is pertinent not just to Frank Bascombe's state, but also to a moment in American history in which both absorption and immediacy, as qualities opposed to the reproductions of self-reflection, seem particularly seductive. As William Chernecky puts it: 'Ford's Frank Bascombe novels reflect the contemporary American cultural climate where people no longer yearn for personal salvation, let alone any return to some earlier epoch, but for the sense, the ephemeral illusion, of well-being, good health, and psychic security.'[87] Representing thought's rebellion against thought, and emotion's rebellion against emotion, is a mimetic hall of mirrors in which a hypothetical true feeling – like the mythical Minotaur of the 'true self' – becomes increasingly hard to distinguish among its own reflections. The dream of an original affect, in accord with an immediate experience of pure being, cannot exist, for the reason that the quest for an unmediated state of non-imitative existence is itself a mediation. In this context, the practical uselessness of reflection – coded as imitative, self-reproducing and mimetic – is its perceived inadequacy to prepare one to live. As Frank's case makes clear, however, the profound irony is that all preparation for living is itself living, and all thinking about life is life itself.

## Affective Artifice: An Expansion of Mimetic Models?

To divide between causes and effects, origins and imitations in the realm of affect is once more to insert categorical barriers in a realm of dynamic force. What appeared mere moments ago to be caused or causal may not only shift, but utterly alter its role in an ongoing maelstrom of affective flow. To isolate one current of this incalculable fluidity is to create an illusion of authority where pure dynamism often reigns. In the same way, if we attempt to locate feelings' initial incarnation – the ur-emotion that constitutes their mythical ancestry – we necessarily embark on a linear model of causation, in an unattainable quest to locate such feelings' subsequent inferior copies.

This vision moreover presumes, with regard to aesthetic representation, a lack of porosity between literature and life: between internal diegesis and an extra-diegetic real. It implicitly postulates the existence of a non-mimetic affective space – alternately termed life, experience or being – which remains somehow untouched by the corruptions of representational processes. It is precisely the existence of such a naturalised space that the fiction analysed in this chapter disputes. It follows that metatextual fictionality does not necessarily question mimetic emotion more fully than more conventional realist modes. For while the latter may appear to embrace a simplified distinction between originals and copies, origins and ends, they are frequently involved in a sophisticated questioning of the hegemonies of affective truth. Emotional negotiations, we come to realise, all rely in different ways on the conventions of mimetic adhesion and belief. Rather than denying such codes, it is perhaps in the effort to extend and challenge their conventions – their heart of imitable artifice – that a possible response to the absolutes of affective causation may lie.

CHAPTER 4

# Myths of Emotional Equilibrium

It is difficult to overestimate the extent to which the concept of emotional equilibrium has become a cultural cliché. From self-help seminars to sport, from traditional to alternative medicines, and even encompassing creative practice itself, the belief in a beneficial stability has come to dominate much thinking on the affects, wherein the latter are seen to resemble other biological processes of homeostasis – such as the regulation of temperature in the body – and represent a constant striving for an optimal mean between excess and restraint.[1]

There are important problems, however, related to emotional equilibrium as an aspirational ideal. Firstly, balance applies a quantitative model to affective intensities characterised not only by constant alterations in magnitude but by incessant qualitative transformations. With anger fading into sudden tenderness, only to blossom into an unexpected joy, how may a supposed equilibrium be found between contrasting energies, themselves subject to unremitting metamorphosis? Secondly, are so-called negative emotions a vital part of this affective equalisation? If so, to what extent? In spite of the fact that they may produce a radical endangering of the social order, can violence and aggression, overwhelming suffering or unbridled desire, make up part of a positive stabilising system? If certain 'extremes' are excluded from such equities of antitheses, the 'tolerant' criterion of balance, in reinforcing consensual and conformist values, may in fact represent a covert apparatus of hierarchical control. For very often, a paradigm of apparent self-management is in fact one of self-restraint, in which instances of intense affect are perceived as dangerous outliers on a spectrum of emotional norms. Lastly, emotional equilibrium recurrently implies the existence of a unified self, whose internal stability would be proof of its overwhelming coherency. In promoting an aspiration to inner unity, the notion risks neglecting those iconoclastic aspects of a sceptical and self-questioning identity – those which, for both epistemological and emotional reasons, stubbornly refuse to cohere.

As we will see throughout this chapter's analyses of the fiction of Richard Yates and Paula Fox, emotional balance begins to morph from a philosophical ideal to a criterion of social and subjective limitation: a normalising pressure or injunction which characters alternately idealise and abhor. From the cultural valuation of affective 'control' in the 1950s, to the often irreconcilable demands for simultaneous 'sincerity' and 'stability' from the 1970s on, the work of Yates and Fox allows us to trace a more general cultural shift from a paradigm of post-war self-discipline to a world of ever-present fabrication, full of unavoidable emotional deception and traps. In all of these theatricalised environments – most often claustrophobic interiors and domestic spaces – the positive and negative artifices of fiction become increasingly impossible to either ignore or negate.

## Aristotle, Galen, Confucius: A Brief Archaeology of a Concept

Before arriving at this analysis it is first necessary to ask why, in the presence of such risks, is the model of affective balance so culturally prevalent? In contrast to the classical heritage of Plato and Aristotle, the modern version of such subjective wholeness does not serve primarily to attain the Good or the True, but rather to delimit the borders of the feeling subject's self-identity and, from this point of unity, to achieve a clichéd 'empowerment'. It is in part for this reason that equilibrium has become a cultural trope not only of affective well-being, but of secular spiritual harmony: a contemporary incarnation and popularisation of Confucius's Zhongyong or the Buddha's famed Middle Way.[2] In the context of Western philosophy, the notion's nominal lineage stretches back to the Pre-Socratics, and ranges from Pythagorean means to the earliest of medical theorists such as Alcmaeon, who first associated the state of bodily health with the equality (or *isonomia*) of opposing interior humours, subsequently extending to the later humourism of Hippocrates and Galen. Beyond the body, the stable existence and appropriate governance of the body politic is often reliant, in Plato for instance, on the restriction of passionate excess via philosophical logic and dialectic.[3] For Aristotle, right action is similarly dependent on a model of passionate control. As we read in *The Nicomachean Ethics*: 'moral virtue is a mean . . . between two vices, the one involving excess, the other deficiency . . . because its character is to aim at what is intermediate in passions and in actions.'[4] Crucially, having affirmed that 'there are also means in the passions', Aristotle even associates truth with the quality of internal equilibrium: 'With regard to truth, then, the intermediate is a truthful sort of person and the mean may be called truthfulness.'[5]

What these canonical conceptions have in common, beginning with the Pythagoreans and extending through Platonic and Aristotelian moral philosophies, is the establishing of affective balance with regard to a rational order. It is this baseline that allows for the positing of emotional equilibrium as an ethical principle of the well-lived affective life. *Mēdén ágan* (μηδέν άγαν), 'nothing in excess', was famously carved over the entrance to the Temple of Delphi, becoming as important as its fellow inscription, 'know thyself'. Moreover, 'nothing in excess' is explicitly linked to this epistemological venture in a chain of strict causality. For this Hellenic tradition, to know oneself is a process not only of expansion, but of limitation: a curbing of the body's passionate deviations so that it conforms not just to society, but to a ratiocentric ideal.

Affective control – if not yet emotional equilibrium in its modern sense – is throughout this tradition a guarantee of moral integrity, and a primary condition for the striving after Plato's Good, Aristotle's *eudaimonia* (well-being) or Aquinas's Virtue.[6] But these lineages lack a peculiarly modern conception of the self as a uniquely sentimental subject, fashioned by what Charles Taylor has called the condition of modern 'inwardness': the sense, emerging out of Augustine's *'in interiore homine'*, that 'awareness is always that of an agent'.[7]

In this lineage, the reason of *logos* is the constant baseline of an inner affective harmony. What happens, however, when such a rational ideal begins to be questioned, no longer seeming as stable or desirable as it once appeared? In the case of emotional equilibrium, the change is radical: the goal is no longer to be balanced with respect to Reason, but to make the self attain a measure of harmony with regard to itself. This search for an inner coherency no longer anchored in transcendent Reason remains an attempt to invest emotion with authenticity, so that the modern subject, as Taylor puts it, may proclaim that 'undistorted, normal feeling is my way of access into the design of things, which is the real constitutive good, determining good or bad'.[8]

Equating sentiment not merely with a variable subjective sensation – which shifts from one individual and moment in time to the next – but with higher values of a fundamentally moral nature means that ethical judgements come to be founded on sentiment's power of perceptive discernment, and its new capacity to show us the way things are. When, as in a Platonic hierarchy, we become dependent on emotional balance to show us the path to the Good, we witness the emergence of a new paradigm of truth – one which falters only if we become unsure what the notion of balanced feeling may in fact imply.

## Intensely Feeling a Lack of Intensity: The Crisis of Emotional Balance in Post-War America

It is in many ways the crisis of this modern conviction which we witness in the work of the post-war American authors under discussion in this book. For many, 'normal feeling' is precisely not Taylor's 'access into the design of things', but on the contrary an indeterminable abstraction by which dominant sociopolitical orders come to regulate the affects of a repressed modern self. In this perspective, the normal feeling of ideal equilibrium is rather a spectre which haunts emotional lives. At once an impossible and damaging archetype, it confuses inner harmony with social conformity, and peaceful consensus with forced restraint. The modern quest for emotional balance thus incessantly underlines a particular epistemological crisis, namely the extent to which we do not know our feelings, and cannot know them, at least within the context of a philosophical tradition sceptical of a hierarchically dominant Reason, and a social body – that of twentieth-century capitalism – that ineluctably commodifies affective well-being.

Increasingly omnipresent across an array of cultural discourses during the immediate post-war period, the link between emotional balance and emotional control is tightly bound to the regimes of affective limitation that were initiated or expanded in the face of the perceived risks of nuclear 'hysteria'.[9] As so often in equilibrist models, what came to be valued in the Cold War United States was not a particular type of stability, but the mere notion of stability itself. For behind these images of balance are medicalised visions of the body – which flourish in the post-war era after a long period of gestation – as a primarily equilibrating climate. Though the term 'homeostasis', for example, was coined by Walter Bradford Cannon in his 1926 book *The Wisdom of the Body*, the idea of internal bodily regulation which strives to maintain a stable 'internal environment' was first outlined in 1865 by the French doctor, physiologist and founder of experimental medicine, Claude Bernard.[10] In these initial formulations, homeostasis was a biological concept exclusively describing the maintenance of constant levels of blood sugar or oxygen supply. Far from explaining sophisticated self-reflexive processes such as emotionality, homeostasis was related solely to the preservation 'of a constant "milieu intérieur" ... in the face of changing environmental stimuli'.[11] Accordingly, Cannon's *The Wisdom of the Body* is structured into chapters with titles such as 'The Constancy of the Salt Content in the Blood' or 'The Homeostasis of Blood Proteins', which assort and classify a range of stabilising organic systems.

In spite of the general limiting of the notion to primary corporal systems, even in these earlier contexts bodily regulation is occasionally extrapolated, in a quasi-Platonic gesture, to the regulation of society and the nation state. In his epilogue entitled 'Relations of Biological and Social Homeostasis', Cannon relates bodily homeostasis to what he terms 'social homeostasis'. Transparently comparing the body's 'fluid matrix' to the state's 'processes of commerce', he extends the metaphor into a political ideology, affirming: 'It is of considerable significance that the sufferings of human creatures because of lack of stability in the social organism have more and more stimulated efforts directed towards improvement.'[12]

Though applied to modes of social organisation, what is absent from these earliest formulations of homeostasis is their application to complex emotional processes. In the context, however, of post-war ideologies of affective control, the concept of internal balance provides a powerful organic anchorage for visions of self-stabilisation. Indeed, emotional balance, supported by the conviction of the body's homeostatic vitality, seems an authoritative foundation for equilibrist models of affect, in that it provides a positivistic 'basis' for what before resembled a mere product of ancient medical theories.

Given this heritage, it is unsurprising that the application of the criterion of emotional balance to literary texts frequently results in its transformation from a positive idea of order to a negative regulation by force. In many post-war realist novels, characters therefore wonder whether their rebellion against interior balance inevitably constitutes a rejection of stifling social values. How is one to distinguish, moreover, between true and false balance, meaningful and meaningless calm? We may imagine that emotional equilibrium is critiqued in order to value a contrastive affective intensity; but this is not always the case. Instead, those who condemn docility often experience a deadening stasis, wherein meaningful intensity remains out of reach.

To be unbalanced is thus not necessarily to be intense. Instead, artifices or simulacra of intensity – such recurrent realist devices as alcohol, sex or sport – act as stopgaps for characters' lack of emotional fervour, the most recent example of which, for many, is associated with traumatic memories of war. Such counterfeits of intensity often cause them to remain in a state at once unbalanced and unintense: a situation mirrored by the suffocating social order of bourgeois American suburbia.

## Affect as Claim to Semantic Agency: Emotional Excess in Richard Yates

In an extension of the paradigm of imitative affect analysed in the preceding chapter, the novels of Richard Yates present us with individuals who intensely feel their lack of intensity. It is hardly surprising, in this context, that the epigraph to *Revolutionary Road* comes from John Keats: '*Alas! when passion is both meek and wild!*'[13] This apostrophe eloquently captures the intractable emotional and political problem with which Frank and April Wheeler find themselves faced, namely that their efforts to break restrictive emotional norms only end up reinforcing them. Crucially, the Wheelers' rebellion against stultification does not disrupt it: it enhances it. It is in fact an integral part of it, providing them with the sense that they, at least, are affectively intense, even if others in their surroundings are not. If one claims for oneself, however, the status of emotional exception, how to account for the fact that affect is necessarily a social mechanism, founded in part on communal values and beliefs? The disturbing possibility that Yates suggests is that the Wheelers' feeling of being unique in their emotional intensity – they alone are 'painfully alive' – is what fuels their affective disconnect.

Conformity is in this way composed of the desire not to conform, and the two poles of meek and wild exist in a feedback loop. It is the simultaneous intensity of affect and its lack – the threat that it may be outwardly intense and inwardly meaningless – which threatens emotional sense. Appropriately, we are confronted in Yates's fiction with instances in which emotional calm shifts into intensity without either of the two states appearing more or less meaningful. The following passage from 1975's *Disturbing the Peace* – in which Pamela, the lover of the novel's alcoholic protagonist John Wilder, announces that she is leaving him – is in this way representative:

> 'I'm moving,' she said. 'I'm quitting the job and I'm giving up the apartment and I'm leaving New York, probably for good. It does mean the end of things between you and me, and I'm sorry, but we always knew it couldn't go on forever, didn't we?'
>
> 'Yeah,' he said, surprised that his voice was low and calm. 'Yeah, I guess we always did know that.' He wanted to spring to his feet in fury and say 'Who's the man?' or to go down on his knees and throw his arms around her thighs and beg her to stay, but he did neither of those things because it seemed important to play the scene her way. And one small, irrational part of his mind suggested that if he did this well, if he was 'civilized' and

kept his emotions under control, she'd be so impressed that she might still change her mind.[14]

The effort to be 'civilized', with its imperialistic echoes, is an attempt to incarnate the social values of regulation and discipline that American modernity has imposed upon normative masculine comportment. Attempting to 'play the scene her way', John, in a moment of divided self-awareness, recognises this behaviour as performative. His awareness of the performativity of his apparent calm, far from weakening the grip of an equilibrist ideology, only reinforces it, for he clings to the hope that this self-control will lead to a rewarding of his virile bravado. In spite of this temporarily 'calm' façade, it is his fragile hold on emotional balance which, when informed by Pamela that there is another man, he is unable to maintain:

> The hell with being civilized; the hell with everything. He was on his feet and bearing down on her in a jealous rage.
> 'How long have you been sleeping with that bastard? Huh? I asked you a simple question: how long?'
> 'John, I don't see any point in losing your temper. There's really –'
> 'How *long*, God damn it. Answer me!'
> 'It's not a question that deserves an answer.'
> And suddenly he passed from anger to an agony of self-debasement and pleading.
> 'Oh, baby, don't go.' He touched her shoulder with one hand. 'Please don't go. I need you; I need you . . .'
> He had done both the things he'd sworn not to do – he had shouted and he'd begged – and there was nothing left.[15]

As a counterpoint to hysterical mythologies, a woman here embodies emotional restraint in the face of 'excessive' masculine feeling. But such feminine calm is again a perpetuation of an alternative trope, namely that of a caring maternal placidity. For John, the justified shift into masculine excess is not liberating, but is on the contrary a further restriction of his behavioural freedom. Having begun with a purely constructed serenity, only to progress to the extremes of shouting and begging, he soon exhausts the limited range of his gendered emotional inventory. In this quantitative model, there is 'nothing left' because his affective options extend not from meaningless to meaningful, but simply from less to more. More intense, but not more meaningful: John depletes his emotional options for the reason that questions of magnitude have replaced those of hermeneutics.

This dialectic between inner intensity and expressive restraint is, to a greater or lesser extent, always at play in our interactions with emotional force. In the context of post-war American realism, however, the degree of conflict within this dialectic is so heightened that neither emotional balance nor intensity is able to be transparently associated with affective truth. In a social context conceived as merely limiting of authentic interior energies, it is all the more disturbing if such intensities are not able to be recognised as incarnations of the affectively true.

Is restraint or the breaking of restraint thus more true? Given such nascent scepticism regarding emotional stability, it is unsurprising that we remark a consistent distrust in such texts of the nascent categories of clinical psychology, with its positing of affective balance as a lack of deviation from standard norms. The following exchange from Yates's 1984 novel *Young Hearts Crying*, in which the protagonist Michael Davenport resists analytic nomenclature, is in this sense revelatory:

> 'Oh, Michael. Are you going to start this nonsense about being "crazy"?'
> 'How is it nonsense? Would you prefer the kind of words the shrinks use? "Psychotic"? "Manic-depressive"? "Paranoid schizophrenic"? Listen. Try to understand this. Way back when I was a kid, before anybody in Morristown had ever heard of Sigmund Freud, we recognized three basic categories: there was sorta crazy; there was crazy; and there was crazier'n hell. *Those* are the terms I trust.'[16]

Michael's nostalgic reference to an era before psychological categorisation, while nominally opposing reductive labels, nevertheless establishes an affective hierarchy and emotional sliding scale. 'Sorta crazy', 'crazy' and 'crazier'n hell' are ironically terms one can trust precisely because they are more, not less, structuring and stratified than the new clinical definitions. We may also note that one crucial category is here missing, namely the baseline of zero psychological affliction. We may think that, in Michael's summary, this absence is implied; but his insistence on 'three basic categories' encourages a more surprising reading, namely that if the best one can ever hope for is 'sorta crazy', and if everyone within the larger social body is in fact an outlier, then the fight to attain affective neutrality is vain, and must be replaced by a common-sense, anti-psychologising attitude of stolid masculine strength.

It is not unimportant, given this revolt against psychosocial reductivism, that the 1950s and 1960s in America saw the rapid outgrowth of pharmaceutical companies keen to profit from the emerging promise of medical intervention as a solution to the problem of emotional extremes. The 1960s were marked by the flourishing of pharmaceutical advertisements, published in medical journals aimed at psychiatrists and general practitioners, which recommended pharmacological intervention for the problem of affective excess. 'Stabilise' was one of the recurrent slogans for this problem of the 'up and down' subject.[17] The domestic sphere, and in particular women, were especially targeted: 'Her kind of pressures last all day . . . shouldn't her tranquilizer?' asks one advertisement for the anxiolytic Meprosan depicting an overwhelmed mother struggling to give her child a bath, while another for the benzodiazepine Serax shows an 'anxious, tense, irritable' woman behind an array of scrubbing brushes, mops and brooms, and advises doctors: 'You can't set her free. But you can help her to feel less anxious.'[18] Renouncing all possibility for systemic change, pharmacological stimulants and depressants were explicitly employed to ensure the equalised maintenance of the domestic hierarchy and consumer economy.[19] Self-coherency and stability were again seen to lead to private 'efficiency', with the limiting of excessive affect – couched in the pathologised euphemisms of 'stress' and 'nerves' – a mode of reinforcement of repressive social and gender norms.

The ideological message of such advertisements is not even a subtext: if women can be 'calmed' by taking such novel inhibitors, they can better be made to accept their roles as docile guardians of domestic peace. As a contemporaneous campaign for Butisol made clear: 'When nervous tension augments family problems', the drug 'restores composure without loss of responsibility'.[20] There is no question of addressing such 'tension' beyond a system of pharmacological management. On the contrary, the 'stress' of these women is both quotidian and 'situational': that is, it is dependent on the social environment that post-war American society promotes as both a normalised and a beneficial state. As another campaign for the anxiety medication Serentil proclaimed: 'Serentil: For the anxiety that comes from not fitting in.'[21] Being emotionally balanced is a way to 'fit in' in the sense that it has the potential to quell revolt against intolerable social repression and malaise.[22]

So-called emotional balance is here an intentional reinforcing of a social status quo. To return to the literary context, such critiques of psychological and clinical categories are repeatedly undermined in Yates's novels by the fact that the very characters who espouse them are themselves victims of their own excesses, which they seek to code as non-pathological. Uncontrollable anger, depression or desire may not be explained away by new clinical terms, but the old nostalgia for a time before such categories – in a protected provincial America – is equally contentious. Both the reductive categories and their absence are similarly inappropriate solutions to the problem of affective control. This double-bind, wherein categorisation and its lack engender differing forms of a debilitating reductivism, frequently leads to a questioning of the ideal of emotional balance itself.

The familiar concept of hysteria, so prevalent in nineteenth-century realist traditions, again rears its head, and provides us with a revealing case study.[23] In this instance, as was already the case for Emma Bovary or Anna Karenina, hysteria is treated as a pathological condition which transcends its social instantiations, and becomes more generally representative of imposed demands of emotional limitation. A further example from *Revolutionary Road*, in the wake of a violent argument between April and Frank, casts the problem in a distinct light:

> She was hysterical. Watching her as she swayed and staggered from the support of one piece of furniture to another and then to the wall and back again, laughing and laughing, he wondered what he ought to do. In the movies, when women got hysterical like this, men slapped them until they stopped; but the men in the movies were always calm enough

themselves to make it clear what the slapping was for. He wasn't. He wasn't, in fact, able to do anything at all but stand there and watch, foolishly opening and shutting his mouth.[24]

In Frank's inherited, limited emotional arsenal, formed out of cultural commonplaces and cinematic clichés, feminine hysteria is meant to be corrected by a masculine gesture which would be at once calm and violent. He seeks a violent balance, but a balance nonetheless. The problem, however, is not merely that he is not calm, but that in failing to attain this state he abandons the possibility of communicating the moral sense of his acts. Revealingly, for Frank, maintaining calm imbues the vehement act in question with sense. Being emotionally balanced is laying a claim to semantic agency. Frank's impotency is of emotional meaning as much as of self-control.

If emotional balance seems impossible to establish without some idea of an affective norm, it is no surprise that the question of hysteria becomes intimately linked with that of representation and artifice. In *Young Hearts Crying*, for instance, Michael's wife Lucy, playing the role of Blanche Dubois in an amateur theatre production of *A Streetcar Named Desire*, is faced with the emotional prejudices of their director Jack:

'When you let hysteria come up into your face and your voice that way, you're robbing us of a lot of tension and suspense. You're kind of giving the whole show away, if you see what I mean.

'Well, of course I see, Jack,' she said. 'It's just that I wasn't aware of any – hysteria, that's all.'[25]

Importantly, hysteria here dissipates theatrical tension, rather than the inverse, as though its emotional pathways were ingrained in a predictable determinism of codified feminine excess. Rather than an increase in affective complexity, it is framed by Jack as a reduction, creating the pathologised simplicity of a symptom and syndrome. In this sense, it is 'giving the whole show away', a statement which implies that the theatrical form is dependent on an economy of affective oversight. Lucy subsequently rejects this limiting label:

'Jack,' she said, 'if you start talking about "hysteria" again, I honestly don't think I'll be able to –'

'No, that part was okay. You had good control on that tonight. This is nothing specific; it's more a general thing. And it's more important.'

His arm was around her, but it didn't bring much comfort. 'What I'm getting at,' he said, 'is that your whole performance tonight was – stagey. You were acting almost as if none of the rest of us were there. You kept kind of upstaging everybody else, all the way through, and the point is that's never a good idea because it shows. The audience can see it.'[26]

Not only, according to Jack, is emotional excess unbelievable, it is distracting. It attracts the audience's attention to one individual, 'upstaging' other actors in a theatricalised version of the danger of affective excess to social cohesion. In broader terms, the fear is that of the increasing primacy of the self, and of the unique intensity of that self's emotional expressions. Balance is crucial – especially for women – in order not to stand out too much in a society of increasing spectacle, thus emphasising the self's external valuations: 'It was all a matter of balance,' we later read, 'of going far but not too far'.[27]

In an extension of this meta-drama, the theatrical model is subsequently contrasted with that of literature, in which the processes of emotional excess involved in literary creation are nominally hidden from the receptive audience. When Lucy later abandons amateur theatre for the creative writing class, it is precisely because of emotional excess's less evident display:

When you wrote it didn't matter if hysteria sometimes came up in your face and voice (unless, of course, you let it find its way into your 'literary voice') because writing was done in merciful privacy and silence. Even if you were partly out of your mind it might turn out to be all right: you could try for control even harder than Blanche Dubois was said to have tried, and with luck you could still bring off a sense of order and sanity on the page for the reader. Reading, after all, was a thing done in privacy and silence too.[28]

The greater temporal and physical distance provided by the literary text shelters the creative woman from claims that she is emotionally unbalanced. Ironically, the calm and seclusion required for literature mirror that of the domestic sphere, wherein women such as Blanche strive to limit their emotional 'profusions'. However, the parenthesis is eloquent: 'unless, of course, you let [hysteria] find its way into your "literary voice".' The active voice of the verb – 'unless *you* let' – implies that it would be the fault of the woman writer for not sufficiently veiling her emotional intensity in the appropriate garb of literary style.

By not rendering her writing or acting sufficiently neutral, the woman artist dissipates 'tension' and 'suspense', as though the repression of affective extremes were required for not only social but also aesthetic success. It is as though the form of art itself – with distinct echoes of repressive models of literary realism – depended on the constant limitation of emotional excess, framed in highly gendered terms. Providing the 'unstable' writer with a gamut of literary techniques, the genre of realist fiction affords the ambivalent opportunity to hide unacceptable emotional instabilities. The point is not, as in the affective luxuriance of certain Romantic poetics, that such states may provide a positive Rimbaldian derangement, or an opening on to the revelatory experiences of a De Quincey, Coleridge or Baudelaire. Physical and emotional excesses do not reveal new worlds; rather, the recourse to such derangement must be masked in a prose which gestures to a veneer of normality, of the same type which pressures the characters of Yates's novels into increasingly restrictive social codes.

The usage of realist techniques is in this sense bivalent: it is beneficial in that it allows women who are creative artists to be taken seriously, but it is deleterious in that it precludes a wide-ranging examination of emotionality's justifiably 'excessive' aspects. Rather than being foregrounded, such exorbitance must be glossed over in order to ironically create the realist mythology of ordinariness and omniscience. As Yates's narrator later states concerning the creative writing workshop: 'Reticence was important in a room where any amount of emotional nakedness might soon be on display.'[29] Women creators are explicitly targeted by this problem. But men and women are caught in an enduring affective trap. Men must not be excessive because they are men, the ideal masculine image being one of affective containment; and women must not be prone to such affective surplus at the risk of being accused of hysteria.

In both cases, emotional excess is condemned. It is not a simple case of men being allowed instances of excess, while women are denied such privilege. Though the social perils are far more prevalent for women, fighting as they are against a patriarchal tradition which equates emotional intensity with inauthentic extravagance, both genders remain imprisoned within specific affective norms. In the end, realist tropes and techniques of diegetic control are an aid and a curse, in that they preclude an expansive treatment of the feeling subject's full affective breadth.

The same demand for emotional balance, replete with its curbing of excessive affect, is equally present in *Revolutionary Road* in the characters of John Givings and his parents, Helen and Howard. Previously interned in a psychiatric institution for his immoderate displays, John initially appears to be the only individual who, like the Shakespearian fool, is able to speak the truth, because his status as 'madman' implies his exemption from acceptable society's limiting speech. 'I just wish he'd keep his God damn opinions in the God damn insane asylum where they belong,' Frank revealingly exclaims at a moment of threatening crisis.[30] Excess and emotional disequilibrium are linked with 'madness' only when they are seen to undermine consensual norms. Rather than a long-desired revelation of ecstatic truth, Frank frames John's accusations in the terms of psychological instability. Clinical diagnosis is a mode of personal protection, with the institutionalisation of John's rebellion serving to inoculate others from his violent critiques. Why, after all, should one be offended by a madman? John's opinions belong in the 'God damn insane asylum' not only because they threaten a collective equilibrium, but because they cause in Frank such uncontrollable intensity that he too begins to lose his grip on the privileged rank of the 'sane'. Unreason thus undermines his masculine authority and his semantic claims. For in his blind rage that attains no truth, Frank's mixture of 'defiance and humiliation' indicates how the fight for the meaning of emotional excess is over who has the right to disrupt collective norms, and who must submit to a consensual accord.[31] Such anger on the part of both men aims at establishing both the rules of an emotional semiosis and who has the authority to decide them, without being forever excluded from the affective communality of the balanced.

Affective meaning is therefore rendered impossible by the very excess which sought to reveal it. Moreover, John's emotional extremes are interpreted as signs of instability less for their excess – for Frank's own are never qualified as 'insane' – than for the iconoclastic positions they defend. His speech is constrained by his parents' constant reminders that his modes of action are 'inappropriate', even when they give voice to compelling affective truths. After such outbursts, the attempted return to composure is a way of sugar-coating disruption beneath a dismissive apology. John's mock 'sorry, sorry, sorry' is a sarcastic summation of the refusal to address such anger on its own terms.[32] It demonstrates the power of processes of social normalisation, attempting to artificially assuage the disruptions of excess rather than address the interrogations they have provoked. In shifting the object from his inappropriate anger to the sadness of his own life, John indicates the twisted priorities of valuing emotional balance above an uncomfortable affective integrity.

We encounter a highly similar attempt to dissipate a problematic intensity, rather than understand it, in John's mother, Helen Givings. Confronted with the emergence of intense emotional pain – 'holding on to the bedpost with both hands and keeping her jaws shut very tight' – Helen attempts to dissipate feeling by focusing her thoughts on the soothing but imprisoning world of domestic order.[33] In the midst of her desperate sobbing, she thus concentrates on her 'sensible country clothes' and 'slipper-socks', now characterised in a cloying rhetoric as 'really the nicest things in the world for knocking around the house'.[34] When her crying subsides there emerges only a moment of self-infantilisation – 'Silly, silly, she scolded herself' – in which any potentially revealing intensity is lost in an unmeaning calm. 'But soon it was over,' Helen reassures herself, implying that all she must do is wait, or perhaps make use of the regulation of bodily rituals and hygienic realignments – 'blow her nose and wash her face and brush her hair' – to guarantee the passing of disruption. Affective disorder fading into immediate unanalysed order relegates such excess to the status of insignificant interruption. This state is, moreover, symbolically represented by the darkness – metaphorically an epistemological obscurity – into which Helen then plunges both her husband and herself: '"There," she said. "That's much cozier. Really, Howard, my nerves were just like *wires* after that business with the Wheelers. You can't imagine how it upset me."[35] The resumption of this normalised emotional tranquillity after such affective pain means that the suffering itself is not for a moment interpreted or explored. Viewed as a momentary, superfluous emergence, it becomes the mere crest of a wave which, once absorbed again into an ambient quiescence, need be considered no more.

The problem therefore lies less in the return to apparent calm than in the fact that there is not, in this state of renewed 'equilibrium', any opportunity for hermeneutic or subjective interrogation. In attributing such disruption to her 'nerves', and comparing them with the mechanist image of 'wires', Helen Givings provides a neurasthenic vision of the body rooted in earlier conceptions of nervous physiologies.[36] This image of the body as automaton, formed of nervous filaments, is indeed so physicalist that, once this nervous irritation has calmed, the questions it elicits may be similarly dismissed as just another symptom of a transitory corporal state. To conceive of Helen's prior sadness as a somatic disturbance is a defensive mechanism geared towards such an affect's non-analysis. Just as, after their subsiding, one would not think to interpret the subjective traces left by a common cold, Helen, having identified her sadness as a 'nervous' condition, does not feel it worthy of further comment.

As though it could have no meaning or value, Helen's intense sorrow in this way slips once more beneath the surface of a reassuring domestic peace. For the Wheelers and the Givingses, excess's use as a tool for revelation frequently ends with either a minimising return to superficial calm or a maximising movement into an equally vapid rage. In both instances, intensity and equilibrium are deployed as charged values, whose minimisation or maximisation allow for the avoidance of crucial emotional investigation. Rather than the revelatory Romantic tranquillity endorsed by Wordsworth's 'Preface', Yates's characters have recourse to a type of emotional acceptance as a mode of protective stasis.[37] Conversely, rather than conceiving of affective intensity as inherently epiphanic, it becomes empty of wider sense.

Throughout Yates's fiction, affective excess and restraint come to constitute a broader inquiry into the nature of emotional meaning.

For if meaning is not to be found according to a spectrum of intensity – merely increasing or decreasing by degrees of perceptible force – then feeling must be imbued with sense in some other way: one which recognises the value of affects not just by their intensity, but by their conceptual richness, formal complexity and creation of alternate ideals. Far more a questioning of the self than an affirmation of that self's convictions, it may be necessary to free emotionality from equilibrium's stultifying demands. For such valuing of balance, as Yates's fiction intimates, is always potentially a way to turn one's gaze from the disquieting contemplation of troubling subjective depths.

## 'She was ruled by impulse, he, by constraint': Agonistic Tensions in Paula Fox

As though no governing state of equilibrium were in fact possible, the characters in Paula Fox's fiction alternate between affective absence and excess. Because of this, they are recurrently accused by others of being either emotionally extravagant or dulled, both of which are seen as modes of contrasting egotism: as a narcissistic self-absorption in the case of excess, and as a hindrance to empathy in the case of affective lack. Convinced that they are conversing with mere social masks, Fox's characters spend so much time interrogating feelings' authenticity – at once other people's and their own – that they appear more preoccupied with determining their truth than with grappling with the underlying questions of identity and the self that such affects desperately pose.

In Fox's 1976 novel *The Widow's Children*, the central drama turns around Laura, a woman who, as her alcoholic husband Desmond puts it, is prone to 'thrilling displays of temperament'.[38] For those close to her – notably her reserved daughter Clara, her increasingly estranged friend Peter Rice and her troubled brothers Carlos and Eugenio – such unbridled emotional force is alternately energising and debilitating. At the novel's outset, Laura receives a phone call to inform her that her mother, Alma, has died that morning in a nursing home, spurned by a family who does not forgive her for a heritage of poverty and emotional neglect. Rather than revealing this news to those around her, setting off a process of open communal mourning, Laura chooses to keep this secret bereavement to herself:

> The news was that her mother, Alma, had died in midafternoon in a home for the elderly where she had been living for the past two years. Laura had turned to Desmond, even smiling when he asked her who was on the telephone, replying it was Clara asking directions to the hotel, would he unwrap the liquor bottles now? Then, returning to the official gravity of the voice at the other end of the wire, certification of death, it was saying, given by the chief doctor on the staff – heart failed . . . quiet death – asking about burial arrangements . . .[39]

Even in this initial revelation we remark the dichotomy between competing emotional registers. Revealingly, Laura's immediate reaction is not neutral, but consists in an affected 'smiling', asking her husband to prepare the omnipresent alcohol in an effort to deaden affective impact. Just as the novel's title transforms individual identities into familial roles – Alma reduced to a 'widow', Laura, Carlos and Eugenio to her 'children' – this disembodied bureaucracy is referred to as a neutral 'it', which in its dry announcement wraps emotional power in institutional nomenclature, prefiguring Laura's own repression of this news. For in spite of her renowned extravagance, the news of her mother's death leads immediately to an absence of 'deep' feeling and thought:

> Her mind had been empty of thought; she had known only that something implacable had taken hold of her. And she had felt a half-crazed pleasure and an impulse to shout that she knew and possessed this thing that no one else knew, this consequential fact, hard and real among the soft accumulations of meaningless events.[40]

Focused on her mother's passing as a 'fact', death is for Laura, from the outset, a paradoxical source of stability among affect's fluctuating variations. As a transcendent and enduring value, it is not for Laura open to doubt or to the infinite modulations of subjectivity, alterity or time. Though painful, such stability underlines a contrast between the dependability of her mother's death and the chaos of affective repercussions which, in their irradiation, will influence all. To state that death, at least, is 'hard and real' is to initiate a disturbing tension wherein only the negation of existence has solidity. Laura's 'half-crazed pleasure' derives as much from an egotistical status of exception as from the exhilaration of finally possessing a 'true' event.

Following the Maldonada family during the brief time between Alma's death and her funeral several days later, *The Widow's Children* presents a universe of supreme and omnipresent artifice. Motifs of falsity and unreality in the narrative's environs are moreover constantly mirrored by cases of emotional deception. Taking place in a series of claustrophobic interiors, the novel's settings are explicitly theatrical. From the outset, these environments, like a range of sets – a hotel room, a corridor, a restaurant – are filled with manifestations of duplicity and subterfuge. Even apparently living objects are in fact lifeless, rendering impossible all desire for connection: 'She passed an enormous potted fern and, reaching out to touch it, found it to be made of plastic.'[41] Throughout the text, such objects are suspended in the same ambiguous state as characters between authenticity and inauthenticity, vitality and apathy. In a binary logic associating artifice with death and truth with life, such surroundings are invariably framed in terms which equate affective balance with the quest for an unmediated real. As Laura's friend Peter puts it regarding the furniture of the hotel room where she receives the news of her mother's death:

> 'So pretentious, this fabric. Fake brocade, isn't it? Why not be plain? Why not a plain, decent chair? Why is music played in elevators? And what music! And those revolting gold tassels on airline menus, and what are those designs stamped on your bedspreads? Coats of arms, no less! I mean –'
>
> 'Peter,' Laura said. 'Don't waste your nerves on trivia. The world is wrecked, my dears. There's no point at all in being sniffy about the corpse's low taste in winding sheets.'[42]

With the use of the term 'decent', the aesthetic characteristic of being 'plain' is associated with a moral quality. Conversely, the notion of embellishment, far from a purely formal judgement, becomes linked with both affective falsity and immoral intention.

Elevator music, gold tassels, designs stamped on bedspreads, are all presented as extrinsic ephemera – 'trivia' in contrast to what is essential, but entirely undefined. Beneath this talk floats of course the unspoken truth of Alma's death: an ultimate condition and event-horizon which renders unnecessary the world's transient objects as much as our feelings about them. Linked to the ancestral heritage of 'coats of arms' – a lineage which, with Alma's death, has been irrevocably severed – artifice and death are again linked in Laura's affirmation on the futility of deploying aesthetic 'taste' for the enshrouding of the dead. Not to waste 'nerves on trivia', as Laura puts it, is another way to ask: why concern ourselves with truth if we necessarily die? Why worry about the falsity of feelings or the world's ingrained artifice if death is an immutable constant, able to eliminate all others with the intensity of its glare?

Throughout the novel, the secret of Alma's death has an array of emotional repercussions, which ripple out from Laura to affect each member of the family in turn. As the origin of extravagant outbursts, Laura is alternately the prime source of affective artifice and the individual who, by way of these same devices, cuts through the reserved falsity of social niceties. Indeed, her husband Desmond's fascination for her is rooted in his desire 'to track down and discover what it was in her nature that led her to such thrilling displays of temperament'.[43] The unpredictability of this excessive feeling is constantly linked to the question of emotional truth. How may we know whether Laura's excesses, by virtue of their brutality, force the revelation of repressed verities or merely perpetuate still more artificial deceits? As Desmond puts it regarding his wife in a highly equivocal formulation: 'Laura told the truth – whatever it was at the moment.'[44] In this self-cancelling logic, Laura is held up as the truth-telling Fool whose veracity will always morph, often incarnating its contrary. She may cut through the veils of decorum, but her ferocious truth will have only a passing legitimacy, appearing, in the next instant, like a deformed falsehood warped by the unveiling of time.

To each member of the Maldonada family, all emotion, including their own, seems somehow inauthentic, torn between unreal lifelessness and the chaos of vital histrionics. As though Alma's death rendered all unreal, Laura's non-reaction at the news of her mother's passing, combined with her melodramatic displays, repeat this dichotomy in varying forms. Asked by Carlos how their mother is faring in her nursing home, for instance, Laura's reaction is eloquent:

> They were all staring at Laura. She had clasped her drink to her forehead frantically as though an ache there must be pressed away. Her eyes were closed. In the tension of her raised arms, the loosened curls tumbling forward, legs lifting toward her stomach, one shoe beginning to slip from a foot, she was like the personification of calamity.[45]

As a literal *tableau vivant*, Laura reproduces tropological gestures, incarnating a clichéd image of overwhelmed emotional pain. Crucially, the narrative voice is also exterior to this diegesis: a mere spectator to Laura's inner processes, this voice is able only to speculate – 'as though' – on the reality of her inner states. Faced with this melodrama, others are entirely unable to determine the degree to which it 'corresponds' or not to a hypothetical inner truth:

> Desmond cried out incoherently, Peter stood up, Carlos backed away toward the windows, and Clara, remembering a glass of whiskey hurled at her by Laura so many years before she could not recall the place, only the arc of the glass, crouched in her chair.
> The legs came down, the foot found the fallen shoe and inserted itself, the drink was held out to be appraised by the now wide-open eyes, and Laura grinned at them like a rogue.[46]

As though the descent back into 'balance' were just as theatrical as the preceding unease, this subsiding into supposed normality, where each element of Laura's *tableau* reassumes its prior appearance, is an extension of her artificial play. Memory of her past actions means that her pose is interpreted according to a tradition of paradoxically predictable transgressions, of which she too is highly aware. Moreover, in this syntax's curious active voice, it is the divided parts of her body, rather than Laura herself as unified identity, which assume once more their original states. Her roguish grin is similarly deceptive: though implying that all was mere play-acting, it does not mean that her display of pain was unequivocally false. There is no way of deciding whether Laura's return to equilibrium is at last an authentic face behind the mask, or simply, on the part of a consummate sentimental actor, another performative posture.

Ingrained in the Maldonada family's artificial heritage is also their status as Spanish emigrants. Through the characters' central obsession with atavism, they view their own histrionic tendencies as the product of 'an ancient ooze, the true elements of that Spanish blood, *sangre pura*'.[47] Alma's death further cuts ties with a past of perceived Hispanic intensity, now exchanged for the conformity of a White American reserve. Indeed, emotional power itself is identified at various points not as a universal aspect of affective interactions, but – as previously seen in James Baldwin's explorations of White society's efforts to curb a 'threatening' African American intensity – as a fundamentally racialised trait. As Laura's daughter Clara puts it regarding her own heritage:

> In no other company more than among these Spaniards was Clara so conscious of a discrepancy between surface talk and inner preoccupation. They sped from one posture to another, eliciting with amused cries each other's biases, pretending to discover anew the odd notions each harbored, amusing themselves nearly to death! Until Laura, with a hard question, thrust a real sword through the paper props, and there would be for a second, a minute, the startled mortified silence of people caught out in a duplicity for which they could find no explanation.[48]

Revealingly, the metaphor of the fight for truth is rendered by the image of stage combat, as though the distinction between Laura's 'real sword' and the 'paper props' of her adversaries were also subsumed within a generalised emotional spectacle. The irony of Clara's claim is that for her to speak of adopted 'postures' is to establish herself as a neutral spectator of such role-play, one able to distinguish, if not between true faces and false masks, at least between variant theatrical avatars.

Though Laura is, throughout the novel, the focal point of questions of emotional excess and truth, the entire history of the Maldonada family is haloed by intensity's blinding glow. As though they were deprived of emotional balance by a genetic mechanism, the cause of their excess is retraced to such biologically predetermined, congenital 'blood'. As we read regarding Laura's brother Eugenio:

> For there was a man whom 'pure blood' had driven crazy ... It was said that Eugenio never touched anyone's hand – fear of contamination, perhaps. Once, when he'd stayed at Alma's old apartment, sleeping on the studio couch among the rattletrap furnishings of the living room, Clara had heard him scream in the middle of the night like a horse pitched onto barbed wire. And once he had kicked a hole in the plaster of the wall, waking to find his foot covered with blood. Alma had pasted over the hole a picture of an ape she had found in a copy of *Life* magazine.[49]

Contamination is related to a fear of both emotional and physical infection, evident in the constant interplays of affect's mutual influence. Eugenio is compared by Clara to a suffering horse and by Alma to an ape, with his screams viewed not as extremes on a human emotional spectrum, but as abnormalities which diverge into the realm of the animal 'other'. Kicking 'a hole in the plaster' is not without metaphorical importance as an affirmation of destructive escape, though this literal breaking through accomplishes Eugenio's transformation from feeling man into uncontrollable beast. Alma's pasting of the image of an ape over this breach is finally a reduction of the possible meanings of Eugenio's act, as though it revealed nothing else besides an underlying brutish will.

Laura justifies her persistent infliction of emotional pain by her role as iconoclastic dissident, engaged in an enduring assault against reason's hypocritical lies. As a self-proclaimed herald of truth, she deploys the weapon of theatrical excess to cut through the artifice of the world. 'To destroy certainty' is, in Clara's words, her mother's antinomical project. It is a project which, far from allowing her to freely move among emotional variations, leads to the permanent confusion of conflictual states. For though the undermining of certainties may appear liberating, the 'equivocal' state which Clara describes, 'as close to weeping as to laughter', is one of affective relativism in which all points of the emotional compass, unbridled by excess, seem equally distanced from a higher sense.[50] Such temporal dynamism is one of the primary problems of associating intensity of feeling with truth, for as Peter Rice observes, 'such dramatic summations' could surge up 'with what seems to be all the truth of a thing, falling away as a great wave falls, into the trough of daily life and its unthinking motion'.[51] Absorbed once more into a quotidian flux, these intensities never attain a status of permanent legitimacy.

Though a constant source of conflictual anxiety, however, Laura is also a source of lived intensity. For many of the characters, she is a potential antidote to both apathy and unreality, even though her excesses cause real carnage. The problem is again that such vigour, after jolting one from complacency, goes so far that it begins to seem utterly performative:

> She actually can't judge her own behavior, Peter thought; she explodes, then wonders at the flying glass ... He had always counted on Laura to rescue him, for a little while, from shallow custom, to revive in him a memory of the life of feeling, but this night, the constantly erupting flames of temperament he'd always thought to be without calculation or prudence seemed merely a mechanical display.[52]

We realise the central philosophical question regarding emotionality that lies within Laura and Peter's bond. For Peter, Laura is valuable as a being who excites within him 'a memory of the life of feeling', save that he needs to feel that these 'erupting flames' are spontaneous, 'without calculation'. For a culture in which true feeling is so often associated with intensity, a central paradox arises when this fervency is infused with orchestration. But can emotional intensity remain intense without harnessing the powers of artificial play? Indeed, as an energy which 'explodes', Laura is at once uncontrollable in her outbursts and profoundly in control of her performative range.

Having attributed to her such fire, Peter may remain passive in his mild-mannered conviction that he simply does not possess the 'flames' of 'Spanish blood'.[53] For if he did to some extent recognise affect's artifice, he would also need to accept the degree to which it may be altered by the self, falling under the scope of its agency and will. There is here no middle ground between a vision of emotions as authentic, unchecked, pure bodily fire, and as mere 'mechanical display'. In an imagology of organicity and mechanicity, temperament's naturally 'erupting flames' may lead to a moment of emotional revival; but as soon as such flames' spontaneity is questioned, and the possibility of their intentional cultivation proposed, they are banished to the status of mechanistic device.

No longer connected to a deeper authenticity, Peter begins to feel that such affective flames burn vainly, fed by no true inner fuel. And this is indeed the risk with all emotional excess, namely its delicate oscillation between poles of concealment and revelation, nonsense and sense. With the revelatory power of her transgressive excesses, Laura can, as Carlos puts it, '[gather] up in one intuitive flash the whole sum of his feeling', focusing her skills for violation and heterodoxy on the production of an 'astonishing discernment'.[54] Just as often, however, such transgressive violence, meant to cut through to provocative truths, results in passionate transports exhausted of intrinsic worth. Laura's transgressive behaviour may then appear empty: mere unbridled destruction without any higher aim. Even more mysteriously, these meaningful and unmeaningful modes may arise concurrently, or be exceedingly difficult to distinguish.

In spite of this appearance of expressivity, we recall that throughout all these displays Laura has been repressing the spectre of her mother's death. There begins to emerge the image of Laura as a simultaneously repressed and excessive figure (or excessive because repressed). For against the background of her extravagant comportment, she is consistently accused of affective detachment, as though a deep coldness were in fact the origin of her vehement outbursts. Viewed as passionate and passionless, she represents a dichotomy of interior apathy and exterior frenzy. After Clara, for example, is finally informed by Peter of her grandmother's death, she remarks of Laura: 'I don't pretend that she didn't feel anything. But Jesus! She's dead cold inside, half born. She doesn't really know that anyone else is alive.'[55] In accepting that Laura feels, all the while affirming that she is 'dead cold', Clara's logic appears contradictory, save that, as she goes on to affirm, Laura's limited feeling remains within the contours of her own self. She may feel, but she does so, in Clara's vision, with herself and for herself, with any emotions revealed to the outer world like ripples spreading from her ego's inner stone. Ironically, and in a further perpetuation of emotional equilibrium's impossible quest, this same critique of absent feeling is later levelled at Clara. 'She looked composed, cold,' remarks Peter when Clara refuses to attend her grandmother's funeral. 'He disliked her suddenly; he was chilled by her callousness. Let her play dead then! . . . She had a hard nature. She was arranging her face to show indifference.'[56] In 'arranging' her face as one may arrange a decorative surface, even Clara, a primary critic of Laura's emotional apathy, becomes an embodiment of both coldness and performativity, infected by a 'callousness' at once real and feigned.

Affective absence, it seems, is thus a frequent impression received by others in their attempts to interpret exterior social displays. In an inquisitional cycle, those who feel others to be unfeeling are accused of being unfeeling themselves. The circulating nature of such accusations indicates that empathy has difficulty thriving in a context based on quantitative conceptions of emotional force. For it is not only Laura whose emotional excesses lead to suspicions regarding affective truth. Her brother Carlos too, as a typological incarnation of the Maldonada 'pure blood', is also a subject of speculation on the insincerity of his emotional displays. In an important extension of these normalising paradigms, Carlos's homosexuality casts a further pall over feelings deemed by other characters to be excessively 'dramatised'. When he learns from Peter of his mother's death, for instance, Carlos's reaction is framed in terms which seek to render it abnormal, or even morbidly pathological:

> 'Your mother died.'
>
> Carlos looked straight up at the ceiling, then burst into clamorous violent sobs. His mouth fell open, enormous tears flowed down his chin, his hands thrashed the air. Lance flew to him and threw his arms around Carlos's massive shoulders. 'Poor old thing . . .' he murmured. 'Poor old thing has lost its mama.'[57]

In this succession of maximising qualifiers, the narrative voice makes plain the exceptional nature of Carlos's reaction, coding it not merely as eccentricity but as disruptive anomaly and affective deviance. Sobs are not just sobs but are 'clamorous' and 'violent', and tears are spatialised as 'enormous', beyond the bounds of quantified norms. As though to underline a position of narrative disapproval, the intensifiers multiply: Carlos does not look up, but 'straight' up; he does not produce identifiable gestures but uses his hands to '[thrash] the air'. Similarly, his partner Lance does not simply move towards him, but 'flew to him and threw his arms around Carlos's massive shoulders': a corporal presence which, like his oversized emotion and tears, is gendered as socially and biologically incongruous.

As though it were in fact his perspective filtered through this narrative bias, Peter's reaction to such expressivity is far from empathetic:

> He was being persecuted by the sounds of lamentation in the other room; those explosive heated sobs seemed operatic and profligate, as though Carlos were desperately simulating grief in order to ward it off. But what had he expected? Indifference? Irony? Ritual gravity?[58]

Peter does not believe in the genuineness of Carlos's grief because of the intensity of its expression. It is, however, precisely the same intensity which in other contexts would be taken as a distinct sign of emotional truth. Peter's accusation of 'simulating grief in order to ward it off' is in this sense a complex allegation. He does not accuse Carlos of feigning grief that he does not feel, but rather of embellishing an inchoate, rising agony, in order to protect himself from that very affect's swelling force. The fake intensity of Carlos's sobbing is, Peter hypothesises, a protection from the true intensity of an emergent inward pain. By this torturous rationale, Peter escapes the conclusion that, in this particular case, he lacks all empathy, and is simply unwilling to accept that such suffering is sincere.

For how, if we follow this reasoning, may Carlos ever express suffering without it being coded as extravagant 'lamentation', and therefore false? Further reinforcing the gendered prejudices at play, a term such as 'profligate' carries strong echoes of a licentious immorality. At the same time, Peter recognises that no other position adopted by Carlos, even if it appeared to correspond to the codes of restrained masculine stoicism – 'Indifference? Irony? Ritual gravity?' – would seem any more appropriate. Situated outside the spectrum of affective expression, it is as though Carlos's emotional manifestations, whatever they may be, will necessarily be deemed unbalanced and thus untrue, due to his alterity with regard to certain heteroaffective norms.

In a further extension of these paradoxes of emotional limitation, Laura is often the one who demands affective regulation: 'Now, Carlos, a little stoicism, please,' she asks at one point of her brother, betraying no irony.[59] This apparent contradiction is in reality imbued with a contorted logic: if Laura exerts no control over her impulses, then she also exerts no control over her desire that others be controlled. Her existing in the crux of hypocrisy, as in the paradoxes of pure desire, is a by-product of her dwelling in the currents of passionate flux. As a contrastive basis to their friendship, this is perhaps why Peter Rice views himself as an ideal image of restraint: 'I am the only sensible person in this place.'[60] Imbued with a parodic rationality, he is recurrently presented, in contrast to Laura's artificial excess, as a repository of deep feeling which is forever concealed:

> 'I don't know,' Peter said with such utter disaffection that Clara wondered if she was not hearing the accents of his real mood, a prevailing truth over which he drew a thin cover of amicability, not, she thought, to deceive, but to avoid an indelicate show of some suffering, some estrangement she sensed in him. He was so unlike the Spaniards; everything about him – his different stance, his hands, so clean, so fleshless, so little given to gesture, his plain suit – spoke of a central idea of manners from times past, a strict intention to keep the solitary wounded self where it belonged, in the private dark.[61]

This dialectic between an outer show of socialised 'manners' and the world of the 'private dark' establishes a fantasy of a unified subjective truth, as though somewhere within Peter, as within us all, lay a definable 'real mood', 'a prevailing truth' of emotional being untouched by an ambiguous performative haze. Peter's cleanliness and his lack of gestures establish a rhetoric of legibility and transparency, contrasted to deceptive embellishment. In Clara's fantasy, it is as though the inner self were not also equivocal, but primary and unified. In such authentic depths, the 'solitary wounded self' is seen to lie like a governing truth, of which Peter's 'clean' public face would be at once concealment and sign. At least in this vision, Peter does not escape the dichotomy between exterior and interior, surface and depth, artifice and truth; only for him, in contrast to 'the Spaniards', it is seen to derive not from a desire for deception, but from a veridical source. Any time Peter hides his feelings, this act becomes, in Clara's mind, not dissimulation but the protection of a deeper truth. Hiding oneself may, in this sense, become a claim to a truth of inner feeling which, for a variety of reasons, can never be expressed.

Neither emotional intensity nor restraint, for Peter and Laura, are thus any more or less artificial. But strangely, in a world where all feeling is infected with falsity by virtue of its distance from a primordial self, suspicion becomes a paradoxical comfort in that it demonstrates one's awareness of social disguise. As Peter observes, it is because Laura is suspicious of everyone – including herself – that he can feel, in his own words, 'safe' with her: 'she was ruled by impulse, he, by constraint. And each pitied the other for their subjugation to opposing tyrannies. And this opposition between them – wasn't it the reason for the durability of their connection?'[62] Those 'less suspicious of themselves', in their increased ability for direct action, pose a greater threat than Laura's self-reflexive excess. Peter implies that impulse is not a rebellion against dominant powers, but a dominant power itself. Excessive feeling is in turn not a liberation but an alternate mode of submission. Supposed enemies, impulse and restraint are thus not at all opposed; instead, they function in much the same way, alternately directing and limiting the whims of an always desiring *conatus*. For Peter to attribute 'the durability of their connection' to their shared enslavement is to insist on a fundamental similarity between modes of emotional expression and repression: that both represent an inner division with regard to the quiddity of the self.

Throughout Fox's fiction, the self is endangered by feeling both because it may reveal a 'private dark', and because there may in fact be no 'deeper' self to reveal. As Clara observes: 'She told them what she thought would amuse them, but kept herself out of it. She feared, without knowing why, that the weight of one word of personal feeling would sink them all.'[63] How, we may wonder in response, is feeling ever not 'personal'? Clara's fear expresses the extent to which she seeks to define emotionality as a question of coded sociality far more than subjective engagement. No such binary is possible, however, for the reason that 'personal feeling' is at once social and of the self. It is not an isolated essence of an inviolable core. This suspension, like that between excess and absence, is part of the self's vulnerability, which the recourse to true feeling strives to dismiss. When Laura suddenly calls Peter 'darling', for instance, he is struck by the possibility that the word reveals within him, for an instant, 'a true state of feeling', rendering him simultaneously fragile and thrilled:

> But *was* it his distress which had elicited from her the thrillingly spoken endearment? He was not comforted, he was alarmed. Was it not that he had revealed, for an instant, a true state of feeling, had abandoned the posture of being her temperate adversary? And if it was that she had recognized, what difference did it make whether she called him *bastard* or *darling*?[64]

Like other postures of emotional excess, Peter's role as 'temperate adversary' may indeed be a role, but this does not mean that any supposed end to his performance implies the discovery of an enduring truth. In placing truth of feeling upon a pedestal of epiphanic resolution, Peter fails to recognise that this 'true state' which he so ardently desires would be merely another fixed image of affective flux. Subject to transformative change, it would in no sense resolve his tensions with Laura. Postures are not 'abandoned', they morph; and in spite of what Peter may claim, being called 'bastard' or 'darling' seems far more important than whether a hypothetical 'true state of feeling' has been reached. Such terms, after all, are the explicit signs of a human connection, and of a meaningful love or hate. For Peter to even question the importance of this distinction – 'what difference did it make' – is evidence, if any more were needed, of the dangers of sacrificing the quality of affective intimacies on the altar of emotional truth.

## Balanced Fixity: Emotional Equilibrium's Problematic Stasis

In these various mythologised quests for emotional stability, true feeling is intuited as a possible solution to the dilemma of a balance which is always absent or failed. Again and again, the impossibility of locating such elusive equilibrium, equated moreover with a lost authentic self, leads to a sense of errant identity beset with acute affective distress. If only, according to this mythology, emotional truth could at last be reached, such swaying between alternate poles of excess and absence could end, for an imperious truth would provide the long-sought counterweight of calm. Truth as equilibrium in this way places a demand of limitation upon the necessarily excessive self.

Frequently condemned as a restrictive normality, emotional balance, in the context of modernity, is a concept which displays a surprising degree of fixity in spite of its multifarious circulations across disciplines and cultural spheres. In spite of the categorisations of modern clinical psychology, we find everywhere in these discourses echoes of Plato's condemnation, in the *Republic*, of Achilles' excessive grief, for the reason that it endangers the moral solidity and coherency of the greater body politic.[65] If emotional balance is to have value, however, it can never be as an imposed ideal of social or subjective stability, but only as a vision of affect's infinitely unstable – because plural – equilibriums, each charged with an inherent excess at their core.

CHAPTER 5

# Medicalisation, Pathologisation and the Intoxicated Self

The growing cultural valuation of true feeling throughout the American post-war period was accompanied by an increasing medicalisation of bodily states. Like the fostering of emotional equilibrium, the goal of maintaining a pure corporal condition, uncorrupted by exterior agents, was sustained by the conviction that the emotions felt while under the influence of altering factors were less 'true' than those which derive from a condition of organic purity. Feelings experienced in the presence of psychotropes were thus negatively viewed as less authentic than those seen to be the product of an uncorrupted corporality. Simultaneously, a range of countercultural discourses sought to elevate psychotropic perceptions – during psychedelic experiences, for example – to a status of phenomenological superiority, because they would be more penetratingly insightful than the everyday emotions of banal somatic neutrality.[1] Such a tendency even extended to the condemnation of emotionality itself, with a writer such as Timothy Leary arguing: 'Emotions are the lowest form of consciousness ... Did you imagine that there could be emotions in heaven? Emotions are closely tied to ego games. Check your emotions at the door to paradise.'[2] What Leary terms 'bliss or ecstasy' is subsequently defined as an 'absence of emotion', and 'higher' modes of being – such as love – dissociated from affective experience. 'Love cannot exist', affirms Leary, 'in an emotional state.'[3]

As we will come to understand through this chapter's analyses of the fiction of John Updike and Raymond Carver, in cases of both countercultural alteration and its conservative resistance, the logic is the same: the feelings of an altered self are either superior or inferior because of their increased or decreased quotient of subjective veracity. For reasons we will see, alcohol plays this altering role in both Carver's and Updike's work, and will form this chapter's central case study. But behind this dichotomous relegation or elevation of feelings lies a powerful ideological conviction concerning emotionality more generally: not only that an 'unaltered' self may exist, but that its feelings could be trusted more or less than its supposedly altered incarnations. Whether the body is seen to be purified by psychotropes or to attain purification by the elimination of their influence, a logic of expiation governs this cathartic process. In the modern mythology of this paradigm, where greater corporal purity is seen to result in greater emotional truth, the desire for true feeling within the body as sanitised essence becomes a mechanism for the inoculation of exterior affects viewed as invading contagions. This rhetoric of contamination leads to a strong degree of separation between interior body and exterior world, with the limits of the corporal membrane seen not to be porous, but to constitute finite borders of defence. In such a vision, the organic body, like the wider American social body affected by a climate of post-war anxiety, assumes a role of protective structure against a vast range of altering mechanisms of malfeasance.

## True Until Disrupted: Psychotropes, Corporal Purity and Emotional Truth

Both causally and conceptually equated with true feeling, such a model of corporal purity instigates an impossible quest for non-influence, where each time a stimulus from the world reaches the body it is seen to disrupt the neutrality of an authentic interior state. Feelings are not, however, true 'until' they are disrupted by the world. They are literally formed of the outer world, woven of its forces as much as by interior chemical and semiotic processes. Since Michel Foucault's *The Birth of the Clinic* (1963) or Georges Canguilhem's *The Normal and the Pathological* (1966), this identification of a corporal normality has been seen in historical terms as intimately linked, since at least the eighteenth century, with the emergence of the legitimacy of modern medical institutions, founded on an array of rationalising epistemologies.[4] While pragmatically central to epidemiological protocols, the pathologisation of behaviours – with their requisite diagnostic classification as addictions, disorders or syndromes – is also part of the way medical professions defend their own claims to cultural and epistemic authority.[5] At the other end of this spectrum, the decriminalisation or liberalisation of substances, with an associated abandoning of psychiatric categorisations, has been viewed as a path of triumphant return to an unaltered bodily normality. Such a state is seen to lie beyond the strictures of medicalised nomenclature and capitalist pharmacologies, whose diagnoses render their own products and disciplines integral to the treatment of disorders which they themselves have 'invented'.[6]

In discourses of both medicalisation and anti-medicalisation, logics of true feeling often reign. The altered body is viewed as a site of purity or corruption, whose emotional authenticity is ultimately harmed or ameliorated by processes of institutional pathologisation. As we will see, however, models of affective purity encounter significant problems when convictions related to the body's base neutrality and normality begin to break down. If we may locate no such stable grounding, may 'intoxicated' feelings still be evaluated according to affective falsity and truth? Like equilibrium, the conceit of the body's unsullied essence becomes increasingly difficult to maintain in the face of conceptual interrogations regarding the nature of such an apparent 'resting state'. Encompassing continuities and ruptures, the notion of altered states structures our experience of the world, and forms an integral part of our constructed narratives of consciousness. But to speak of an altered body is necessarily to ask: altered with respect to what? To a norm or baseline which, like homeostasis, presupposes a hypothetical quiescence? To a graduation of changes extending across various spectrums? As we exist in time, and are conditioned by the experience of change, our consciousness, bodies and very existences are inevitably and continually altered. In the same sense as for Canguilhem the concept of health integrates and necessitates the threat of disease, to conceive of an uninfluenced emotional purity is to live always in the shadow of its impending corruption by the forces of intoxicating alteration.[7]

What then are the limits to the psychotropic? Are all substances and energies deemed to be exterior, altering 'others', able to engender changes within an internal organicity?[8] If so, is food an altering psychotrope? Is water, or air? Where are the borders of the body's unaltered normality if such a state is constantly shifting, being shaped by the eddies and currents of a permeable world? Equating emotional truth with an organic purity makes emerge a range of new problems, especially if we come to suspect that the body is always characterised by a condition of altered becoming. These interrogations are multiplied if we in turn wonder whether such states can even be conceived of as 'states' at all, but rather as dynamic variations for which no categorical differentiation may be found. Indeed, if alteration implies disruption, it may be improper to refer to states at all, to the extent that this implies a degree of stability and dependability, rather than the indistinguishable continuity of multivalent flux.

Does it make sense then to speak in terms of normality and pathology, neutrality and alteration with regard to affective paradigms? Should emotions generated or influenced by altering forces be considered somehow lesser or fake? Or is the value of such experiences distinct from their causation? In the light of these interrogations, this chapter asks whether emotional truth is threatened when feelings are seen to have an artificial or psychotropic origin. Is the deep sadness or unbridled joy that may emerge, only to suddenly morph or pass, when drunk, on drugs, in a fever or during dreams less 'true' than those emotions which occur in moments of alert consciousness, deemed to be statically neutral? Conversely, what occurs when individuals begin to equate their normal waking lives with a condition of artificial distortion? How to understand one's own affective integrity when the simple fact of existing in the world seems imbued with less reality than the powerful emotional actualities of intoxication or derangement?

From the development of pharmaceutical industries in the 1950s and 1960s to Richard Nixon's War on Drugs in the early 1970s, the context of the post-war years provides a particularly charged environment not only for the enforcement of notions of bodily purity, but for their association with paradigms of affective truth.[9] The extent to which Nixonian policies were based on the implied true feelings of the 'silent majority' – which Nixon, in his television and radio address of 3 November 1969, used as justification for the United States' ongoing involvement in the Vietnam War – is a crucial aspect of specific psychotropes' post-war repression.[10] As Dan Baum outlines, though supported by a voter base which was in reality 'quaking with rage and fear', Nixon continually underlined the extent to which this base's tranquil neutrality, nevertheless framed in terms of a 'war', would win out against the forces – racial, sexual, political – of social disruption:

> [Nixon's] administration would restore 'the peace forces as against the criminal forces' and ask little else of the 'forgotten Americans' who 'go to work and pay their taxes and support their schools and churches'. Rather than argue with the critics of either racial discrimination or the Vietnam War, Nixon and the Republicans were learning to discredit them indirectly. Rather than debate policy, they denounced conduct.[11]

This moralisation of personal responsibility – also typical of post-war policies on narcotics – places the calm of an affective majority on the side of bodily and emotional purity, and opposes it to the altering forces of 'criminal' defilement. In a symbolic paradigm wherein the maintenance of the body's unadulterated borders is extensible to the exclusory divisions of the nation state, true feeling comes to sanction the repression of a disruptive heterogeneity, with such 'peace forces' an incarnation of an affective and political purity.

This chapter will explore the ramifications of such ideological conflicts by focusing on one key post-war substance: alcohol. Viewed as both a corrupting psychotrope and an everyday aliment, alcohol was in many ways the drug of choice for American realist writers, characters and even readers, condensing a range of social paradigms such as normalisation and pathologisation, transgression and repression, rebellion and control. In contrast to countercultural valuations of psychedelics, alcohol throughout the post-war years was used less as an iconoclastic means of liberating perception than as a way to tolerably persist within established norms. In doing so, and in contrast to a potentially rebellious impetus, alcohol established itself as a curiously 'neutralised' substance, deceptively invisible in its altering effects and banalised in its transparent integration into social environments. The way emotional truth comes to be viewed under alcoholic influence is all the more striking because of alcohol's cultural normalisation. For the fact that alcohol is framed as a personal problem – either of the individual will or as a generic disease – means that it no longer semiologically constitutes, as for periods of prohibition, a radical threat to either communal cohesion or the moral order. It remains, however, a threat to an even more fragile, solipsistic structure: the emotional truth of the self.

## Drunk on Truth: Alcohol and Authenticity in Post-War America

Since at least Plato's *Symposium*, the tripartite concepts of intoxication, emotion and truth have maintained a long and troubled history.[12] Even before questions of causal interactions in the body's physiology, alcohol and emotionality share certain related traits. They are commonly conceived according to a fundamental dynamism, being associated with fluidity, unpredictability and impermanence. As figures of a Dionysian irrationality, alcohol and affect are viewed, in a ratiocentric tradition, as giving rise to an inner subjective disquiet. Viewed as internalised agents of delirium, both are framed as operatives which hinder perception, leading the subject further from the real and deeper into the shadows of Plato's cave. Appropriately, diverse philosophical traditions of a revelatory drunkenness concentrate on the idea of frank expression, with *in vino veritas* – already quoted by Pliny the Elder in the first century AD – as their motto.[13] Though it is considered an agent which liberates expression, what is less common throughout this tradition is the notion that alcohol may facilitate not only sincere declaration but also the discernment of the real. In stark contrast to the epiphanic dimension accorded in the post-war period to peyote, psilocybin or LSD, alcohol is often seen to dull the perceptive faculties, preventing a more profound phenomenological encounter via a deepening anaesthesis.

There are, however, important counter examples to this heritage. The American novelist Patricia Highsmith argues that alcohol is integral for the artist as it 'lets him see the truth, the simplicity, and the primitive emotions once more'.[14] This points to a Rimbaldian derangement as a way of attaining a true affective candour beneath limiting social veneers.[15] In this vision, alcohol is a substance which strips away the manners of an inhibiting decorum, providing access as much to an expressive sincerity as to an ontological real. But such alternative propositions are rare; for what is surprising, in the context of modern American literary history, is the near absence of positive visions of intoxicated revelation from the 1950s on. In writers of this era, from Shirley Jackson to Norman Mailer, alcohol is a much darker substance than for the prior generation of equally 'alcoholic' American realists.

Though the texts of these post-war authors are just as alcoholically saturated as those of the interwar years, literary depictions of the substance come to be cloaked in a new lexis of pathologisation, and emerging psychotherapeutic conceptions of the addicted self.[16] We may remark the almost total evacuation from post-war realist fiction of scenes of 'happy' intoxication. From Chaucer to Boccaccio and later Joyce, scenes of congenial sociable drunkenness and jubilant abandon are a ubiquitous literary trope, as present in Greek poetry as in medieval sagas or Renaissance theatre. This modern shift towards depression, anxiety and death in the literary depiction of alcohol marks an important change regarding not only the substance's social consideration, but its link to affective intensity. While certainly not always positive, alcohol in the work of writers such as F. Scott Fitzgerald or Ernest Hemingway carries the potential for romantic ideation, affective intensification and a movement into truth. This dimension is frequently absent from post-war literatures in which both alcohol and the feeling body are beset by paradigms of addiction and clinical care.

## From Alteration to Addiction: The Shifting Paradigms of Deranged Experience

Post-war America in this sense represents a continuation of the disciplinary and sociopolitical process – initiated in the nineteenth century and intensifying throughout the movements of American Temperance and Prohibition – of alcohol's expanding medicalisation. 'Medicalization', as Peter Conrad notes, 'describes a process by which nonmedical problems become defined and treated as medical problems, usually in terms of illnesses or disorders.'[17] Historically, this development took the form of what sociologists have termed a shift from a rhetoric of alteration, inebriation and intoxication, to one of addiction, disorder and disease.[18] The post-war medicalisation of alcohol, and the rise of the notion of 'alcoholism' itself, was thus a central social and academic controversy.[19] Throughout American history, and most notably in Temperance rhetoric, the practical usefulness of alcoholism's pathologisation was clear, for as Joseph Schneider puts it: 'Such a characterization allowed temperance leaders to draw on a cultural universal. Disease, however defined, is undesirable. It should be opposed, controlled, and if possible, eradicated.'[20] In the context of the twentieth century, medicalisation was significantly enhanced by the post-Prohibition development of clinical research, and the medical establishment's growing cultural authority. Impotence, stress or sunlight similarly enter into evolving medicalising discourses.[21] As Paul Starr outlines, the invention of clinical conditions such as alcoholism is further bolstered by a process of legitimisation in which 'Americans, who were wary of medical authority in the early and mid-nineteenth century, became devoted to it in the twentieth'.[22]

Whether alcoholism or a variety of other types of addiction do or do not constitute a pathology is of course not here at stake. What is pertinent however is the observation that emotions felt under the influence of supposed altered states are increasingly delegitimised. Because such pathologisation led to certain altered feelings being inscribed in a symptomology issuing from 'disease', they were no longer culturally invested with the same degree of affective authenticity, much less with the revelatory dimension accorded to them by countercultural movements.

All of this culminates in the concept of intoxication (as distinct from our modern understanding of addiction) being, as Marty Roth puts it, 'a "lost object" of social and cultural history'.[23] In turn, intoxication's omnipresence in literary texts, along with its semantic implications, is underplayed or ignored. We find in a variety of works, as Roth remarks, a 'constant hum of alcoholic reference that should dominate all other indicators of meaning and yet can be apprehended only as cultural white noise'.[24] In spite of its semantic and symbolic saturation, few critics would venture that *The Great Gatsby* (1925) is a novel literally 'about' alcohol; framed in these terms, it seems like an unworthy semantic centre around which the novel's diegetic machinery would turn. Notions such as authenticity, materialism or the unstable modern self are presented as bearers of semiotic weight – but drinking? What are we to do, however, with the fact that essentially every one of the novel's key scenes occurs under alcoholic influence? Merely literal or purely symbolic, alcohol is relegated to the status of a qualifying environment: like the weather, it is simply there, forever in the background, composing a fictional medium but deprived of the power to truly mean.

This hypothesised shift in twentieth-century literature from a paradigm of intoxication to one of addiction eloquently captures the transition from a climate of socialised revelry to one of isolated pathology. In *The Sun Also Rises* (1926) and *The Great Gatsby*, alcohol consumption is invariably communal, extroverted and ideational, devolving into rare violence only in exterior social space. In contrast, within the cramped environments of Yates, Carver or Updike, alcoholic consumption foregrounds a world which is invariably asocial, introverted, domestic, and plagued by intimate violence within the family unit. Implicated in the emerging pathologies of clinical addiction, alcohol is no longer the froth of champagne – the effervescence of existence – but rather the dark unreality of a distorted affective life. Something has changed since Fitzgerald's praise of the fusional qualities of champagne's fizz. As Nick Carraway observes during Gatsby's garden party, not without a certain irony: 'I had taken two finger-bowls of champagne, and the scene had changed before my eyes into something significant, elemental, and profound.'[25] We may compare this description to Ina's reflection some fifty years later in Truman Capote's 'La Côte Basque': 'Champagne does have one regular drawback: swilled as a regular thing a certain sourness settles in the tummy, and the result is permanent bad breath. Really incurable.'[26] By 1975, Capote's formulation has transformed champagne's effects into a medicalised condition. Pathologised in its repercussions, it is the drink's propensity to create an 'incurable' corporal state which is emphasised over any other alteration. Whether or not this condition describes a physiological reality is of course beside the point: what matters is that only rarely in Hemingway or Fitzgerald is there talk of alcohol, or any other intoxicating substance, in such uniquely medicalised terms. In the space of a half-century, much of the romantic froth has faded from the drink which, for the Roaring Twenties, was an ideal symbol if not of joy, at least of uninhibited festivity.

Mirroring the arc of alcohol as a face of twentieth-century medicalisation, the diagnostic term 'alcoholic' is also conspicuously absent from this prior fiction, but ever more present in post-war texts from the 1950s on. Indeed, a language and semiotics of addiction begins to permeate, integrating alcoholic consumption – and the emotions felt under its influence – into contemporary medicalising discourse. Stripped of a rhetoric of liberating *jouissance*, alcohol is rendered clinical, and becomes a generalised code for the isolation and spiritual detachment of the modern subject, unable to find her place in a world of bourgeois conformity and emergent consumer capitalism. Linked with a range of antisocial behaviours, the substance becomes a simultaneously distorting and revealing lens through which to interrogate the myth of true feeling and its widespread penetration of cultural discourses.

## 'Everybody who tells you how to act has whisky on their breath': Interiority, Isolation and Addiction in John Updike

Incarnating derangement's darker side, alcohol is thus linked in an array of realist texts with motifs of limitation and control. As Saul Bellow observed of John Berryman in 1973: 'Drink was a stabilizer. It somewhat reduced the fatal intensity.'[27] And as Rabbit Angstrom affirms early in the first novel, *Rabbit, Run*, of John Updike's tetralogy: 'Everybody who tells you how to act has whisky on their breath.'[28] In the place of champagne's interwar charms, post-war whisky becomes representative of a new alcoholic paradigm. Rather than a source of liberation, alcohol in this way becomes both a tool and a symbol of the conformist subservience to social rules.

Updike's 1960 novel begins with Harry 'Rabbit' Angstrom, a twenty-six-year-old middle-class salesman of kitchen appliances, who returns home one evening after work to find that his wife Janice, though seven months pregnant, has relapsed. In the wake of the ensuing explosive argument, Rabbit leaves their suburban abode and impetuously decides to drive out of the small town of Mt. Judge on to the interstate, leaving his home, his wife and his two-year-old son Nelson, apparently for good. After living for several months with Ruth Leonard, a woman who occasionally works as a prostitute, Rabbit returns to Janice following the birth of their daughter, Becky. Attempting to re-establish a life of domestic normality, Harry and Janice's existence quickly deteriorates as Janice, recovering from childbirth, is unable to respond to Rabbit's insistent sexual desires. In order to remedy the problem, Harry tries to coerce Janice into sex, in spite of her history of alcoholism, by fixing her drinks:

> He persuades Janice to have a drink. He makes it – he doesn't know much about alcoholic things – of half whisky and half water. She says it tastes hateful. But after a while consumes it.
>
> In bed he imagines that he can feel its difference in her flesh. There is that feeling of her body coming into his hand, of fitting his palm . . . He rubs her back, first lightly, then toughly, pushing her chest against his, and gathers such a feel of strength from her pliancy that he gets up on an elbow to be above her. He kisses her dark, hard face scented with alcohol. She does not turn her head, but he reads no rejection in this small refusal of motion, that lets him peck away awkwardly at a profile.[29]

In its invading saturation, alcohol suffuses Janice's body, altering its outer 'texture' and inner constitution, until Harry 'can feel its difference in her flesh'. Its influence, which renders inactive a body deprived of agency, is compared to the insistent touch which asseverates its power by way of a manipulative mock tenderness. Meant to prepare her for the unwanted sexual encounter, alcohol generates simultaneous vulnerability and resistance, an incongruent 'pliancy' and 'dark, hard face'.

Establishing an association between alcohol and a deeply negative affective artifice, this connection only deepens when, after the rejection of Rabbit's advances and his typical flight once more, Janice is left alone with her whisky as an intimate replacement for his absence. As she wakes alone after her husband's departure, alcohol's return in Janice's existence is fraught with symbolic sense:

> The last hours are like some narrow turn in a pipe that she can't force her thought through. Again and again she comes up to the sound of him saying Roll *over* and can't squeeze through it, can't not feel panicked and choked. She gets out of bed and wanders around with her one tight breast the nipple stinging and goes into the kitchen in her bare feet and sniffs the empty glass Harry made her drink whisky out of. The smell is dark and raw and cozy and deep, and she thinks maybe a sip will cure her insomnia. Make her sleep until the scratch at the door awakens her and she sees his big, white body ramble in sheepishly and she can say *Come to bed, Harry, it's all right, do me, I want to share it, I really want it, really.*[30]

In spite of the preceding sexual violence, the lexis used – 'dark and raw and cozy and deep' – is one of homeliness and interiority. From the 'last hours' being 'like some narrow turn in a pipe', however, to the literal bodily constriction of choking, the passage is rife with images of claustrophobic confinement, contrasting with the whisky's evocation of domestic sanctuary. Appropriately, the cramping panic of Janice's existence is assuaged by the imminent swallowing of her drink; the substance is moreover medicalised, framed as a sleep-inducing sedative. Her subsequent encounter with the external environment beyond such private suffocation will pose the question of the affective reality of her intoxicated world:

> She puts just an inch of whisky in, and not much water because it would take too long to drink, and no ice cubes because the noise of the tray might wake up the children. She takes this dose to the window and stands looking down past the three tar roofs at the sleeping town. Already a few kitchen and bedroom lights show pale here and there . . . The highway, half-hidden by the silhouettes of houses like a river between banks of trees, this early swishes with traffic. She feels the workday approaching like an army of light, feels the dark ridged houses beneath her on the verge of stirring, waking, opening like castles to send forth their men, and regrets that her own husband is unable to settle into the rhythm of which

one more beat is about to sound . . . Anger at Harry begins to bloom, and to stifle it she drains the glass and turns in the dawn to look where she lives: everything in the apartment is a shade of brown.[31]

In a recurrent trope of calibration and measurement, the act is calculated so that the drink will not take too much time, nor make too much noise: so that this tool of emotional repression will itself remain stifled. In these images of half-tones, nothing is bright nor distinct. Throughout, the contrast between domestic interiority and suburban exteriority is explicit; but which is the more 'real'? Forcing one to accept, in this 'army of light', a normative existence of martial regulation, the pragmatic world of active effort is also somehow unreal. If it too is shade-like, then how is one to believe that the sober, diurnal world indeed corresponds to the real? Transformed into the homes of a fairy story, 'opening like castles to send forth their men', the lines between the worlds of waking and sleeping, transparency and alteration become profoundly blurred. In a waking landscape of 'silhouettes', Janice's drunken awareness is perhaps closer to an unpleasant truth than the blind functionalism of a societal 'rhythm' that Rabbit is unable to accept.

In a crucial inversion of accepted values, the 'army of light' of the outside world, with its erroneous promises and misplaced dreams, is somehow less real than the shadow-world offered to Janice by her whisky. This inner realm is not simplistically separate but has rather, by the passage's end, come to mirror the drink itself: 'everything in the apartment is a shade of brown.' Fusing altering substance and altered real, this standardising colour unites cause and effect in a new homogeneity which destabilises perception. As Janice's downward spiral deepens, alcohol, rather than an anaesthetising paralysis, produces an extreme degree of self-conscious awareness. Struggling against the limitations of her state, she occupies an ever more externalised perspective, especially in her accomplishment of parental 'duties':

When she picks up the baby again she feels its wet legs and thinks of changing it but cleverly realizes she is drunk and might stab it with the pins. She is very proud of thinking this through and tells herself to stay away from the bottle so she can change the baby in an hour.[32]

This undermining of ratiocentric processes, wherein Janice becomes a doubled identity, shows the extent to which alcohol is not an escape from rational discernment, but rather a plunging into the tortuous networks of reason's simulacra. In a spiralling semantics, Janice's feelings become not so much disconnected from the world of sense as involved in the extreme connectivity of their hermetic logics.

It is indicative that such alteration takes place exclusively in the domestic sphere, where Janice's duty as housewife, mother and carer increasingly resembles a theatrical role which she is less and less able to play. For the result of all this mental calculation is that the baby will remain unchanged. Though Janice appears to strive to preserve a maternal ideal, alcoholic excess allows her to elide her functions, without expressing this refusal in the terms of an ideological critique. A range of affective qualities coded as feminine – notably patience, empathy and nurture – are in this environment instruments of repression. Alcohol thus provides a paradoxical rebellion not merely because it makes Janice less able to fulfil her custodial role, but because it immerses her in the rationalising contradictions at the heart of this affective restraint. In causing her to perform incomplete parodies of repetitive chores, drinking limits Janice to this function in the midst of her attempts to free herself from it. Unable to assume a spectrum of emotional norms, she nevertheless still aspires to them and is able only to generate an intoxicated, ersatz version of maternal care.

Alcohol confronts the problem at its heart: when reason, reality and truth become devices of oppression, their disruption aims at a transgressive liberation. Rather than a true emancipation, however, drinking leads Janice to the mimicking of her precise modes of enslavement. Homely scenes – such as sitting with Nelson on the living-room rug, playing with colouring books – become occasions for affective derangement:

> She smiles in the delight of coloring her page, a barnyard, so well, of feeling the little rods of color in her fingers make such neat parallel strokes and her son's small body intent and hard beside hers. Her bathrobe fans out on the floor around her and her body seems beautiful and broad. She moves to get her shadow off the page and sees that she has colored one

chicken partly green and not stayed within the lines at all well and her page is ugly; she starts to cry; it is so unfair, as if someone standing behind her without understanding a thing has told her her coloring is ugly.[33]

Janice's suffering is not unreal simply because of her advancing inebriation, nor because its stimulus is the 'unimportant' fact of not staying 'within the lines', with the myriad symbolic echoes of this regimentation. Rather, her sadness, like her initial delight, is as real as any other state – and indeed it may be precisely because these affects seem caused by a substance, rather than her surrounds, that Janice is able to penetrate deeper into her matrix of emotional pain. What matters is not a binary of a revelatory or distorting pharmacopoeia – whether alcohol takes Janice deeper into true feelings, or constitutes their twisted perversion. Such dualism ceases to be meaningful as soon as we remark that alcohol gives rise to an anguish which is both epiphanic and illusory, with no inherent contradiction.

Though a literal cause of endangerment, alcohol promises the maintenance of the feminine calm and capability valued by a certain patriarchal morality. For if inebriation has encouraged the emergence of tears, it also promises their disappearance in the flux of affective energies, and the resumption of maternal action:

> Nelson looks up and his quick face slides wide and he cries, 'Don't! Don't, Mommy!' . . . She pushes herself up from the floor with a calm smile and goes into the kitchen, where she thinks she left her drink. The important thing is to complete the arch to the end of the day, to be a protection for Harry, and it's silly not to have the one more sip that will make her capable. She comes out of the kitchen and tells Nelson, 'Mommy's stopped crying, sweet. It was a joke. Mommy's not crying. Mommy's very happy. She loves you very much.' His rubbed stained face watches her.[34]

Though proof of her affective distress, such dynamism nevertheless serves a purpose. In their vigorous transitions from pleasure to pain, such shifts resist hierarchies of normalising stability. It is appropriate then that the simulacra of logical processes again affirm their presence, with this parody of reason also infecting Janice's internal rhetoric. For in claiming that her crying 'was a joke', she seeks to comfort not only her son, but also herself, by professing that such mutability is part of a ludic artifice. Phrases such as 'Mommy's not crying' and 'Mommy's very happy' are similarly idealistic projections: they are not merely lies that Janice tells herself but also assert a desired reality. They are what she desperately wants to believe, and are in this sense as much emotional ideations as her obvious malaise.

Such an interpretation is an alternative reading to critics who see in Updike's fiction, as Tony Tanner put it in a 1972 *New York Times* review, portraits of 'the terrible inner hollowness' of individuals who remain 'emotionally deadened'.[35] Comparing Updike's characters to Plyushkin in Gogol's *Dead Souls* (1842), Tanner finds them affectively deficient and expresses the feeling of 'reading about people in whom the capacity for a key emotional response or experience has been omitted or eradicated, leaving a small central void that diminishes or undermines the authenticity of their other emotional experiences.'[36] In such a model, an affective essentialism is required for characters to be viewed as lacking with regard to it. We may not, however, declare that Janice feels emotions that are inauthentic – that are, as she herself puts it, a mere 'joke'. Her emotional life is less Tanner's 'central void' than a highly charged concentration of ambiguous valence, poised between representation and reality, strategies of repression and terrible pain.

Throughout this process, alcohol remains a substance which incites a new disequilibrium, in which the balance of normalised feeling is disrupted, no matter the risks. When Janice cuts short a concerned phone call from her father, for example, such volatility takes bodily form:

> Feeling dizzy, she hangs up. This is a mistake, but she thinks on the whole she's been clever enough. She thinks she deserves a drink. The brown liquid spills down over the smoking ice cubes and doesn't stop when she tells it to; she snaps the bottle angrily and blot-shaped drops topple into the sink. She goes into the bathroom with the glass and comes out with her hands empty and a taste of toothpaste in her mouth. She remembers looking into the mirror and patting her hair and from that she went to brushing her teeth. With Harry's toothbrush. She discovers herself making

lunch, like looking down into a food advertisement in a magazine, bacon strips sizzling in a pan at the end of a huge blue arm.[37]

Janice's state is symbolic of a general loss of orientation with regard to a stable real. Crucially, this destabilising does not render impossible her domestic performance, but merely distorts such tasks, transforming them into awry simulacra. Unmoored from both time and space, Janice is able to seize their occurrence only when they are past. Puppet-like, her actions awkwardly re-enact habitual gestures, as though they too were part of an addiction.

Though within her homely jurisdiction, Janice no longer controls the objects and ephemera of her world. The poured alcohol 'doesn't stop when she tells it to', and spilt drops escape their container. However clumsily reproduced, all of her actions either seek to take care of her appearance or complete rote chores. Her dissociation is so radical that she is mentally absent not only from activities, but also from her self. Like this life's standardised ephemera, her arm no longer belongs to her, but is likened to the advertisements of market consumerism: she becomes at once part of such images and their ironic deformation. Accompanying this dissociative effect are the dynamic powers of the psychotropic, which allow her to move far more quickly (but chaotically) across an affective spectrum:

> Nelson says the bacon is greasy and asks again if Daddy go away and his complaining about the bacon that she was so clever and brave to make at all annoys her so that after his twentieth refusal to eat even a bit of lettuce she reaches over and slaps his rude face. The stupid child can't even cry he just sits there and stares and sucks in his breath again and again and finally does burst forth. But luckily she is equal to the situation, very calm, she sees the unreason of his whole attempt and refuses to be bullied. With the smoothness of a single great wave she makes his bottle, takes him by the hand, oversees his urinating, and settles him in bed. Still shaking with the aftermath of sobs, he roots the bottle in his mouth and she is certain from the glaze on his watchful eyes that he is locked into the channel to sleep. She stands by the bed, surprised by her stern strength.[38]

We realise the extent to which Janice's emotional existence escapes the reductive criteria of authentic or inauthentic, false or true. For if ever we were tempted to see this outburst as less rational than the ensuing state of serenity, we discover here their mutual mimicry. Incarnating all maternal postures at once, she is able to impose, after her aggressive action, an equally constructed calm. In a disturbing reversal, Janice adopts a position of emotional evaluator, judging Nelson's terror as unreasonable. 'With the smoothness of a single great wave' she begins again her habitual activities, as though none of these fluctuations caused any lasting disruption in the ideological weft of her world. In this sense, Janice's renewed composure is no less artificial than her anger. It is not a return to reason after the excesses of affective intensity, but a shift into an equally ambiguous state wherein reason and unreason continue to act out their shared theatrical roles. Her intoxicated state is not one of unreasoning violence interrupted by lucid quiescence; it is a fluid spectrum in which calm and reason, as oppressive authorities, generate as much suffering as their more vehement antagonists.

These scenes all foreshadow the novel's dreadful climax in which Becky, Rabbit and Janice's newborn daughter, drowns in the bathtub while a drunk Janice attempts to give her a bath. In desperately trying to maintain the natural rhythms of her existence in the judging eyes of others, Janice involuntarily destroys the very entity that made such rhythms a pragmatic need. Domestic responsibility is removed along with the being who made such responsibility a requirement. In this immeasurable loss, framed according to an ideology in which 'the worst thing that has ever happened to any woman in the world has happened to her', Janice's conclusive refusal of a stifling role as maternal protector is traumatically accomplished.[39] Alcohol is the means of this terrible rebellion, whose 'liberating' distortions could find no other emancipating space.

Becky's death is in many ways the tragic result of Janice's emotional existence having no other modes of enactment beyond the true and false binary of imposed social functions. We encounter a final instance of this paradigm in the last novel of Updike's tetralogy, *Rabbit at Rest*, which provides a contrasting case to Janice's experience through her son, Nelson. Now an adult in the late 1980s, and in accordance with societal shifts in American psychotropic consumption, Nelson is addicted to cocaine, with his dependence causing Rabbit and Janice to lose the family car-dealership. In a conversation with his golfing friends, Rabbit demonstrates the degree to which questions of alteration are linked to those of true feeling, establishing a dichotomy between the true and false happiness which psychotropes create:

> 'I don't know about Sanders,' Bernie says, 'but a lot of it's drugs. Cocaine. The stuff is everywhere.'
> 'You wonder what people see in it,' Rabbit says.
> 'What they see in it,' Bernie says, stopping the cart and resting his cigar on the edge of the plastic ledge for holding drinks or beer cans, 'is instant happiness.' He squares up to his second shot with that awful stance of his, his feet too close together, his bald head dipping down in a reverse weight-shift, and punches the ball with a four-iron: all arms and wrists. It stays straight, though, and winds up within an easy chip in front of the elevated green. 'There are two routes to happiness,' he continues, back at the wheel of the cart. 'Work for it, day after day, like you and I did, or take a chemical shortcut. With the world the way it is, these kids take the shortcut. The long way looks too long.'
> 'Yeah, well, it is long. And then when you've gone the distance, where's the happiness?'[40]

Several interacting senses of the term 'happiness' are here at play, for in the notion of 'routes to happiness', further tied to the pragmatic ethics of 'work', we realise that the word is used as much to describe the 'successful life' of economic prosperity as an emotional quality of the self. In a metaphorical mirroring, the flight of Bernie's golf ball, which in spite of surrounding obstacles 'stays straight', recalls this linear teleology towards contentment conceived as static accomplishment. Bernie's rhetoric – 'work for it, day after day' – mirrors a particular corruption of Emersonian self-reliance into the mantras of mercantile self-help, with its credos of American independence, personal initiative and entrepreneurial achievement. Opposed to the 'hard work' which guarantees success in a mythology of egalitarian meritocracy, the 'chemical shortcut' implied by pharmacology is as much anti-capitalistic as it is anti-natural. Even worse, such 'happiness' via intoxication is seen to be inauthentic precisely because it is anti-capitalistic: easy to achieve, it has not respected the accepted path to accrued emotional joy. In doing so, it bypasses the laws not only of emotional accretion, but of a capitalistic worth.

Drug-induced happiness is thus not unreal in itself, but because of its corruption of the stable benchmarks of social standing. As a shortcut to an unchanging goal, these 'two routes' underline the implicit binary between nature and artifice, labour and chemistry, which informs this ideology throughout. In this context, Rabbit's final phrase is poignant, for having accepted a vision of the world in which 'hard work' and self-reliance allow for the attainment of an emotional ideal, he unwittingly undercuts this fantasy by implying that all such work does not result in any idealised well-being. 'Where's the happiness?' is a question which hangs over the entirety of this exchange, and over Updike's work more generally. With its echo of an unfair bargain, the question equates happiness with a return on investment, a salary for labour or a reward for sufferings past. But there is here no dividend at the end of one's emotional expenditure. Instead, happiness is forever elusive within a model which conceives it only as an intoxicated immediacy or a capitalistic reward.

Far from a simple division between the natural feelings of a balanced body and the constructed excesses of an artificial pharmacopoeia, we find in Updike's fiction a constant inversion of such binary logics. Indeed, alcohol frequently leads to a type of behaviour seen to be 'instinctual' which may only be repressed via a return to the 'reason' of the self. In these contexts, the criteria of a revelatory or distorting psychotrope begin to break down, as does the coherency of right feeling. In its sociohistorical longevity, extending from the post-war 1950s to the late 1980s, Updike's tetralogy confronts us with the lasting hold of reductive paradigms of true feeling, which stake their claim to the value of the uncorrupted body and elevate such purity to the status of righteous virtue. For the hypothetical condition of non-influence imposes a further stricture on an already limited moral world. In such a paradigm, the choice is no longer between the artificial and the natural, psychotropes and their absence, but between altering intentionalities of various qualities and degrees. Such a vision confers a greater measure of agency to eternally altered subjects, with dominion over the body's transgressive affects related not merely to exterior agents, but to the modifiable dynamics of a durably plastic self.

## 'I'll tell you what real love is': Deranging Feelings in Raymond Carver

As for a range of other post-war writers, alcohol is omnipresent in the fiction of Raymond Carver. In myriad stories, characters are either in rehab ('Where I'm Calling From'), fresh out of rehab ('Kindling'), or desperately needing to attend ('Vitamins').[41] It is a substance which permeates virtually the entirety of Carver's work, as literal cause and symbolic reflection of an array of emotional misunderstandings, and a constant reminder of the epistemological difficulty of ever knowing others or oneself.

If alcohol is linked in Carver to the problem of knowledge, this is partly due to its function as that which simultaneously reveals and obscures. Alcohol is seen to cut through the artifices of repressed niceties, reaching unexpressed truths which may seem, in the end, as artificial as social civility. As the narrator puts it in the story 'Gazebo', alcohol's self-referentiality is a primary cause of its creation of epistemological aporia:

> Drinking's funny. When I look back on it, all of our important decisions have been figured out when we were drinking. Even when we talked about having to cut back on our drinking, we'd be sitting at the kitchen table or out at the picnic table with a six-pack or whiskey.[42]

Drinking in order to decide to stop drinking establishes a semantic loop, with alcohol again encouraging a parody of rational processes. In a mirroring of such circular logic, we encounter characters who, in discovering 'more' about each other under alcoholic derangement, realise that they in fact know less. In a negative hermeneutics, which mirrors an increasing bodily instability, an absolute verity is at once revealed and undercut in an ongoing rhetoric of divulgation and concealment.

In the story 'What We Talk About When We Talk About Love' from Carver's 1981 collection of the same name, the unstable link between alcohol and emotional knowledge takes on a radically sceptical form.[43] Such scepticism questions the very possibility of staking claims to knowledge, whether experiential or abstract, with regard to affective force. Narrated by Nick, a generally featureless everyman, the story begins one evening in a typical suburban kitchen, where two couples – Nick and Laura, Mel and Terri – are having rounds of drinks. In an ironic echo of the *Symposium*, the conversation soon turns to a central interrogation on love's essence. In contrast to Socratic method, the discussion does not ascend via the propositions of a cogent dialectic, but soon descends into a spiral of inebriated disarray. At the story's beginning, the aims of the exchange are nevertheless clear:

> My friend Mel McGinnis was talking. Mel McGinnis is a cardiologist, and sometimes that gives him the right ... There was an ice bucket on the table. The gin and the tonic water kept going around, and we somehow got on the subject of love. Mel thought real love was nothing less than spiritual love. He said he'd spent five years in a seminary before quitting to go to medical school. He said he still looked back on those years in the seminary as the most important years in his life.[44]

From the outset, epistemological claims are central, with Mel's status as medical doctor – specialist of the heart, no less – curiously establishing him as a respected arbiter with regard to emotional affairs. His status as rational scientist is undercut, however, by the tonal ambiguity of the narrator's potentially sardonic 'sometimes that gives him the right'. His 'right' to speak on such spiritual topics as love is endorsed by his role as specialised analyst of bodies. McGinnis's past hesitation regarding a career in the seminary further confirms his role as representative of a logocentric right to knowledgeable speech. Rather than instigating a binary opposition to scientific positivism, his assertion that this period constituted 'the most important years in his life' reinforces his claim to structures of institutional knowledge, whether religious, philosophical or scientific. Later, all of these institutionalised authorities on love's essential qualities will be put into question by the group's descent into alcohol's doubt-inducing helix.

Is love thus a potential target of applied knowledge, like engineering, botany or logic? If so – to frame the problem in Platonic terms – is knowledge about love a techne or episteme, an aspect of experiential acquisition or abstract reasoning? This question is reflected in the story's title, for the phrase 'What We Talk About

When We Talk About Love' assumes that there is indeed a 'what' to discuss, as a coherent focus of analysis. In the same vein, 'Mel thought real love was nothing less than spiritual love' becomes comical in its pithy condensation of an exceedingly complex philosophical quandary, in which a concept such as 'real love' is predicated without any attempt to define it. Subsequently contrasted with an equally fuzzy 'spiritual love', these two indeterminate categories are in no way able to mutually illuminate one another.

We are in the heart then of a profound epistemological dilemma, which alcohol both mirrors and magnifies, further complicating the interactions between 'rational' processes and 'irrational' beliefs. Already there is something automatic in alcohol's influence, for Nick, in a notably active construction, observes that the gin and the tonic water 'kept going around', as though invested with an innate energy. With the instinctive gestures of drinking, consumption is equated with an unconscious activity, occurring alongside the analytic process of determining love's composition. Faced with this disconnect, various participants in the discussion provide experiential data in support of their contrasting views:

> Terri said the man she lived with before she lived with Mel loved her so much he tried to kill her. Then Terri said, 'He beat me up one night. He dragged me around the living room by my ankles. He kept saying, "I love you, I love you, you bitch." He went on dragging me around the living room. My head kept knocking on things.' Terri looked around the table. 'What do you do with love like that?'[45]

Here, as throughout Carver's story, 'love' as coherent semantic unit is never declined into various senses, but treated as an essentialistic unity. No distinction is made, for example, between love as a personal feeling, a type of behaviour, a claim to value or a situational interaction. Indeed, Terri unwittingly refers to just such an unexplored divergence when she claims that 'he loved me. In his own way maybe, but he loved me. There was love there.' In such a formulation, the initial sense of the verb – love as relation between subject and object – is distinct from the ensuing sense of love as an autonomous construct, imbued with its own ontology. Whether such violent abuse can be 'called' love is in this sense a different question to whether it can be part of love, or alongside love, or opposed to it. It is an interrogation which, in grouping into one category love as feeling, act, state, interaction and event, concerns language far more than love as an isolated concept. Rather than proceeding, however, to this type of conceptual fragmentation, the characters of this modern *Symposium* take alternating paths, insisting either (in the case of Laura and Terri) on an absolute relativism, or on a universalising essentialism: 'My God, don't be silly. That's not love, and you know it,' Mel said.[46] The apparently anodyne call to God's higher power not only gestures towards love's invariable nature, but implies that knowledge about what love 'is' or 'is not' – in the story's ever-present binary – is ultimately something we all know. A shift occurs in the sense of the second-person pronoun which, from referring to Terri, morphs to become the 'you' of a universalising collective: 'I don't know what you'd call it, but I sure know you wouldn't call it love.'[47] To question what it may mean to 'call' something love is to insist on a central controversy between essentialism and nominalism – whether love may be said to exist in a noumenal state, beyond its semiotic incarnations – and is recurrently marked by the text's obsession with paradigms of linguistic reference. Shifting, moreover, from the singular to the collective as a reinforcement of a rationalising totality, Mel calls on the notion of a generalised agreement – at once social and transcendent – on love as a fixed truth.

This totality is countered in the story by an equally radical relativism. 'With Laura's remark "But who can judge anyone else's situation?"', argues Arthur F. Bethea, 'the text suggests that no one can know "the particulars" of another's experience, because experience is inextricably bound to consciousness, which is unique and, to some extent, unknowable.'[48] Such unknowability is not a sufficient justification, however, for complete axiological disengagement. When faced with an exclusionary truth, the only option available cannot be the absolute relativism of subjective inscrutability. Similarly, the utter failure to instantiate knowledge cannot be the only alternative to its violent imposition.

In this dialectic of extremes, alcohol is of course crucial. For these sequences of brief interspersed gestures – 'he held his glass', 'he finished his drink and reached for the gin bottle' – occur alongside

Mel's hieratical claims to a universally accepted truth, and his criticism of his wife's 'romanticism'. In participating in a wilful self-derangement, Mel disrupts his own claims to stable rationales while in the very process of making them. One reason for this, as Charles E. May has argued, is the prevalence in the story of interlocking layers of diegesis, demonstrating 'the inability of people to talk about love in any way except by telling stories, which, inevitably, listeners do not understand'.[49] Sentences and syntax become fragmented, more unstable versions of previous dogmatic claims: 'Mel said, "The kind of love I'm talking about is. The kind of love I'm talking about, you don't try to kill people."'[50] As the discussion progresses, Mel continues to oscillate between various claims to understanding which, as the drinking too goes on, enact the disintegration of foundational claims to a rational truth.

'When [Mel] was sober,' we read in a series of ratiocentric adjectives, 'his gestures, all his movements, were precise, very careful.'[51] If alcohol deranges Mel, as it eventually does all of the conversation's actors, it also abstracts him from his calm claims to a dominant epistemology, which soon become anxious recognitions of knowledge's lack. This shift notably occurs in the following exchange on the suicide of Terri's ex, Ed:

> 'He was dangerous,' Mel said. 'If you call that love, you can have it.'
>
> 'It was love,' Terri said. 'Sure, it's abnormal in most people's eyes. But he was willing to die for it. He did die for it.'
>
> 'I sure as hell wouldn't call it love,' Mel said. 'I mean, no one knows what he did it for. I've seen a lot of suicides, and I couldn't say anyone ever knew what they did it for.'
>
> Mel put his hands behind his neck and tilted his chair back. 'I'm not interested in that kind of love,' he said. 'If that's love, you can have it.'[52]

What was once a dogmatic claim to categorical mastery has subtly shifted into a recognition of incomprehension ('no one knows') and a purely personal preference ('I'm not interested'). Labelling such behaviour 'abnormal', however, is not sufficient to dispel its destabilising effects.

It is all the more appropriate that Mel should be the one to blindly continue this anti-rational process of derangement: '[Terri] poured the last of the gin into her glass and waggled the bottle. Mel got up from the table and went to the cupboard. He took down another bottle.'[53] In this wordless rite, it is Mel who administers the alcohol like a *pharmakon* – poison and panacea – which will intensify both their collective derangement and their apparent quest towards truth: '"A toast to love. To true love," Mel said. We touched glasses. "To love," we said.'[54] Alcohol is symbolically called upon to sanction the very category which it will soon chaotically undo. This ritualised tribute progresses from the idea of a singularised 'love' to an even more restrictive concept: 'true love'. Crucially, the others do not follow Mel's ceremonial lead, with Nick, Laura and Terri, as though in instinctive resistance, all omitting the epithet 'true'. In this climate, embroiled in the question of emotion's wavering extremes, Mel begins to oscillate wildly between intense certainty and doubt:

> 'I'll tell you what real love is,' Mel said. 'I mean, I'll give you a good example. And then you can draw your own conclusions.' He poured more gin into his glass. He added an ice cube and a sliver of lime. We waited and sipped our drinks.[55]

This dogmatic opening is immediately undermined by affirmations of ever-diminishing certainty, which culminate in the weakest possible appeal to subjective opinion: 'you can draw your own conclusions'. Recalling Mel's utilitarian perspective, his next claim that 'it seems to me we're just beginners at love' is to conceive of the notion as an object of technical mastery. Like a practical skill, one could thus approach love with the aim of linear improvement, with its value to be determined not by recondite speculations but by mere iterative rote.

This too is the desire for a firmer grounding for emotional states beyond the fluidities of affective force. Throughout the story, neither Mel's moral absolutes nor Terri's vacillating relativism are able to provide such an anchorage. Alcohol similarly promises and denies such stability, leading to both confident assertions and their immediate subversion. Each gesture here – pouring more gin, adding ice cubes, waiting, sipping – introduces a further interruption to Mel's increasingly incoherent diatribe. In the movement towards incoherency which this drinking escorts, it is unclear if what is being searched for is love's true definition, or rather proof that true love is ultimately impossible to define.

Attached to various 'objects' over time – now to Terri, but before her to Mel's first wife – love is seen, like alcohol and affect, to be disturbingly dynamic, altering utterly depending on its instant of temporal apprehension:

> '[I]f something happened to one of us tomorrow, I think the other one, the other person, would grieve for a while, you know, but then the surviving party would go out and love again, have someone else soon enough. All this, all of this love we're talking about, it would just be a memory. Maybe not even a memory. Am I wrong? Am I way off base? Because I want you to set me straight if you think I'm wrong. I want to know. I mean, I don't know anything, and I'm the first one to admit it.'
>
> 'Mel, for God's sake,' Terri said. She reached out and took hold of his wrist. 'Are you getting drunk? Honey? Are you drunk?'[56]

Terri's 'are you drunk?' is ironically similar to Mel's dichotomous interrogations, such as 'does that sound like love to you?'. For this sliding towards instability and disquiet is more a continuous spectrum than a binary of clarity and derangement. Now he has been designated as 'drunk', Mel's conviction has been reduced to a Socratic affirmation of ignorance which, while it avoids the dogmatism of love's definition, is hardly more helpful in forging a valuable approach. 'Am I wrong?' is the sign that we have reached a new stage of uncertainty, where reality itself – and above all love's emotional essence – is no longer a simple matter of assertion based on entrenched beliefs. Love, whether as concept, experience, interaction or word, has now escaped the limits of its reductive categorisations. But such a movement is not a simple liberation. Indeed, Mel's defensive reaction to Terri's question, which he takes as an accusative insult, demonstrates that such derangement risks deepening the schism with the knowable real:

> 'Honey, I'm just talking,' Mel said. 'All right? I don't have to be drunk to say what I think. I mean, we're all just talking, right?' Mel said. He fixed his eyes on her.
>
> 'Sweetie, I'm not criticizing,' Terri said. She picked up her glass.

'I'm not on call today,' Mel said. 'Let me remind you of that. I am not on call,' he said.

'Mel, we love you,' Laura said. Mel looked at Laura. He looked at her as if he could not place her, as if she was not the woman she was.

'Love you too, Laura,' Mel said. 'And you, Nick, love you too. You know something?' Mel said. 'You guys are our pals,' Mel said.

He picked up his glass.[57]

To insist on the innocence of the act of 'just talking' is to limit language's role both in establishing potential truths, and in undermining acquired verities previously taken as given. No one is 'criticizing' Mel for the reason that all are searching for an agreed communion on love's nature, taken as singular, non-contextual category. Pronounced here to one's friends, 'love you too' is a phrase divested of all pretension to spiritual sense. Evoking *in vino veritas*, Mel's objection that 'I don't have to be drunk to say what I think' is paramount to the claim that the more troublesome aspects of love do not need derangement to surge forth. These aspects, however, were in no way evident in the confident beginnings of Mel's speech.

This insistence that alcohol, with regard to truth, is neither a hindrance nor a help, but a neutral factor which plays no role, is again to posit a unified real, and a united emotional disposition related to it. As though to support this harmonising attempt, Laura's 'Mel, we love you' is a solipsistic use of 'love' as social analgesic. Indeed, in a discussion about its very nature, the word has become reduced to an expression of superficial intimacy far removed from the 'spiritual love' of the story's incipit. In a context where the phrase 'I love you' has become equal to 'you guys are our pals', drinking's repetitive gestures further ritualise this bathetic descent. It is unsurprising that such insistence on harmony rapidly gives way to conflict:

> Mel said, 'I was going to tell you about something. I mean, I was going to prove a point. You see, this happened a few months ago, but it's still going on right now, and it ought to make us feel ashamed when we talk like we know what we're talking about when we talk about love.'
>
> 'Come on now,' Terri said. 'Don't talk like you're drunk if you're not drunk.'
>
> 'Just shut up for once in your life,' Mel said very quietly.[58]

The didactic effort to 'prove a point', therefore establishing a unique truth, is contrasted with an exploratory desire to map love's various forms. Mel's 'point' is ironically that our pretension to affective knowledge is fundamentally misguided (though this is the precise same pretension that he has continually displayed). Alcohol again intervenes as a symbolic nexus of questions of belief and the affective real. For like the condition of being drunk or not drunk, asking what love 'is' or 'is not' is to collapse into binaries a continuum of utter flux. Moreover, such binaries themselves become confused. 'Don't talk like you're drunk if you're not drunk' confirms that it has become difficult to distinguish between alteration and neutrality, conceived now as performative poles.

For in a context where there is no neutral end to affect's ceaseless flow, both love and intoxication transcend their abstract quotients of truth. Mel's violent response to Terri's insinuation demands an end not only to discordant speech, but to the shifting uncertainties that have come to plague his altered state. Even Nick as narrator is soon affected by similar doubts: 'Terri looked at us and then back at Mel. She seemed anxious, or maybe that's too strong a word. Mel was handing the bottle around the table.'[59] In such self-correction, Nick betrays an expressive hesitation previously absent from his telling. Language itself has become similarly affected by the semantic fluidities of acategorical affects and their intoxicating modes.

The flagrancy of this derangement, which the characters nevertheless strive to ignore, is further proof that undermining stable taxonomies cannot easily create a new fluidity. As the story nears its end, the difficulty of focusing on phenomena, combined with the couples' frozen stasis in an ever-darker room, begin to explicitly echo the immovable positions expressed throughout the story regarding emotionality and the real:

> Maybe we were a little drunk by then. I know it was hard keeping things in focus. The light was draining out of the room, going back through the window where it had come from. Yet nobody made a move to get up from the table to turn on the overhead light.
>
> 'Listen,' Mel said. 'Let's finish this fucking gin. There's about enough left here for one shooter all around. Then let's go eat. Let's go to the new place.'

'He's depressed,' Terri said. 'Mel, why don't you take a pill?'
Mel shook his head. 'I've taken everything there is.'
'We all need a pill now and then,' I said.
'Some people are born needing them,' Terri said.[60]

No radically altering light can here be illuminated because the process of obscuring alteration must be pursued to its end. There is no conceivable conclusion suggested beyond 'let's finish this fucking gin'. Though a series of reductive classifications are continually undone, we witness the emergence of new typologies. Now labelled as 'depressed' – without this label ever opening on to a discussion of what it may mean – Mel becomes the object of a proposed pharmacological solution. With intoxication calling for further alteration, Terri's final sentence frames Mel's condition in the restricted category of a pathology. For the stark difference between Nick's 'we all need a pill now and then' and Terri's 'some people are born needing them' is that between a model of environmental variance and an immutable congenital core.

Psychotropes thus become a central vector of the question of essentialism and dynamism, nature and culture, inherency and acquired characteristics. In spite of alcohol's ambiguously liberating influence, limiting diagnoses ('He's depressed') impose an end to all hermeneutic exploration. In this downward spiral, the darkening kitchen is transformed into a disturbingly claustrophobic cocoon, where all options seem the same. Or in Nick's formulation:

'Eat or not eat. Or keep drinking. I could head right on out into the sunset.'
'What does that mean, honey?' Laura said.
'It just means what I said,' I said. 'It means I could just keep going. That's all it means.'[61]

Keep going, however, towards what? Towards utter derangement? Towards language's disintegration? Towards death? For the questions 'what is love?', 'what is feeling?' and 'what is truth?' trace a horizon line that infinitely recedes. To 'head right on out into the sunset', like the romantic hero of a nostalgic American West, will at least put an end to the interminable fluctuations of feeling which, if one desires a stable truth, may be the cause of unbearable distress. Though the bottle may appear to end, there is always, somewhere, another drink, even if to 'keep drinking' means ultimately to accept the finality of a projected death.

At the story's close, we enter into a timeless state where the condition of emotional suspension will eternally endure: 'I could hear my heart beating. I could hear everyone's heart. I could hear the human noise we sat there making, not one of us moving, not even when the room went dark.'[62] The heart, as the home of human feeling, is transformed from its symbolic role as love's locus into its mere biological function. With the cardiologist Mel McGinnis reduced to a despondent wreck, this 'human noise' of hearts beating – basal, anatomical, elementary – constitutes an organic reality, contrasted to the abstractions of affective constructs. In this motif of sanguine circulation, these last lines open on to a terrifying stasis whose tension cannot be resolved. What could potentially be a moment of communion – 'I could hear everyone's heart' – insists rather on a primal resemblance of recurrent cycles, categories and types. For what is one to do if no definition of love has been reached? Continue the discussion, endlessly? Keep talking and, above all, drinking, until the ever-receding final word or drop? In this never-ending abeyance, the slow passing of the light mirrors the passing of all hope for illumination, foreshadowing death as 'solution' to affective uncertainties. As though the discussions to define love were, like drinking, inexhaustible, this process never arrives at a definition, for the object of its investigation is always, like Deleuze's 'last drink', eternally deferred.[63] Elusive and yet inevitable, it recedes into the simulacra of its own alterations.

Throughout 'What We Talk About When We Talk About Love', it is unclear if we are ever penetrating deeper into true feelings via derangement, or perusing a new range of intoxicating masks. And in the end, to ask whether alcohol and affect are revelatory or distorting is specious. For it is not an issue of distinguishing between clarity and obscurity, between feelings' perversion and their exposure. Fixated on deceptively stable 'objects', this binary – like all efforts to attain love's 'definition' – furnishes a reductive vision of an always intoxicating emotional life. If these characters at first appear to drink their last drink, this finality is in fact as illusory as any accession to love's truth. A sentimental ruse, such truth as unchanging absolute will also, at some point, be swathed in a settling dark.

## Intoxicating Spectrums: Literary Realism against the Stable Real

In spite of its historical reputation as a tool for emotional sincerity, alcohol frequently increases the impression of the artificiality of all affect, and not merely of those emotional states under an intoxicating influence. It follows from the analyses of this chapter that affect and altering psychotropes often pose an endless interrogation: in order to establish their valency, both engender states which refer always to other states, within the body and the ambient world. For emotions are not imbued with a standardised truth, but refer to other reactive processes in a never-ending and reflexive self-definition. Within such an accretion, the fact that there may be no 'definition' of love implies a new, if disturbing, liberty. For affects, like other altering substances and states, do not deal in established categories, but rather in blurred spectrums of dependencies. It is for this reason that they never cease to refer to other points along a continuum, dynamically defining themselves by contrasts of degree.

In the wake of American post-war culture, the shift from a paradigm of intoxication to one of addiction occurs in the midst of intense questionings of the form and modes of literary realism itself. This provides a complex metafictional dimension to the questions at hand, in which psychotropic alteration becomes a generalised metaphor for literary processes. To remark the transition in this semiotics is to recognise a more general shift in the understanding of the feeling body, with the 'disruptive' elements of both affect and alterity entering into increasingly pathologised visions of both corporality and the self.

# Conclusion: The Theatre of the Affective Mind

Myriad modern defences of literature have argued that literary texts allow us privileged access to profound emotional truths. This contention unites discourses as diverse as Victorian efforts to legitimise literature's moral value, modernist disquiet regarding its 'unscientific' epistemologies, and contemporary anxieties over its supposed cultural decline. Otherwise difficult to reach, such true feeling, at once nested in the inner folds of subjectivity and deployable as a transhistorical charge, is seen to straddle immense societal and philosophical divides. In doing so, it unites visions of fiction, on the one hand, as an intimate encounter with the self in a realm of authentic private essences and, on the other, as the transcultural alliance of a communal sentiment, sympathetically shared.

Simultaneously universal and highly particular, the mythology of literature as the ideal aesthetic incarnation of true feeling has been omnipresent throughout the emergence of literary studies as a distinct discipline in the modern university. In this lineage, literature is invested with the role of ultimate bulwark in a culture-wide defence against the uncivilised armies of emotional untruth. This is more widely, we may suspect, a Romantic paradigm, with the self's communion with true feeling always under threat by the instability and vulnerability of a revelatory ontological state. But what is different in post-Romantic iterations is the association of literature as true feeling not with primarily spiritual or metaphysical principles, but with utilitarian goals. In the modern age, the true feeling of literature can make us more empathetic, more intelligent, more sensitive, more cultured: new and improved human beings. Both Thoreau in his woods or Emerson as 'transparent eye-ball' ('I am nothing; I see all') risked slipping back into the continuity of the everyday, out of the numinous sublime.[1] But this did not imply, or not to the same extent, depriving literature or philosophical exploration of their reason for being; it was rather a stage in an ongoing dialectic, wherein the power of epiphanic emotion provided a temporary penetration into the heart of the invisible world. The supposed endangerment of literature throughout modernity – its perpetual existence in a state of imminent or actual peril – is a platitude which, if certainly present throughout nineteenth-century Romantic discourse, comes to characterise literature's post-Romantic entrenchment, ever more reliant on the myth of true feeling as its mode of cultural legitimisation.

## Why Resist Legitimising Literature through True Feeling? Utilitarianism, Liberalism and the Reign of Market Rationalisms

Today, in this third decade of the twenty-first century, this conception of literary texts as true feeling's proper home is used in problematic ways to justify literature's legitimate place in modern liberal economies. Such efforts are indeed far more concerted and widespread than in the twentieth-century post-war period, when the disciplinary value of literary studies, though never economically or ideologically assured, was nonetheless supported by a range of cultural convictions – the importance and hegemony of national canons, for instance, or the role of the liberal arts education in the formation of a cohesive *civitas* – whose viability came to be questioned. In the vacuum left by such necessary critiques, however, growing numbers of journalistic articles and academic studies, from the disciplines of cognitive psychology to sociology and the neurosciences – and in this sense in utter concord with the utilitarian justifications of the humanities in vogue in the politics of the contemporary academy – argue the extent to which reading fiction increases empathy, reduces loneliness, makes one smarter and improves one's mental and physical health.[2] Whether as a facilitator of the 'emotional intelligence' of self-help discourses and popular psychology, or in academic arguments that it improves students' 'emotional quotient' or 'EQ', fiction is seen to foster a wealth of personal affective benefits. For a variety of these models, the implication is that literature 'helps' because it allows us to harness an affective universality; and as an advocate for our emotional similitude, the myth of true feeling is of immense help in this project. Indeed, one of the most widespread tropes concerning literary value, namely that literature allows us to develop and cultivate empathy, is tightly woven with true feeling as universalising myth.

The question, of course, is not whether any of these social functions of fiction 'work' or do not work. The fact that many individuals feel both their lives and selves enriched through engagement with literary texts is an important pragmatic aspect of literature's multifarious modes of valuation. But it is not the only one, and the problem lies in elevating such personal enhancements to the status of moral justifications. Like Victorian fears that reading certain types of fiction could lead to the degradation of principled or decorous behaviour, contemporary neuroscientific claims that fiction makes us more emotionally intelligent, thus more empathetic, are profoundly extrinsic foundations for literary value.[3] Attributing no inherent value to literature itself, such claims are involved in ameliorative teleologies of self-improvement, structured, albeit implicitly, according to market logics of social utility, efficiency, investment and return.

Nuclear physics also, one may presume, improves 'brain connectivity', but this is hardly seen as an appropriate subject for myriad journalistic articles and studies in cognitive psychology. Literature is seen to be in need of these defences because its value is precisely not assured. Such contemporary discourses often attempt to legitimise literary texts – and their apparent emotional 'improvement' of individuals – as though they required legitimising. In this way, commentators not only contribute to the reputation of literature's cultural fragility, but perpetuate beliefs regarding its connection to, and incarnation of, a standardised emotional truth.

Such proponents remain convinced that they are doing literature a favour, when they are in fact condemning it to a societal niche of emotional coach, wherein fiction would forge the simplified empathy of an affective universality in much the same way as 'sensitivity training' creates a superficial 'harmony' in the modern workplace. In this paradigm, the regime of true feeling attributes to literary texts the subaltern status of messenger for underlying emotional verities. 'Among critics, scholars, administrators, and casual readers, there is an odd and unsettling consensus,' observes Rachel Greenwald Smith:

> We read works of literature because they allow us direct contact with individuals who are like us but not us; they allow us to feel what others feel; they provoke empathy; and they teach us how to understand what it means to be a unique human being. What could be wrong with that? As it turns out, plenty.[4]

Tracing the links between this conception of literary emotion and the rise of modern neoliberalism, Greenwald Smith exposes the array of problems associated with what she terms the 'affective hypothesis', in which the reading of literature is tied to such neoliberal values as privatisation, self-amelioration and the profit motive.[5] In insisting always on modes of harmonisation over disruption, this framework is profoundly limiting, reducing both emotionality and fiction to a range of affective intensities deemed to be socially useful and thus justifiable within neoliberal economies.

I have argued in this book that such utilitarian visions depend to a large extent on the notion that literature can initiate the self to a higher true feeling, in an epiphanic deliverance seen to constitute its greatest communal and spiritual good. Many current interdisciplinary approaches to literary texts, from cognitive psychology to sociology and neurobiology, further 'the tendency for fundamental literary meaning to be equated with the production of recognizable emotional content'.[6] Recognisable and, I would add, recognisably 'true' – for behind this containment of its potentialities to the production of fellow feeling and affective universals is a strong heritage of imagining literature merely as a vehicle for a transhistorical emotional veracity.

It is also for this reason that so many of the authors discussed in this book, in the post-war period through to the 1980s, create characters with whom it may be difficult to enter into relationships of traditional emotional engagement. How, we may ask, are we to feel sympathetically fused with the depraved Mickey Sabbath, the erratic Laura Maldonada or the hypocritical Rabbit Angstrom?[7] This is not, of course, to emit a reductive judgement of such individuals' moral quality or comportment; but it is to recognise that our reactions to them, and in particular our emotional commitments, may run the gamut from bored to distant, amused to denunciatory. Never necessarily incarnating the fused feeling of empathetic mythologies, we may therefore enter into critical interrogations regarding their emotional being and our own, which are all the more challenging for their lack of homogeneity.

Breaking down simplistic models of sentimental amalgam in an attempt to lessen the cultural hold of true feeling as a criterion is part of a wider post-war literary project. For indeed, since the close of the nineteenth century brought Tolstoy's well-known formulations in *What Is Art?*, empathy has been viewed not just as an essential component of realist ideations, but as their defining characteristic. Underlining a central tenet of the myth of realist fusion, Tolstoy affirmed:

> The activity of art is based on the fact that a man, receiving through his sense of hearing or sight another man's expression of feeling, is capable of experiencing the emotion which moved the man who expressed it . . . And it is upon this capacity of man to receive another man's expression of feeling and experience those feelings himself, that the activity of art is based.[8]

So closely associating literature and true feeling means that, when emotional authenticity is seen to be failing, literature too will appear forever under threat. Widespread calls for its always imminent 'death', as a gesture repeated throughout literary history, insist on each specific era's lack of affective authenticity and recommend a return to a time when works were in touch with a ubiquitous emotional quintessence.

But literature should not be seen to re-affirm a static matrix of feeling which we recognise in others and ourselves. It should on the contrary question it, if necessary destabilise it, setting it once more into motion. To destabilise is not necessarily to oppose, for there is nothing gained by replacing the conservative maintenance of universal values with the equally static idea of literature as always iconoclastic, perpetually disrupting the mind's previously stable processes. For regarding emotionality as regarding ideology, literary texts are neither inherently conservative nor dissident, for the reason that they do not 'naturally' divide, in the sense of moral hierarchies, between true and false feelings which intrinsically confirm or disrupt. Fiction rather places such feelings within its own space of representation and processes of diegesis – those which, within both our bodies and our minds, are also at the heart of emotionality itself.

## The Material Fallacy: Literary Emotions as an 'Unexplored Body of Data'

Many contemporary interdisciplinary approaches to literary emotion thus inadvertently proceed as though literature were not in fact a symbolic artifice, made of inestimable representational layers, but rather a transparent experience of emotional connection within the self and the wider social world. We thus encounter arguments from cognitivism to moral philosophy which insist on what literature may 'teach' or 'tell' us about feeling, enlightening us of its universal truths. The cognitivist critic Patrick Colm Hogan, for instance, lamenting the fact that 'the vast pool of data supplied by literature remains underutilized in emotion research', seeks to justify the use of literary characters in cognitive research.[9] The terms of this engagement become clear in Hogan's outlining of the debate between cognitivists and experimental psychologists as to whether literature yields revealing emotional 'data' or mere 'anecdotes':

> Literature provides a vast and largely unexplored body of data for emotion research. On hearing this general idea, experimental psychologists sometimes reply that literature is not data. It is just anecdotes. But this is a bizarre response. Certainly, one cannot establish a science based on a researcher's private tales. But the existence and vast emotional influence of literary works are simply not private tales.[10]

We may be tempted to respond that literature is neither 'data' nor 'anecdotes'.[11] In its processes of symbolisation, subjectivation and representation, literature engages aspects of emotional being that are so self-reflexive, symbolic and semiotically complex that they can never be deemed either anecdotic or data-like, as they forever escape such materialising narratives. In these visions, fiction supplies us with emotional material, imbued with an affective content. This presumption underpins many models of literary utility based on empathetic precepts, in which literary texts are seen to contribute to an ethical and emotional common good.

To debate whether literature may constitute an untapped well of feeling on which cognitivists and psychologists may draw is tantamount to equating feelings with the pinned butterflies of the entomologist's alluring display. If scientific discourses seek to justify literature by proving its validity as scientific material – valued because it makes procurable a universal true feeling which may then be science's privileged object – then something terribly wrong has occurred in the articulation of many of our contemporary interdisciplinary methodologies.

## 'Universal Longings' and 'Truths of the Heart': True Feeling's Modernist Roots

This book has proposed that, throughout the second half of the twentieth century, a fundamental shift occurred in the way emotionality was seen to relate to the concept of truth. This change was especially pronounced both in the United States and in the realist fiction which emerged out of the post-war period. From the modernist lamentation of the retreat of true feeling from an abandoned world, to the post-World War II critique of this same notion's sovereign rule, a radical alteration is felt in the ability of the criterion of truth to adequately describe the representational complexities of emotional processes. From a nostalgised ideal to a suffocating imperative, the literary-historical evolution of true feeling traces a path which mirrors that of the questioning of authoritarian truths within the movements of modern critical theory.

But the contemporary persistence of the reputation of true feeling as an edifying and ennobling value should make us question the effectiveness of this post-war rebellion. For even in the heart of modernism's formal and thematic experiments – up to and including the way these texts continue to be taught in the contemporary university – the hegemony of true feeling has asserted its lasting cultural hold. 'That is part of the beauty of all literature,' F. Scott Fitzgerald is reputed to have declared, in the record of Sheilah Graham, towards the end of his life. 'You discover that your longings are universal longings, that you're not lonely and isolated from anyone. You belong.'[12] What if you discover through literature, however, that your longings are not always universal? Are you meant to fashion them so that they cohere to an ideal pantheon of affective energies and emotional states? What if literature in fact attests to the extent of your alterity: your non-belonging, your difference and your distance from others, finding in this realisation an opportunity for epistemological exploration and renewal?

In his acceptance speech for the 1949 Nobel Prize for Literature, William Faulkner declared that 'the young man or woman writing today has forgotten the problems of the human heart in conflict with itself'.[13] Faulkner went on to propose that, with regard to such now neglected but age-old affective truths, the writer of the post-war generation should have only one approach:

> He must learn them again. He must teach himself that the basest of all things is to be afraid; and, teaching himself that, forget it forever, leaving no room in his workshop for anything but the old verities and truths of the heart, the old universal truths lacking which any story is ephemeral and doomed – love and honor and pity and pride and compassion and sacrifice. Until he does so, he labors under a curse. He writes not of love but of lust, of defeats in which nobody loses anything of value, of victories without hope and, worst of all, without pity or compassion. His griefs grieve on no universal bones, leaving no scars. He writes not of the heart but of the glands.[14]

If these were the words of a reactionary realist, immediate accusations of jaded traditionalism would be easily upheld. And indeed, reading this passage out of context, with no indication of its origin, we would be forgiven for thinking that it was penned by the staunchest of literary conservatives, bent on a vision of literature as a faithful rendition of human universals, allying moral purity with a range of static 'truths of the heart'.

But emotionality, as is so often the case, somehow finds itself located outside these traditional strictures of ideological appraisal of the aesthetic. This new literature, deprived of either 'pity or compassion' and abandoning empathy, is seen by Faulkner to eschew the heart's 'universal truths', which he identifies as the primary value not only of the writing of the prior generation, but of all literature in an undefined historical continuum. Faulkner's conclusion revealingly warns against a literature purely of 'the glands': one which would not be grounded in the body's sentimental essences, consecrated by a defined Romantic heritage, but merely in those corporal centres devoted to a chemical reactivity. The message is clear: the false emotions of the 'glands' are emotions which, based in the body's superficial layers of worldly reactions, do not represent the deeper true feelings of the 'heart'. The latter are seen to transcend, subjectively and historically, the sham imitations of 'ephemeral' affect, confined to the particularity of subjective alterity. Writerly 'griefs' which 'grieve on no universal bones, leaving no scars' are detached from a living 'natural' body, on which they leave no imprint. They are not the product of an organic affective totality, but of a deterministic mechanism, focused on 'lust' rather than 'love'. Like the Romantics for Ezra Pound or T. S. Eliot and the Augustans for many Romantics, bad writing is again made of fake feelings, with the underlying conviction that literature must express the quintessence of an eternal heart.

Faulkner, bolstered by his reputation as aesthetic iconoclast and staunch defender of innovative form, proceeds to trot out a selection of categorical emotional values: 'love and honor and pity and pride and compassion and sacrifice'. In its insistence on lost universals which must be relocated if the coming generation should wish to overcome a paralysing fear, there is little to distinguish Faulkner's speech from the discourses of emotional containment of the Truman and Eisenhower administrations. Faulkner's notion that the Cold War fear of annihilation should have clouded the new generation's contact with a base reserve of emotional verities is tantamount to labelling post-war anxieties a mere passing historical delusion.

This technical vision of the modern artist labouring 'in his workshop' is a further conservative nod to an art which attempts to preserve the consecrated emotional values of yore, in a quasi-Heideggerian gesture towards the artisanal preservation of a seeping modern Being. In this static affective catalogue – and just like Walker Percy's Aunt Emily in her lamenting of the modern absence of 'recognizable' joy, pity and fear – Faulkner indeterminately mixes moral values such as honour and sacrifice with emotional 'essences' such as love.[15] The implicit meaning is clear: the 'truths of the heart' are made of both universal moral values and universal sentiments, fused into a union wherein their truth refers simultaneously to their proved endurance as humanist principles, and to their socially approved didactic worth.

We may not be surprised by such a statement from an Arnoldian cultural critic, who thought of literature as a path to right behaviour. But William Faulkner? Of course, like all modernists, Faulkner's integration into a homogenously iconoclastic canon is itself reductive, with a conflict always evident in his work between the foregrounding of innovative processes and what critics like Daniel J. Singal have called his 'post-Victorian self'.[16] We are perhaps reminded too of Raymond Williams's insistence on the deep roots of bourgeois universalism at the sentimental heart of modernism, which manifest here in the way profoundly static conceptions of emotional value remain a touchstone even in the most 'radical' of modernist enterprises.[17]

What this new generation, as Faulkner calls them, later sought to achieve with regard to such 'truths of the heart' must not have been to the liking of the 1949 Nobel Laureate. For far from seeking to 'learn again' these truths, such writers, I have argued, came to occupy a paradoxical position, wherein quests for true feeling were dramatised, in the specific mode of realist diegesis, precisely in order to performatively interrogate their structures of moral and social oppression.

## Truth and Totalitarianism: On the Post-War Resistance to Emotional Artifice

In many ways, this developmental arc in how much American fiction came to view the social and aesthetic imperatives of true feeling mirrors that which occurred in twentieth-century visions of truth more generally. For if truth, in the wake of the modern era's totalitarian movements, came increasingly to be critiqued as a domineering principle, totalitarianism itself was considered to instil ideologies in which systematic modes of ontological distortion ultimately severed ties between what was representation and what was real. The Cold War climate of identitarian paranoia is a later incarnation of the political dangers of masks, alter egos and hidden selves beneath an outer veneer. Emotionality, and the generalised myth of true feeling of which literature was to be the highest expression, are tightly interwoven with the dual conception of truth-regimes which these historical tensions imply. As Hannah Arendt observed in 1951, in *The Origins of Totalitarianism*:

> Just as terror, even in its pre-total, merely tyrannical form ruins all relationships between men, so the self-compulsion of ideological thinking ruins all relationships with reality ... The ideal subject of totalitarian rule is not the convinced Nazi or the convinced Communist, but people for whom the distinction between fact and fiction (i.e., the reality of experience) and the distinction between true and false (i.e., the standards of thought) no longer exist.[18]

Arendt's remonstrance is testament to the degree to which the post-war distinction between true and false, fact and fiction, reality and representation, was intricately bound up in the loss of ethical and perceptual stability under the oppressive weight of malicious ideologies. Of course, distinguishing between 'fact and fiction' with regard to political ideology is not the same as in the realm of literary diegesis. But the fear of confusion between these polarities nevertheless engendered a complex dialectic between true feeling as an authoritarian pressure, and the need for stable notions of emotional value in order to prevent the ethical aberration – replete with its unfeeling de-subjectivation – of totalitarian catastrophe.

To locate feeling outside of ideology, in a transcendent emotional truth, is a temptation to which Arendt was herself to succumb in her search for an apolitical affectivity able to treat unhealable wounds. 'Love, by its very nature, is unworldly,' affirms Arendt in *The Human Condition*, 'and it is for this reason rather than its rarity that it is not only apolitical but antipolitical, perhaps the most powerful of all antipolitical forces.'[19] Though this impetus may be to protect love from the machinations of an all-too-human 'inhumanity', its risks, like the yoking of literature to the expression of an apolitical true feeling, are ethically and politically grievous. For such a situating of love as a healing affective universal, though an understandable gesture in the wake of mass historical trauma, effectively depoliticises love, or any other affect granted such transcendent status, making its relation to truth one of a celestial epitome. Rather than enacting systemic changes, love, like literature, risks being called upon as a harmonising intensity, which instead of challenging our ethical limitations merely displaces such energies towards the utopia of an empathetic similitude.

Love, like all affective matrices, is in part profoundly worldly. Like literature, it is not always harmonising, nor is it always based on feeling what others feel. For acting towards others with their own interests in mind, even when we do not share their feelings, is surely a higher ethical imperative than that of a sentimental conjunction. Love, like literature, may also be positively disruptive, insisting not on harmonisation but on the challenges to held convictions, which are also repositionings of our affective and moral compass. This in turn suggests feeling's use as a tool of revelation of difference: an active participant in the processes of affective artifice which make difference visible, rather than glossed over in the invisibility of a universal synthesis. An alternative but more arduous gesture would be precisely to politicise love, to insist not on its unworldly ascension above human values but on its necessary imbrication in the *hic et nunc* imagining of better worlds. If I am making this comparison between the historical consideration of love and literature, it is because neither one nor the other requires our protection. Like all emotional matrices, they are both unworldly and worldly, at once of our particular chronotope and gesturing to an imagined universality beyond.

## Unemotional Critics? New Criticism and Emotional Moralisation

In concentrating on the fiction of the American post-war period, this book has not explicitly mined the territory of whether the literary theory and criticism of these years was engaged in the same reforming process. But the supposed exclusion of emotionality from the primary concerns of movements such as Structuralism and New Criticism has become something of a literary-historical trope. While this boycott is in many ways palpable, it is important to qualify its terms. For in spite of contemporary accusations as to their 'unemotional' nature, an ideology of true feeling is nevertheless present in the writings of many New Critics. This is hardly surprising if we consider that even those critical schools of modernity reputed to be uninterested in emotion, or not interested enough – Russian Formalism, French Structuralism, Anglo-American New Criticism – implicitly rely not only on emotional truth as a concept, but on the assumption that literature's social legitimacy consists in its capacity to reveal it.

It was not so much, then, that New Critics did not believe emotion to be of central importance to literature – as their judgements regarding texts' 'failed' or 'successful' emotionality make plain – as that affect was not, to many New Critics, a potential site for the type of rationalised irony that was their primary interest. As is the case in much of T. S. Eliot's criticism, the fact that literature was the embodiment of true feeling was not even open to doubt; and indeed, the true feeling of 'good literature' was cast by many New Critics as so evidentially paramount that it hardly needed to figure into the types of ambiguous valency which they sought to explore.

Throughout the post-war period, both New Critics and their opponents thus argued, albeit in different ways, that emotional truth was literature's main value claim. Writing in 1977, for instance, the critic Jane P. Tompkins, formulating a fairly standard anti-New Critical argument, observed:

> While the New Criticism's insistence that we look at the text and the text only – ignoring the human beings involved in producing and in reading it – has been under attack for some years now, the general desire of critics to appear detached and scientific remains. The fig leaf of critical objectivity has been removed, but no one has yet looked straight at the consequences. Emotional reactions, whether they occur simultaneously with cognition or a split second after, are the main component of the literary experience.[20]

In the same breath we encounter the condemnation of detached New Critical rationality, and the postulating of emotionality as literary experience's reified 'main component'.

But this is itself an assertion with which New Critics were highly familiar. After all, F. R. Leavis, echoing a moral tenet of Russian Formalism concerning literature's emotional improvement of the self, affirmed that 'literature is the supreme means by which you renew your sensuous and emotional life and learn a new awareness'.[21] In a further example, Leavis reproaches Percy Shelley for his 'wordy emotional generality' and observes of Shelley's play *The Cenci* (1819): 'We are told emphatically what the emotion is that we are to feel; emphasis and insistence serving instead of realization and advertising its default.'[22] The extract is typical of New Critical judgements, not in its ignoring of questions of emotionality, but in its stringent criticism of texts for inappropriately incarnating emotions or influencing those of its readers in turn.

Even second-wave American New Critics such as Allen Tate, Cleanth Brooks, Robert Penn Warren or John Crowe Ransom, more reactionary than I. A. Richards and F. R. Leavis, repeated such standardising gestures. In Brooks and Warren's 1946 anthology *Understanding Fiction* – which June Howard calls 'a classic if forgotten site of New Critical antisentimentalism' – emotion is in no way absent from their concerns.[23] On the contrary, the detection of the corrupting sentimentalism of false feeling becomes one of the attentive New Critics' primary preoccupations:

> The presence of this straining for an emotional effect is one of the surest symptoms that one is dealing with a case of sentimentality (see Glossary). In its general sense sentimentality may be defined as an emotional response in excess of the occasion. We speak of a person who weeps at some trivial occurrence as being sentimental. Such a person lacks a sense of proportion and gets a morbid enjoyment from an emotional debauch for its own sake.[24]

Rather than neglecting to speak of texts' emotional qualities, the New Critical project may rather be seen as a widespread moralisation which, in the guise of analysis of form and style, seeks to impose morally congruent affective parameters. Far from a triumph of scientific rationalism or mere snobbish disdain, the alternate 'evacuation' of emotion from analysis is also a sanctioning of true feeling's predominance.

In this sense, such criticism is in vogue with the general cultural climate of standardisation and repression against which much modern American realist fiction sought to rebel. Moreover, it was to some extent the New Critical desire to isolate literature from its sociohistorical and authorial underpinnings which further meant that affect – as well as literature as true feeling's privileged locus – was further separated, in a transcendent realm of universal truths, from its sociocultural modes of activation in 'real' identities with real political concerns. Rather than being confined to Formalism's unemotional stratosphere, New Critical analyses may be considered as in their own way highly emotional, betraying constant recourse to true feeling as a normalising authority. It is an emotional standardisation which is all the stronger because of, and not in spite of, New Critics' attempts to isolate literary texts from their sociopolitical influences.

## Do Not Lament for Authenticity: Realism as Artifice's Ideal Terrain

In the dominant critical movements of post-war America, the tendency to value literature as the natural vessel of true feeling thrived in spite of the production, as I have argued in this book, of various modes of fiction – both realist and otherwise – that strove to oppose such conceptions. This opposition is, however, often framed by critics as a mere pining for a lost authentic life. A dominant commonplace sees, in the work of Saul Bellow for instance, a recurrent lamentation for the loss of true feeling, and a railing against the emotional inauthenticity of the modern world. We thus encounter a range of literal readings of Bellow's statement: 'One of my themes is the American denial of reality, our devices for evading it, our refusal to face what is all too obvious and palpable', which leads a critic such as Michael K. Glenday to argue that 'there is in Bellow's thought none of that philosophical skepticism about the nature of reality which has so characterised the postmodern literary aesthetic over the past twenty five years'.[25]

Whatever Bellow's extra-diegetic convictions, when these ontological questions are thrown into the maelstrom of his fiction – poised always between excessive melodrama and absurdist picaresque – these anxieties are turned on their head, shown to be comically solipsistic, tragically self-referential and part of infinite rhetorical loops. Spiralling in a world of ever-ambivalent representation, they can no longer be viewed as simple quests for reality or the authentic affective life, of which Bellow and his characters are seen to retain no scepticism. They are, by the very necessity of literature's mimetic techniques, played up and played with, becoming the modifiable potentialities of both imagination and the projected real.

What all this means for realist fiction is a radical change in its claims to emotional apprehension. No longer conceived, as was the case in certain nineteenth-century formulations, as a form which seeks to attain a unifying and universal affective constant, and to re-affirm the empathetic power of literary processes, postwar realist fiction does not merely critique this heritage. Instead, it occupies an ambivalent posture wherein this lineage of true feeling, so intimately linked to the entire history of realism itself, is at once mourned, nostalgised, undermined and explicitly denounced as a hegemonic imperative. Individuals therefore engage in processes of self-interrogation wherein they long for true feeling, analyse the artifice of their own affects, and often end up renouncing oppressive structures of emotional control.

Realism was, I have argued, perfectly suited as the terrain for this equivocal exploration because of the specific history of its relationship to representation and the real. What better form, after all, in which to work against true feeling as powerful mythology than that of its strongest literary-historical proponent? For if postwar American realism allows us to penetrate into the 'heart' of emotional processes, it does so by simultaneously hiding and foregrounding performativity itself. At the same time as it complicates affect's inherent artifice, it also gestures towards impossible ideals of emotional naturalness, purity and perfection. Both ideational and critical, it reflects in this way the constructive dialectics at work in all emotional processes.

For our feelings within the self are always already characterised by infinite mimetic mirrors, which are further complicated by the diegetic layers of literary texts. In this vision, post-war realism no longer resembles a reactionary movement against the formal expansions or ideological perversions of modernist utopias, but establishes a defensive outpost against the more hegemonic aspects of modernism's dominant dreams. Because of its canonical heritage as a mode intricately involved with claims to depict the real and the true, realism is amply invested with the rhetorical tools necessary to theatricalise, and in some cases undo, the priority often automatically accorded in affective existences to the natural, the non-imitative, the normal and the real.

In spite of this, and as I have sought to demonstrate, according stability to particular emotional values was a central project of vast spans of Cold War culture. That much American literature from World War II until the century's final decades should not just constitute an iconoclastic rebellion against such foundational enterprises is one of the intriguing manifestations of this historical moment. For the novels and short stories analysed in this book present myriad characters who yearn for knowable feelings at the same time as they seek to desperately flee their controlling hold. Like the profoundly ambiguous status of the natural body, original emotion or the uncorrupted self, they are concurrently ideals and oppressions, and activate this dialectic in a poignant attempt at social and personal liberation.

Realist literature is furthermore particularly adept in ensuring this ironic valency for the reason that such errancy occurs within the selfsame representational gesture. As Peter Boxall observes, noting the unwarranted exaggeration of a 'realist' and 'anti-realist' binary:

> We have not simply to produce a more accurate, less caricatured model for understanding how the history of prose realism has sought to make pictures of the world. We have also to develop an understanding of how a dissatisfaction with realism, a sense that realism is never really realism, is the result not of an aberration, not of a failure of the mechanisms of realism, but part of its basic condition, and its means of going on.[26]

It follows that the 'precarity' of literature which has defined its status throughout modernity need not be a reason to run to true feeling in literature's defence, for 'this precarity is not a mark of the failure of the novel, not a sign of its demise, but the very condition of its being'.[27] Any desire to accord to literature a status of cultural assurance is thus akin to the desire to accord stability to a range of emotional values which are incessantly conditioned by their own dynamic change.

'People wonder why the novel is the most popular form of literature,' remarked G. K. Chesterton, in a continuation of Victorian moral legitimisations. 'People wonder why it is read more than books of science or books of metaphysics. The reason is very simple; it is merely that the novel is more true than they are.'[28] But literature should not attempt to quantitatively or qualitatively rival other disciplines in its quotient of truth (whether truth as correspondence, coherence or pragmatic success). It should not claim to be 'more true' than science – whatever this may mean – or, in an Aristotelian sense, more universal than history. Rather than a mere conduit to true feeling, literature may on the contrary afford us the opportunity to experience affects' vital, ongoing construction.

The extent to which realist fictions are suspended between the collective and the personal, the public and the private, is in many ways the same dialectic as between our desire for true feeling as universalised collectivity and the need for an emotionality of rebellious personal exclusion. Such rebellion insists on the extent to which our feelings do not readily correspond either to a ratiocentric ideal, or to those uncontrollably circulating intensities of the outer world. We cannot give weight, then, to only one side of this ideation. Even more importantly, we cannot fail to recognise that it is indeed a fantasy, which never ceases to make fictional projections out of an emotional life poised between equally constructed images of affective harmony and discord.

### Affective Fictions: Emotion as Creation of Imaginary Worlds

'Only a literature that cannot be taken seriously', remarked Witold Gombrowicz in 1957, 'attempts to solve the problems of existence.'[29] In deepening the complexities of representation, affectivity and subjectivity, the recognition of the fundamental artifice of affect eschews 'solutions' to the challenges of affective life, erroneously conceived of as problems to be resolved. For like experience, literature's aim is not to solve problems, and it is not a problem in itself. Literature, as Gombrowicz notes, 'does not exist to make life easy, but to complicate it'.[30] In the same sense, the feelings of literary texts question us, challenge us, accuse us even in defiant protest, asking of us that we reflect on what we take to be our self-evident sentimental modes. In doing so, literature leads to other feelings in the same way it continually leads to other lives. These lives are the lives of fiction itself, both those of created characters and those of our own future selves. In this sense, we are interwoven with fictionality, and our emotional lives are better viewed as living projections, on the wall of Plato's cave, rather than the distant rays of a domineering sun.

Asking ourselves, while reading literature or in our daily lives, if our feelings are natural, real or true is perhaps an inevitable part of ongoing affective interrogations, and in no way negative in and of itself. This book has sought not to sententiously condemn such questioning, much less to demonise or pathologise it, but rather to recognise the extent to which it too is part of the play of performative representations – the artifice of all affect – within the heart of the self. 'In the heart of the self' is also, of course, a wilful ideation, which may be uttered only if we recognise that the self may in fact have many hearts, which interact, overlap and contradict one another in an evolving emotional semiosis. No essential core, then, to either emotion or subjectivity, does not mean no meaning; on the contrary, meaning is only enriched by artifice's ever-multiplying iterations.

To wonder if our own feelings, or those of literature, are true is thus not intrinsically a problem, as long as it is conceived as part of a spirited, self-reflexive exploration which does not strive to reach a transcendent end. The problem arises when this process is integrated into socialised institutions, politicised ideologies and personal hierarchies of value, frequently becoming fixed, stagnating into prejudicial assumptions and anchored beliefs. It is at this point that this questioning may begin to cast opprobrium over untrue feelings that do not meet its norms. This occurs not only at a communal level but within the self committed to true feeling as a way of discovering its true nature, and the related nature of the real.

Beginning as a free-thinking inquiry, such a process risks becoming restrictive and prohibitory. In its place, recognising the artifice of all affect does not seek to instigate a reign of absolute relativism – relinquishing jurisdiction over emotional value itself, with all feelings being deemed equal – but rather to take control over feelings' plasticity, interrogating the constructs and concepts that forge them, as they too forge themselves. It is thus not about attributing primacy to the intuitions of the self or the grounding of an objective real, but about admitting the mutual, creative, necessarily synthetic forming of both.

For the artifice of affect in reality makes space for the true, affirming that truth is a vital process of ongoing interrogation, forever shaped, like literature itself, by representation's paradoxical codes. To recognise affective artifice is to value literature not for its proximity to true feeling – or to the mythically natural constructions of the body or the self – but for its transformative fabrication of our perceptive and emotional worlds. If our feelings appear to be fictions, this should not be an occasion for anxiety as to their authentic worth, but rather a celebration of their evolving force. For fiction provides us always with a space of emerging potential and, rather than the enslavement to static values, presents the enduring promise for change.

Literature may then appear not as a lens through which to filter affect's inauthentic rays, in order to attain those purified essences which, by chance or determinism, we all somehow share. It may rather be seen as a performative exploration of feeling's inherent fictionality, locating aesthetic artifices at the heart of affect's conceptual and corporal life. For these ever-shifting affective intensities are as fictional as the diegetic incarnations of literature that they diverge from and reflect. On the stage of emotional being, the traversals of affect contribute to a spectacle in which literature may never be conceived as a mode of access to a range of pre-representational universals, but only as another highly animate site of representation's dynamic unfolding. Engendering fictional realities both within us and beyond us, affects, rather than solutions to the problems of representation, are representation enacted: they are sites of a living diegesis, engaged always in the active creation of evolving emotional worlds.

# NOTES

## Introduction

1. Prior critiques of true feeling which were crucial in the elaboration of this book's central arguments include Lauren Berlant's 'The Subject of True Feeling: Pain, Privacy, and Politics', in *Cultural Studies and Political Theory*, ed. Jodi Dean (Ithaca, NY: Cornell University Press, 2000), 42–62, and Michael Bell's *The Sentiment of Reality: Truth of Feeling in the European Novel* (London: Allen & Unwin, 1983) and *Sentimentalism, Ethics and the Culture of Feeling* (New York: Palgrave Macmillan, 2000).
2. 'Adequational' in this context refers to models of affective authenticity that, as in correspondence theories of truth in the philosophy of language or metaphysics, attempt to equate an emotion's supposed veracity to its degree of concordance with reality, things or facts.
3. Sianne Ngai, *Ugly Feelings* (Cambridge, MA: Harvard University Press, 2005); Rachel Greenwald Smith, *Affect and American Literature in the Age of Neoliberalism* (Cambridge: Cambridge University Press, 2015); Lauren Berlant, *Cruel Optimism* (Durham, NC: Duke University Press, 2011); Sara Ahmed, *The Promise of Happiness* (Durham, NC: Duke University Press, 2010).
4. This conception of truth is closer to Foucault's 'régimes de vérité', established against the abstract truth of idealism or dispassionate contemplation. See Michel Foucault, *The Foucault Reader*, ed. Paul Rabinow (New York: Pantheon Books, 1991), 73. For Foucault's 'conditions of truth', see Michel Foucault, *The Order of Things: An Archaeology of the Human Sciences* (New York: Vintage, [1970] 1994).
5. Berlant, 'The Subject of True Feeling: Pain, Privacy, and Politics', in *Cultural Studies and Political Theory*, 46.
6. Foucault, *The Foucault Reader*, 74.
7. Theodor Adorno, *Aesthetic Theory*, trans. R. Hullot-Kentor (Minneapolis: University of Minnesota Press, [1970] 1997); William James, *Writings 1902–1910* (New York: Library of America, 1987).

8. James, *Writings 1902–1910*, 573–4.
9. Jean Baudrillard, *Simulations*, trans. Paul Foss, Paul Patton and Philip Beitchman (New York: Semiotext(e), 1983).
10. Along with Sianne Ngai's *Ugly Feelings*, see Ann Cvetkovich, *Depression: A Public Feeling* (Durham, NC: Duke University Press, 2012), or *Shame and its Sisters: A Silvan Tomkins Reader*, ed. Eve Kosofsky Sedgwick and Adam Frank (Durham, NC: Duke University Press, 1995).
11. See notably Ahmed, *The Promise of Happiness*; Barbara Ehrenrich, *Bright-Sided: How the Relentless Promotion of Positive Thinking Has Undermined America* (New York: Metropolitan Books, 2009); William Davies, *The Happiness Industry: How the Government and Big Business Sold Us Well-Being* (London: Verso, 2015); *Against Health: How Health Became the New Morality*, ed. Jonathan M. Metzl and Anna Kirkland (New York: New York University Press, 2010).
12. Herman Melville, *Moby Dick*, 3rd edn, ed. Hershel Parker (New York: W. W. Norton, [1851] 2018), 66.
13. Saul Bellow, *The Adventures of Augie March* (London: Penguin Books, [1953] 2001), 402.
14. Ralph Ellison, *Invisible Man* (London and New York: Penguin Books, [1952] 2001).
15. Penguin Random House, 'Teacher's Guide: *Invisible Man*', accessed 6 May 2022: <https://www.penguinrandomhouseaudio.com/teachers-guide/46131/invisible-man>.
16. Ellison, *Invisible Man*, 259.
17. Thomas Jefferson, *Notes on the State of Virginia*, ed. Frank Shuffelton (New York: Penguin Books, [1785] 1999), 146.
18. Ellison, *Invisible Man*, 577.
19. Ibid.
20. Ibid. 573.
21. Ibid. 577.
22. Ralph Ellison, *The Selected Letters of Ralph Ellison*, ed. John F. Callahan and Marc C. Conner (New York: Random House, 2019), 294.
23. Jefferson, *Notes on the State of Virginia*, 146.
24. Ibid. 147.
25. For the modern roots of this controversy, see Silvan Tomkins, 'What Are Affects?', in *Shame and its Sisters: A Silvan Tomkins Reader*, 33–75; Brian Massumi, *Parables for the Virtual* (Durham, NC: Duke University Press, 2002), 28; Ruth Leys, 'The Turn to Affect: A Critique', *Critical Inquiry* 37, no. 3 (Spring 2011): 434–72; Adam Frank and Elizabeth A. Wilson, 'Like-Minded: A Response to Ruth Leys' "The Turn to Affect: A Critique"', *Critical Inquiry* 38, no. 4 (2012): 870–7.
26. Donald R. Wehrs underlines the Cartesian nature of this heritage in the use of the term 'affect' throughout the twentieth century, though not in the context of more recent theory. See 'Introduction', in *The Palgrave Handbook of Affect Studies and Textual Criticism*, ed. Donald R. Wehrs and Thomas Blake (London: Palgrave Macmillan, 2017), 1.
27. Massumi, *Parables for the Virtual*, 28.
28. Ibid. 29.

29. It is just such a tendency toward a 'bipolar analytic framework' in some thinking about affects which was to be an early subject of critique in Eve Kosofsky Sedgwick and Adam Frank, 'Shame in the Cybernetic Fold: Reading Silvan Tomkins', *Critical Inquiry* 21, no. 2 (1995): 500.
30. Eve Kosofsky Sedgwick, *Touching Feeling: Affect, Pedagogy, Performativity* (Durham, NC: Duke University Press, 2003), 2.
31. Brian Massumi, 'The Autonomy of Affect', *Cultural Critique* 31, 'The Politics of Systems and Environments' (Autumn 1995): 83-109.
32. Ronald de Sousa, *Emotional Truth* (New York: Oxford University Press, 2011).
33. For a useful summation of these problems see Mikko Salmela, 'True Emotions', *The Philosophical Quarterly* 56, no. 224 (July 2006): 382-405, 383.
34. Ibid.
35. De Sousa, *Emotional Truth*, 21.
36. Ibid.
37. On this point see Salmela, 'True Emotions', 382.
38. Arlie Russell Hochschild, *The Managed Heart: The Commercialization of Human Feeling* (Berkeley: University of California Press, [1983] 2003), *The Commercialization of Intimate Life: Notes from Home and Work* (Berkeley: University of California Press, 2003) and *The Outsourced Self: Intimate Life in Market Times* (New York: Metropolitan Press, 2012). From a growing bibliography in care ethics, we may mention *The Subject of Care: Feminist Perspectives on Dependency*, ed. Eva Feder Kittay and Ellen K. Feder (Oxford: Rowman & Littlefield, 2002), and Virginia Held, *The Ethics of Care: Personal, Political, Global* (Oxford: Oxford University Press, 2006).
39. Hochschild, *The Managed Heart*, 190.
40. Ibid.
41. Sarah J. Tracy and Angela Trethewey, 'Fracturing the Real-Self ↔ Fake-Self Dichotomy: Moving Toward "Crystallized" Organizational Discourses and Identities', *Communication Theory* 15, no. 2 (May 2005): 168-95, 174.
42. Edward F. Mooney, *Lost Intimacy in American Thought: Recovering Personal Philosophy from Thoreau to Cavell* (New York: Continuum, 2009), 85.
43. For further discussion of the condemnation of emotions experienced under 'altered' states as being necessarily 'artificial' and thus of reduced value, see Chapter 5.
44. Robert Charles Solomon, *True to our Feelings: What our Emotions Are Really Telling Us* (Oxford: Oxford University Press, 2007), 2-3.
45. Ibid. 215.
46. Ibid.
47. Carl Gustav Jung, *Two Essays on Analytical Psychology*, trans. R. F. C. Hull (London: Routledge, [1953] 1966), 192. Though Freud's understanding and use of 'affect' in many ways describes a distinct notion from that of recent critical theory, the link between what Freud terms *die Affekte* and repression (*refoulement, Verdrängung*) is nevertheless a crucial heritage of present true-false emotional binaries. For further analysis see notably Solange Carton and Daniel Widlöcher, 'Émotions et affects en psychanalyse', *Geriatr Psychol Neuropsychiatr Vieil* 10, no. 2 (2012): 177-86.

48. Carl Gustav Jung, *The Spirit in Man, Art and Literature* (London: Routledge, 2003), 143.
49. D. W. Winnicott's key article 'Ego Distortion in Terms of True and False Self' dates for example from 1960. See *The Maturational Processes and the Facilitating Environment* (Madison: International Universities Press, 1987), 140–52.
50. Tracy and Trethewey, 'Fracturing the Real-Self ↔ Fake-Self Dichotomy', 169.
51. Ibid. 168.
52. D. W. Winnicott, *The Collected Works of D. W. Winnicott, Volume 6: 1960–1963*, ed. Lesley Caldwell and Helen Taylor Robinson (Oxford: Oxford University Press, 2017), 167.
53. Ibid.
54. Donald E. Kalsched and Daniela F. Sieff, 'Uncovering the Secrets of the Traumatised Psyche', in *Understanding and Healing Emotional Trauma: Conversations with Pioneering Clinicians and Researchers* (London: Routledge, 2015), 11–25, 19.
55. Ibid.
56. Martin Seligman, *Authentic Happiness: Using the New Positive Psychology to Realize your Potential for Lasting Fulfillment* (New York: Free Press, 2002), 5.
57. See Guillaume-Benjamin Duchenne (de Boulogne), *Mécanisme de la physionomie humaine ou analyse électro-physiologique de l'expression des passions* (Paris: Renouard, 1862).
58. At the opening of his *Mécanisme de la physionomie humaine*, Duchenne quotes Georges-Louis Leclerc de Buffon's identification of the face as a site of transparency for the soul, framing the pathos of facial expressions in decidedly aesthetic terms. See Georges-Louis Leclerc de Buffon, *Histoire naturelle, générale et particulière, avec la description du Cabinet du Roi*, vols I–X, ed. Stéphane Schmitt (Paris: Honoré Champion, 2007–17). Also quoted in Duchenne, *Mécanisme de la physionomie humaine*, v.
59. The concept of theatricality is indeed increasingly central in recent affect theory. See notably Adam Frank, *Transferential Poetics, from Poe to Warhol* (New York: Fordham University Press, 2015).
60. Duchenne, *Mécanisme de la physionomie humaine*, 62.
61. The authentic 'Duchenne smile' is recommended as a behavioural path to happiness in myriad popular self-help books, such as George A. Bonanno, *The Other Side of Sadness: What the New Science of Bereavement Tells Us* (New York: Basic Books, 2009).
62. See for instance Paul Ekman and Richard J. Davidson, 'Voluntary Smiling Changes Regional Brain Activity', *Psychological Science* 4, no. 5 (1993): 342–5; Paul Ekman, E. T. Rolls, D. I. Perrett and H. D. Ellis, 'Facial Expressions of Emotion: An Old Controversy and New Findings', *Philosophical Transactions: Biological Sciences* 335, no. 1,273 (1992): 63–9.
63. It is furthermore revealing that Seligman should choose the profession – flight attendants – whose neglected emotional labour was famously highlighted in the work of Arlie Hochschild (at various points for instance throughout *The Managed Heart*).
64. Seligman, *Authentic Happiness*, 5.

65. Ibid.
66. From Galen's humourism to the purported role of the pineal gland in Descartes, such biological determinism as the basis of fixed affective classifications is part of a specific historical understanding of the passions. See *Galen on the Natural Faculties*, trans. Arthur John Brock (London: Loeb Classical Library, 1952), and René Descartes, *The Passions of the Soul*, trans. Michael Moriarty (Oxford: Oxford World's Classics, 2015).
67. Seligman, *Authentic Happiness*, 5.
68. Jonathan Greenberg, 'Chapter 2: Modernism's Story of Feeling', in *Modernism, Satire and the Novel* (Cambridge: Cambridge University Press, 2011), 21–40, 27.
69. On this omnipresent condemnation, see Louis Menand, *Discovering Modernism: T. S. Eliot and his Context* (Oxford: Oxford University Press, 1987).
70. Ezra Pound, 'A Retrospect', in *Literary Essays of Ezra Pound*, ed. with an introduction by T. S. Eliot (New York: New Directions, [1935] 1968), 3–14, 13.
71. T. S. Eliot, 'The Perfect Critic', in *The Sacred Wood: Essays on Poetry and Criticism* (New York: Alfred A. Knopf, 1921), 1–14, 13.
72. F. T. Marinetti, 'War, the Only Hygiene of the World', in *Futurism: An Anthology*, ed. Lawrence Rainey, Christine Poggi and Laura Wittman (New Haven: Yale University Press, 2009), 84–5, 85.
73. D. H. Lawrence quoted in Hugh Stevens, 'D. H. Lawrence: Organicism and the Modernist Novel', in *The Cambridge Companion to the Modernist Novel*, ed. Morag Shiach (Cambridge: Cambridge University Press, 2007), 137–51, 137.
74. Bell, *Sentimentalism, Ethics and the Culture of Feeling*, 160. See more generally chapter 7, 'Modernism and the Attack on Sentiment', as well as Michael Bell, *Literature, Modernism and Myth: Belief and Responsibility in the Twentieth Century* (Cambridge: Cambridge University Press, 1997).
75. Joyce Cary, 'The Art of Fiction', *Paris Review* 7 (1954–55): 65, quoted in *The Oxford Critical and Cultural History of Modernist Magazines, Volume II: North America 1894–1960*, ed. Peter Brooker and Andrew Thacker (Oxford: Oxford University Press, 2012), 767.
76. See Suzanne Clarke, *Sentimental Modernism: Women Writers and the Revolution of the Word* (Bloomington: Indiana University Press, 1991), or Julie Taylor, *Djuna Barnes and Affective Modernism* (Edinburgh: Edinburgh University Press, 2012).
77. We need only recall Wordsworth's insistence in the 'Preface' that his project is to remain proximate to what he calls 'our elementary feelings' and our 'essential passions of the heart', in contrast to other poets' dividing themselves, by way of 'a far more philosophical language', from 'the sympathies of men'. See William Wordsworth, 'Preface', in William Wordsworth and Samuel Taylor Coleridge, *Lyrical Ballads: 1798 and 1802* (Oxford: Oxford University Press, 2013), 97.
78. Marga Vicedo, 'Cold War Emotions: Mother Love and the War over Human Nature', in *Cold War Social Science: Knowledge Production, Liberal Democracy, and Human Nature*, ed. Mark Solovey and Hamilton Cravens (New York: Palgrave Macmillan, 2012), 233–51, 245.
79. Guy Oakes, *The Imaginary War: Civil Defense and American Cold War Culture* (Oxford: Oxford University Press, 1994), 50.

80. Joseph R. McCarthy, 'Address to the Republican Women's Club of Wheeling, West Virginia, "Enemies from Within" (February 9, 1950)', in *Essential Documents of American History, Volume II: From Reconstruction to the Twenty-first Century*, ed. Bob Blaisdell (New York: Dover, 2016), 232–40, 233.
81. On this question see Eva S. Moskowitz, *In Therapy We Trust: America's Obsession with Self-Fulfillment* (Baltimore: Johns Hopkins University Press, 2001), 218–19.
82. Gore Vidal, *Rocking the Boat* (Boston: Little, Brown and Company, [1951] 1962), 83.
83. George Eliot, *Middlemarch*, ed. Bert G. Hornback (New York: W. W. Norton, [1871–72] 2000), 291.
84. For analysis of minority authors' positions during the Cold War on the question of emotional and national unity, see texts such as Vaughn Rasberry, *Race and the Totalitarian Century: Geopolitics in the Black Literary Imagination* (Cambridge, MA: Harvard University Press, 2016), or Robert J. Corber, *Homosexuality in Cold War America: Resistance and the Crisis of Masculinity* (Durham, NC: Duke University Press, 1997).
85. Keith Wilhite, 'WASP Culture', in *American Literature in Transition, 1950–1960*, ed. Steven Belletto (Cambridge: Cambridge University Press, 2018), 103–16, 114.
86. This is comparable to Greg Forter's argument regarding mourning in modernism as a re-affirmation of White masculine normativity in *Gender, Race, and Mourning in American Modernism* (Cambridge: Cambridge University Press, 2011), 6.
87. Philip Roth, *American Pastoral* (New York: Vintage, 1997).
88. I use the terms 'modern' or 'post-war' realism and realists to distinguish American writers from the Cold War to the end of the twentieth century from the canonical American realism of the late nineteenth and early twentieth centuries.
89. James Baldwin, *Going to Meet the Man* (London and New York: Penguin Books, [1948] 1991); John Cheever, *The Stories of John Cheever* (London: Vintage, 2000); Richard Ford, *The Sportswriter* (New York: Vintage, [1986] 1995), *Independence Day* (New York: Vintage, [1995] 1996) and *The Lay of the Land* (London: Bloomsbury, 2006); Kathleen Collins, *Whatever Happened to Interracial Love?* (New York: HarperCollins, 2016); Paula Fox, *The Widow's Children* (New York: W. W. Norton, [1976] 1999); Richard Yates, *Revolutionary Road* (London: Vintage, [1961] 2007); Philip Roth, *Sabbath's Theater* (London: Vintage, [1995] 1996).

## Chapter 1

1. This is the case whether we consider the notion, in the sense of Peter Brooks, as a conceptual constant transcending its specific historical incarnations or as the codified movements of the nineteenth century. On this distinction see notably Peter Brooks, *Realist Vision* (New Haven: Yale University Press, 2005), and Ian Watt, *The Rise of the Novel: Studies in Defoe, Richardson and Fielding* (Berkeley: University of California Press, [1957] 2001). This binary of realism

as historical movement and realism as representative impulse transcending its programmatic nineteenth-century modes was moreover already a trope in post-war definitions of the term. See for example M. H. Abrams, 'Realism and Naturalism', in *A Glossary of Literary Terms*, 5th edn (San Francisco: Holt, Rinehart and Winston, 1988), 152–4.
2. See Roland Barthes, 'L'effet de réel', *Communications* 11 (1968): 84–9.
3. Gustave Flaubert, 'Letter to Mlle Leroyer de Chantepie', 18 March 1857, in *The Letters of Gustave Flaubert: 1830–1857*, ed. and trans. Francis Steegmuller (Cambridge, MA: Harvard University Press, 1980), 230, and *Correspondance, t. II: Juillet 1851–Décembre 1858* (Paris: Gallimard, Collection Pléiade, 1980).
4. See Virginia Woolf, 'Modern Fiction', in *The Essays of Virginia Woolf, Volume 4: 1925–1928*, ed. Andrew McNeillie (London: Hogarth Press, [1921] 1984).
5. George Levine, *The Realistic Imagination* (Chicago: University of Chicago Press, 1981); Raymond Tallis, *In Defence of Realism* (Lincoln: University of Nebraska Press, [1958] 1998); Katherine Kearns, *Nineteenth-Century Literary Realism: Through the Looking Glass* (Cambridge: Cambridge University Press, 1996).
6. Lilian R. Furst, *All Is True: The Claims and Strategies of Realist Fiction* (Durham, NC: Duke University Press, 1995), viii.
7. For further exploration of the politics of anti-realist positions within the modern academy, see chapter 3, 'The Politics of Anti-Realism', in Gerald Graff, *Literature Against Itself: Literary Ideas in Modern Society* (Chicago: University of Chicago Press, [1979] 1995), 63–103.
8. Geoffrey Baker, 'Introduction', in *Realism's Others*, ed. Eva Aldea and Geoffrey Baker (Newcastle: Cambridge Scholars Publishing, 2010), x.
9. Flaubert, *The Letters of Gustave Flaubert*, 240, and *Correspondance, t. II*, 691. The existence of such a myth is not to claim that various nineteenth-century realist fictions do not maintain highly complex relationships to the value of artifice and the artificial. It is to underline, however, the propensity within *manifesti* (especially by Zola or Flaubert) to make radical claims regarding realist fiction's ability to attain a universal truth. Correlating 'personal emotions' with 'nervous susceptibilities' moreover equates feeling with a pathologised corporal state of psycho-physical agitation.
10. Flaubert addresses these lines to a reader, in an epistolary context, and their programmatic aspect must be kept in mind.
11. Massumi, *Parables for the Virtual*, 28.
12. Eric Shouse, 'Feeling, Emotion, Affect', *M/C Journal* 8 (December 2005), accessed 2 February 2021: <www.journal.media-culture.org.au/0512/03-shouse.php>; also quoted in Leys, 'The Turn to Affect: A Critique', 435.
13. See Jean-François Lyotard, *Discours, figure* (Paris: Klincksieck, 1971), *Le Différend* (Paris: Éditions de Minuit, 1983) and *Des dispositifs pulsionnels* (Paris: Galilée, 1994).
14. Ron Katwan, 'The Affect in the Work of Jean-François Lyotard', *Surfaces* 3 (1993), <https://doi.org/10.7202/1065103ar>.
15. Massumi, *Parables for the Virtual*, 40.
16. Though historically prevalent, this vision of realism as dismissive of alterity is certainly not ubiquitous. For the argument that literary realism strives to

integrate otherness, see for example Lawrence R. Schehr, *Figures of Alterity: French Realism and its Others* (Stanford: Stanford University Press, 2003).
17. Theodor Adorno, 'Commitment', in Theodor Adorno, Walter Benjamin, Ernst Bloch, Bertolt Brecht and George Lukács, *Aesthetics and Politics: The Key Texts of Classic Debate within German Marxism*, ed. and trans. Ronald Taylor (London: Verso, 1977), 177–95, 179; also quoted in Baker, *Realism's Others*, ix.
18. Peter Boxall, *The Value of the Novel* (New York: Cambridge University Press, 2015), 29.
19. Jacques Derrida, 'Plato's Pharmacy', in *Dissemination*, trans. Barbara Johnson (Chicago: University of Chicago Press, 1981), 63, and 'La Pharmacie de Platon', in *La Dissémination* (Paris: Éditions du Seuil, 1972), 79.
20. Walker Percy, *The Moviegoer* (London: Vintage, [1961] 1998).
21. Ibid. 10–11.
22. See Viktor Shklovsky, 'Art as Device (1917/1919)', in *Viktor Shklovsky: A Reader*, ed. and trans. Alexandra Berlina (London: Bloomsbury, 2017), 73–96.
23. Percy, *The Moviegoer*, 11.
24. Ibid. 80.
25. Ibid. 145.
26. Søren Kierkegaard, *Concluding Unscientific Postscript* (Princeton: Princeton University Press, 1974), 179.
27. Linda Whitney Hobson and Walker Percy, 'The Study of Consciousness: An Interview with Walker Percy', *The Georgia Review* 35, no. 1 (Spring 1981): 50–60, 57.
28. Ibid. 56.
29. Michael Kobre, *Walker Percy's Voices* (Athens: University of Georgia Press, 2000), 40.
30. Percy, *The Moviegoer*, 86.
31. Ibid. 98–9.
32. Brian A. Smith, *Walker Percy and the Politics of the Wayfarer* (London: Lexington, 2017), 65.
33. Percy, *The Moviegoer*, 145.
34. Ibid. 121.
35. Ibid. 194.
36. Ibid. 190.
37. Ibid. 220.
38. Ibid.
39. Ibid. 222.
40. Ibid. 223–4.
41. Bertram Wyatt-Brown, *The House of Percy: Honor, Melancholy, and Imagination in a Southern Family* (Oxford: Oxford University Press, 1994), 320.
42. See Percy, *The Moviegoer*, 226.
43. Hobson and Percy, 'The Study of Consciousness: An Interview with Walker Percy', 57.
44. Percy, *The Moviegoer*, 223.
45. Saul Bellow, *Dangling Man* (London: Penguin Books, [1944] 2007), 1.
46. Ibid.

47. Saul Bellow, *Herzog* (London: Penguin Books, [1964] 2003), 125.
48. James Clements, 'Bottomless Surfaces: Saul Bellow's "Refreshed Phrenology"', *Journal of Modern Literature* 33, no. 1 (2009): 75–91, 76.
49. Lionel Trilling, *Sincerity and Authenticity* (Cambridge, MA: Harvard University Press, 1971), 41.
50. Frank D. McConnell, *Four Post-War American Novelists: Bellow, Mailer, Barth, and Pynchon* (Chicago: University of Chicago Press, 1977), xv.
51. Michael K. Glenday, *Saul Bellow and the Decline in Humanism* (London: Palgrave Macmillan, 1990), 66.
52. Ibid. 65.
53. Ibid. 65–6.
54. Brooke Allen, 'The Adventures of Saul Bellow', *The Hudson Review* 54, no. 1 (2001): 77–87, 79.
55. Saul Bellow, *Conversations with Saul Bellow*, ed. Gloria L. Cronin and Ben Siegel (Jackson: University Press of Mississippi, 1994), 95.
56. Ibid. 96.
57. Ellen Pfifer, 'If the Shoe Fits: Bellow and Recent Critics', *Texas Studies in Literature and Language* 29, no. 4, 'Twentieth-Century Fiction' (Winter 1987): 442–57, 444.
58. Ibid.
59. Bellow, *Herzog*, 74–5.
60. Ibid. 240.
61. Bellow, *Conversations*, 96.
62. Bellow, *Herzog*, 266.
63. As we will see, Philip Roth extends this Bellovian dilemma, for as Jonathan Brent argues, Roth's Zuckerman novels 'brutally analyse this naïve quest for happiness through authenticity. What Zuckerman finds is that at the centre of this authentic selfhood is nothing but images, an empty, gravityless void.' Jonathan Brent, 'The Unspeakable Self: Philip Roth and the Imagination', in *Reading Philip Roth*, ed. Asher Z. Milbauer and Donald G. Watson (New York: St. Martin's Press, 1988), 180–200, 192.
64. Bellow, *Herzog*, 266.
65. Bellow, *The Adventures of Augie March*, 384.
66. Ibid. 455.
67. Ibid. 402.
68. Mark Greif, *The Age of the Crisis of Man: Thought and Fiction in America, 1933–1973* (Princeton: Princeton University Press, 2015), 190.
69. Bellow, *The Adventures of Augie March*, 402.
70. Ibid.
71. Ibid.
72. Ibid.
73. Ibid.
74. Saul Bellow, *The Dean's December* (London: Penguin Books, [1982] 2012), 311.
75. Ibid.
76. Ibid. 243.

77. 'New forms for new feelings' was an integral conviction of Eliot, Pound, Lawrence and Woolf. See for example Lorraine Sim and Ann Vickery, 'New Feelings: Modernism, Intimacy, and Emotion', in *Affirmations: Of the Modern* 1, no. 2 (Spring 2014): 1–14.

## Chapter 2

1. In such usages, the term 'nature' often refers both to an objectivised structure of the real (i.e. all that is not 'us') and to internal causes and properties, in the sense of primordial mechanisms of the organic body such as 'drives' or 'instincts'. These two senses are moreover related in a logic of extrapolation and causation, in which natural 'laws' are seen to govern both organic body and inert reality. Though Aristotelian mimesis has been misused to justify naturalising aesthetics, the Greek φύσις (*physis*) is hardly a comparable term to modern acceptations of 'nature'. On this point see Gerard Naddaf, *The Greek Concept of Nature* (New York: State University of New York Press, 2005).
2. Aristotle, *Poetics*, trans. Anthony Kenny (Oxford: Oxford University Press, 2013), 24. For Heidegger's exploration of the historical evolution of this distinction see Martin Heidegger, *Contributions to Philosophy (Of the Event)*, trans. Richard Rojcewicz and Daniela Vallega-Neu (Bloomington: Indiana University Press, [1989] 2012).
3. This is notably the central interrogation of the so-called 'paradox of fiction'. See especially R. T. Allen, 'The Reality of Responses to Fiction', *British Journal of Aesthetics* 26, no. 1 (1986): 64–8; Greg Currie, *The Nature of Fiction* (Cambridge: Cambridge University Press, 1990); James Gribble, 'The Reality of Fictional Emotions', *The Journal of Aesthetic Education* 16, no. 4 (Winter 1982): 53–8, 54.
4. Eva Illouz, Daniel Gilon and Mattan Shachak, 'Emotions and Cultural Theory', in *The Handbook of the Sociology of Emotions*, vol. 2, ed. Jan E. Stets and Jonathan H. Turner (Dordrecht: Springer, 2014), 221–44, 238.
5. Reuven Tsur, *Toward a Theory of Cognitive Poetics* (Brighton: Sussex Academic Press, 2008), 8.
6. Peter Stockwell, *Cognitive Poetics: An Introduction* (London: Routledge, 2002), 2.
7. Tsur, *Toward a Theory of Cognitive Poetics*, 4.
8. Ibid. 25, 4.
9. Ibid. 4–5.
10. For further discussion of this disciplinary formation see Gerald Graff, *Professing Literature: An Institutional History* (Chicago: University of Chicago Press, 1987), or Stein Haugom Olsen, 'The Discipline of Literary Studies', in *Literary Studies and the Philosophy of Literature*, ed. Andrea Selleri and Philip Gaydon (London: Palgrave Macmillan, 2010), 37–64.
11. Otniel E. Dror, 'Dangerous Liaisons: Science, Amusement and the Civilizing Process', in *Representing Emotions: New Connections in the Histories of Art, Music and Medicine*, ed. Penelope Gouk and Helen Hills (Aldershot: Ashgate, 2005), 223–34, 223.
12. Ibid. 225.

13. For an in-depth critique of homeostatic conceptions of affective balance, see Chapter 4.
14. Amélie O. Rorty, *Explaining Emotions* (Berkeley: University of California Press, 1980), 117.
15. See Gorgias, 'On What Is Not, or On Nature', in *The First Philosophers: The Presocratics and Sophists*, trans. Robin Waterfield (Oxford: Oxford University Press, 2009), 222–41; Lucretius, *De rerum natura*, ed. and trans. Cyril Bailey (Oxford: Clarendon Press, 1963); Gilles Deleuze, 'Lucretius and Naturalism [1961]', trans. Jared C. Bly, in *Contemporary Encounters with Ancient Metaphysics*, ed. Abraham Jacob Greenstine and Ryan J. Johnson (Edinburgh: Edinburgh University Press, 2017), 245–53; Friedrich Nietzsche, *Beyond Good and Evil*, ed. and trans. Marion Faber (Oxford: Oxford University Press, 2008), 12; Martin Heidegger, *Being and Time*, trans. John Macquarrie and Edward Robinson (New York: Harper Perennial, [1927] 2008), 100.
16. Maurice Merleau-Ponty, *Phenomenology of Perception*, trans. Colin Smith (London: Routledge, 1965), 169. For further exploration of anti-naturalising philosophies, see Steven Vogel, *Against Nature: The Concept of Nature in Critical Theory* (New York: State University of New York Press, 1996).
17. Merleau-Ponty, *Phenomenology of Perception*, 169.
18. Clément Rosset, *L'anti-nature. Éléments pour une philosophie tragique* (Paris: Presses Universitaires de France, [1973] 1986), 10–11, my translation.
19. Bruno Latour, *Politics of Nature: How to Bring the Sciences into Democracy*, trans. Catherine Porter (Cambridge, MA: Harvard University Press, 2004), 25–6. For Latour's critique of the political ramifications of this transcendent status, see also Latour, *We Have Never Been Modern*, trans. Catherine Porter (Cambridge, MA: Harvard University Press, 1993).
20. Pierre Montebello, *Métaphysiques cosmomorphes. La fin du monde humain* (Dijon: Les Presses du Réel, 2015), 232, my translation. See also Montebello, *Nature et subjectivité* (Grenoble: Millon, 2007).
21. Timothy Morton, *Ecology without Nature: Rethinking Environmental Aesthetics* (Cambridge, MA: Harvard University Press, 2007), 1.
22. Georges Canguilhem, *The Normal and the Pathological, with an Introduction by Michel Foucault*, trans. Carolyn R. Fawcett in collaboration with Robert S. Cohen (New York: Zone Books, 1991), and *Knowledge of Life*, ed. Paola Marrati and Todd Meyers, trans. Stefanos Geroulanos and Daniela Ginsburg (New York: Fordham University Press, 2008).
23. Canguilhem, *Knowledge of Life*, xx.
24. Rosset, *L'anti-nature*, 60, my translation.
25. Elaine Scarry, *The Body in Pain: The Making and Unmaking of the World* (Oxford: Oxford University Press, 1985), 251.
26. Jenefer Robinson, *Deeper Than Reason: Emotion and its Role in Literature, Music, and Art* (Oxford: Clarendon Press, 2005), 196.
27. Merleau-Ponty, *Phenomenology of Perception*, 169.
28. Nietzsche, *Beyond Good and Evil*, 12.
29. Morton, *Ecology without Nature*, 19–20.

30. Though this may seem more immediately evident in his metafictional works such as the Zuckerman novels or *My Life as a Man*, such self-reflexive processes are also omnipresent in Roth's more realist modes. On this, see Lillian S. Kremer, 'Philip Roth's Self-Reflexive Fiction', *Modern Language Studies* 28, nos. 3/4 (1998): 57–72.
31. Roth, *Sabbath's Theater*, 153.
32. Ibid. 143.
33. Ibid. 371.
34. Ibid. 169.
35. Ibid. 258.
36. Jane F. Thrailkill, *Affecting Fictions: Mind, Body, and Emotion in American Literary Realism* (Cambridge, MA: Harvard University Press, 2007), 5.
37. Roth, *Sabbath's Theater*, 135.
38. Ibid. 230–1.
39. Ibid. 231.
40. See Denis Diderot, *The Paradox of Acting*, trans. Walter Herries Pollock (London: Chatto & Windus, 1883), and *Entretiens sur le fils naturel, de la poésie dramatique, paradoxe sur le comédien* (Paris: Gallimard, 2005).
41. See Minsoo Kang, *Sublime Dreams of Living Machines: The Automaton in the European Imagination* (Cambridge, MA: Harvard University Press, 2011), 211.
42. Roth, *Sabbath's Theater*, 158. For further analysis of the implications of Sabbath's puppetry, notably in relation to the historical precursor of Heinrich von Kleist's *Über das Marionettentheater*, see Frank Kelleter, 'Portrait of the Sexist as a Dying Man: Death, Ideology, and the Erotic in Philip Roth's *Sabbath's Theater*', *Contemporary Literature* 39, no. 2 (1998): 262–302.
43. Roth, *Sabbath's Theater*, 247.
44. Ibid. 158.
45. Patrick Hayes, *Philip Roth: Fiction and Power* (New York: Oxford University Press, 2014), 86.
46. Roth, *Sabbath's Theater*, 153.
47. Ibid. 373, 362.
48. Ibid. 160.
49. Ibid. 198.
50. As for Saul Bellow, such interior subjective division has also been interpreted with regard to the sociohistorical contexts of modern Jewish identity. See for example David Brauner, 'Fiction as Self-Accusation: Philip Roth and the Jewish Other', *Studies in American Jewish Literature* 17, 'The Resonance of Twoness: Ambivalent Faith in an Ambiguous World' (1998): 8–16.
51. Roth, *Sabbath's Theater*, 298.
52. Ibid. 219.
53. For further discussion see Conor Cunningham, *Genealogy of Nihilism* (London: Routledge, 2002), or Karen Leslie Carr, *The Banalization of Nihilism: Twentieth-Century Responses to Meaninglessness* (New York: State University of New York Press, 1992).
54. Roth, *Sabbath's Theater*, 319.
55. Thrailkill, *Affecting Fictions*, 16.

56. This is notably Blake Bailey's position in his biography *Cheever: A Life* (New York: A. A. Knopf, 2009), 364.
57. John Cheever, 'The Geometry of Love', in *The Stories of John Cheever*, 594–602, 596.
58. Ibid. 597.
59. Ibid. 595.
60. Ibid. 599.
61. Ibid. 598–9.
62. Ibid. 597.
63. See Kathryn Riley, 'John Cheever and the Limitations of Fantasy', *CEA Critic* 45, nos. 3/4 (1983): 21–6, 24.
64. Cheever, 'The Geometry of Love', 599.
65. Ibid.
66. Ibid. 600.
67. Ibid.
68. Ibid. 595.
69. John Cheever, *The Journals of John Cheever* (New York: A. A. Knopf, 1991), 117.
70. John Cheever, *The Wapshot Chronicle* (New York: Harper Perennial, [1954] 2003).
71. Cheever, *The Journals of John Cheever*, 7.
72. John Cheever and Annette Grant, 'John Cheever, The Art of Fiction no. 62', interview in *The Paris Review* 67 (Fall 1976), accessed 6 October 2021: <https://www.theparisreview.org/interviews/3667/john-cheever-the-art-of-fiction-no-62-john-cheever>.
73. Cheever, 'The Geometry of Love', 596.
74. Merleau-Ponty, *Phenomenology of Perception*, 169.

## Chapter 3

1. Derrida, *Dissemination*, 204. Derrida insists moreover that such 'Platonism' also includes anti-Platonic movements for the reason that, in perpetuating this ontological binarity, they participate in a dominant metaphysical tradition.
2. See Plato, *Ion*, in *Early Socratic Dialogues*, trans. Trevor J. Saunders (London: Penguin, 1987), 39–68.
3. See Wordsworth, 'Preface', in *Lyrical Ballads*, 97.
4. Derrida, *Dissemination*, 201.
5. Ibid. 206.
6. Thomas Dutoit, 'Just . . . Mimesis: Jack Hitt's Act V', *Revue française d'études américaines* 135, 'Mimesis dans les lettres américaines', ed. Richard Anker (2013): 94–109, 100.
7. Though Derrida relates this 'internal division' specifically to mimesis's Platonic role as at once discredited copy in the mimetic arts and the unveiling of truth through remembrance (*anamnēsia*), it is a division which, I argue, may be extrapolated to a generalised model of mimetic negotiations within the feeling subject. See Derrida, *Dissemination*, 204, and *La Dissémination*, 235.
8. Ibid.

9. See Erich Auerbach, *Mimesis: The Representation of Reality in Western Thought* (Princeton: Princeton University Press, [1953] 2003).
10. Émile Zola, *Le Roman naturaliste*, ed. Henri Mitterand (Paris: Le Livre de Poche, [1880] 1999), 84–5, my translation.
11. For further discussion of this Enlightenment heritage see Charles Taylor, *Sources of the Self: The Making of the Modern Identity* (Cambridge: Cambridge University Press, [1989] 2012), Part 2: 'Inwardness', 111–99.
12. For in-depth analysis of these questions, see Bell, *The Sentiment of Reality*.
13. See Chapter 2, especially '"True lives belonged to others": Unknowable Artifice in Philip Roth'.
14. Yates, *Revolutionary Road*, 60.
15. Many aspects of this dialectic in Yates are close to Erving Goffman's notion of social performance. See *The Presentation of Self in Everyday Life* (London: Penguin Books, [1956] 1990).
16. Yates, *Revolutionary Road*, 20.
17. Ibid. 332.
18. The plot of Robert Sherwood's 1935 melodrama *The Petrified Forest* closely mirrors the Wheelers' story. See *The Petrified Forest* (New York: Dramatists Play Service, 1948).
19. Yates, *Revolutionary Road*, 332–3.
20. John Cheever, 'The Swimmer', in *The Stories of John Cheever*, 603–12, 611.
21. Ibid. 611–12.
22. David Castronovo and Steven Goldleaf, *Richard Yates* (New York: Twayne, 1996), 7. See also 56.
23. Though written in the late 1960s and throughout the 1970s, Collins's stories were only published posthumously in 2016.
24. James Baldwin, *Giovanni's Room* (London and New York: Penguin Books, [1956] 2001), 137.
25. Kathleen Collins, 'The Uncle', in *Whatever Happened to Interracial Love?*, 15.
26. Ibid.
27. See for instance Richard Wright, *The Man Who Lived Underground* (New York: Library of America, [1941] 2021).
28. Collins, 'The Uncle', 18.
29. See Christina Sharpe, *In the Wake: On Blackness and Being* (Durham, NC: Duke University Press, 2016).
30. Collins, 'The Uncle', 18–19.
31. W. E. B. Du Bois, *The Souls of Black Folk* (New York: Barnes & Noble, [1903] 2003), 9.
32. Ibid. This dilemma also recalls Frantz Fanon's writings on the construction of Black identity in *Black Skin, White Masks*. See Frantz Fanon, *Peau noire, masques blancs* (Paris: Éditions du Seuil, 1952).
33. Collins, 'The Uncle', 20.
34. Importantly, many of Collins's stories have been read as far more affirmative and optimistic than they may appear on further analysis. One notable case is the unusual interpretation of the collection's title story, which according to a recent review suggests that 'love might soften if not conquer differences between

the races'. In truth, the story's ever-present irony traces recurrent problems and conflicts – political, racial, emotional – inherent in such relationships. See Colin Grant, 'Whatever Happened to Interracial Love? by Kathleen Collins Review – Black Power and Pathos', *The Guardian* (24 February 2017), accessed 1 November 2021: <https://www.theguardian.com/books/2017/feb/24/whatever-happened-to-interracial-love-by-kathleen-collins-review>.

35. See Aida Levy-Hussen, *How to Read African American Literature: Post-Civil Rights Fiction and the Task of Interpretation* (New York: New York University Press, 2016), 6.
36. Kathleen Collins, 'Whatever Happened to Interracial Love?', in *Whatever Happened to Interracial Love?*, 36–7.
37. Beth Hinderliter and Steve Peraza, *More Than Our Pain: Affect and Emotion in the Era of Black Lives Matter* (New York: State University of New York Press, 2021), 3.
38. Ibid.
39. James Baldwin, 'Everybody's Protest Novel', in *Notes of a Native Son* (Boston: Beacon Press, 1955), 13–23, 14, and 'The Black Boy Looks at the White Boy', in *Nobody Knows My Name* (New York: Vintage Books, 1993), 229.
40. See for instance Tyrone S. Palmer's analysis of 'Black affective responses' being 'only legible as signs of pathology, further reifying blackness-as-subhumanity; as a sign of both excess and lack'. Tyrone S. Palmer, '"What Feels More Than Feeling?": Theorizing the Unthinkability of Black Affect', *Critical Ethnic Studies* 3, no. 2 (2017): 31–56, 32.
41. James Baldwin, 'Previous Condition', in *Going to Meet the Man*, 80–99, 92.
42. Ibid. 87.
43. Ibid. 87–8.
44. Ibid. 88.
45. Ibid. 90.
46. Ibid. 91.
47. Ibid. 91–2.
48. Ibid. 92.
49. Ibid.
50. Ibid. 92–3.
51. Ibid. 94.
52. Ibid. 95.
53. Ibid.
54. Ibid. 99.
55. Ibid.
56. Auerbach, *Mimesis: The Representation of Reality in Western Thought*, 486.
57. See Derrida, *Dissemination*, 204–7.
58. Ford, *The Sportswriter*, 19.
59. Ibid.
60. Ford, *Independence Day*, 94.
61. Ford, *The Sportswriter*, 64.
62. See Plato, *Ion*, in *Early Socratic Dialogues*, 39–68, and *Republic*, trans. Robin Waterfield (Oxford: Oxford University Press, 2008).
63. Ford, *The Sportswriter*, 64–5.

64. Romanticism is of course also highly self-reflexive and rife with 'Romantic irony', but this is not its dominant cultural myth. See Lilian R. Furst, *Fictions of Romantic Irony* (Cambridge, MA: Harvard University Press, 1984), or John Francis Fetzer, 'The Evolution of a Revolution: Romantic Irony', *The Comparatist* 11 (1987): 45–53.
65. Ford, *The Sportswriter*, 64.
66. Ibid. 76.
67. Ibid.
68. Ibid. 119.
69. Ibid.
70. Ibid. 139.
71. Ibid. 374.
72. Ford, *The Lay of the Land*, 432.
73. Ford, *The Sportswriter*, 223.
74. Lene M. Johannessen, 'The "Long Empty Moment": Richard Ford's *The Sportswriter*', in *Horizons of Enchantment: Essays in the American Imaginary* (Hanover, NH: Dartmouth College Press, 2011), 78–96, 80, 92.
75. Ford, *The Sportswriter*, 63.
76. David Foster Wallace, *Infinite Jest* (Boston: Little, Brown, 1996).
77. Ford, *The Sportswriter*, 63–4.
78. Ibid. 64.
79. Ibid. 224.
80. L. J. Rather, 'The "Six Things Non-Natural"', *Clio Medica* 3 (1968): 337–47; see also Saul Jarcho, 'Galen's Six Non-Naturals', *Bulletin of the History of Medicine* 44 (1970): 372–7.
81. Ford, *The Sportswriter*, 119–20.
82. Ibid. 120.
83. Ibid. 132.
84. Ibid. 375.
85. Ibid. 133.
86. Ibid. 140.
87. William G. Chernecky, '"Nostalgia Isn't What It Used to Be": Isolation and Alienation in the Frank Bascombe Novels', in *Perspectives on Richard Ford*, ed. Huey Guagliardo (Jackson: University Press of Mississippi, 2000), 157–77, 164.

## Chapter 4

1. For representative examples of this popular material see Roy Martina, *Emotional Balance: The Path to Inner Peace and Healing* (London: Hay House, 2010), or Beth Jacobs, *Writing for Emotional Balance* (Oakland, CA: New Harbinger Publications, 2005).
2. See Book 6 of Confucius, *The Analects*, trans. Raymond Dawson (Oxford: Oxford University Press, 2008).
3. See Plato, *Republic*, above all '4. Primary Education for the Guardians', 70–115, and '5. The Guardians' Life and Duties', 115–33, as well as 'Poetry and Unreality', 344–603, for the heritage of poetry's deleterious influence on the maintenance of emotional stability.

4. Aristotle, *The Nicomachean Ethics*, trans. David Ross, revised with an introduction and notes by Lesley Brown (Oxford: Oxford University Press, 2009), II. 9, 35.
5. Ibid. II. 7, 33.
6. See St Thomas Aquinas, *Summa Theologica*, vol. 2, part II (New York: Cosimo, 2007), 858.
7. Taylor, *Sources of the Self: The Making of the Modern Identity*, 130.
8. Ibid. 284.
9. See Introduction: 'Enemies from Within: Post-War America and Emotional Control'.
10. For Claude Bernard's 1865 concept of 'milieu intérieur' see *Introduction à l'étude de la médecine expérimentale* (Paris: J. B. Baillière et Fils, 1865), 107–12, 206–13. For the coining of the term 'homeostasis', see Walter B. Cannon, *The Wisdom of the Body: How the Human Body Reacts to Disturbance and Danger and Maintains the Stability Essential to Life* (New York: W. W. Norton, [1926] 1963).
11. 'Physiological basis for emotions affecting health', in the *Oxford Companion to Emotion and the Affective Sciences*, ed. David Sander and Klaus Scherer (Oxford: Oxford University Press, 2009), 212.
12. Cannon, *The Wisdom of the Body*, 318, 320.
13. See John Keats, 'Isabella; or, The Pot of Basil', in *Complete Poems and Selected Letters of John Keats* (London: Modern Library, 2001), 209; quoted in Yates, *Revolutionary Road*, 1.
14. Richard Yates, *Disturbing the Peace* (London: Vintage, [1975] 2008), 171.
15. Ibid.
16. Richard Yates, *Young Hearts Crying* (London: Vintage, [1984] 2008), 367–8.
17. See Serpatilin advertisement, *New York State Journal of Medicine* 56 (July–December 1956): 2,047.
18. Meprosan advertisement, *The Journal of the American Medical Association* 199, no. 2 (1967): 226–8; Serax advertisement, *The Journal of the American Medical Association* 200, no. 8 (1967): 206–7.
19. As with the case of electroconvulsive therapy in Yates's *Revolutionary Road*, the debate here is not about the real-world efficacy of specific treatments, but rather the modes of their rhetorical and social presentation, and the underlying ideologies they incarnate.
20. Butisol advertisement, *The Journal of the American Medical Association* 188, no. 7 (1964).
21. For a brief history of Serentil and its consumer marketing, see Allan V. Horwitz and Jerome C. Wakefield, *All We Have to Fear: Psychiatry's Transformation of Natural Anxieties into Mental Disorders* (Oxford: Oxford University Press, 2012).
22. For a general history of psychopharmacology's twentieth-century evolution, see David Healy, *The Creation of Psychopharmacology* (Cambridge, MA: Harvard University Press, 2004).
23. Among the varied studies on hysteria's historical ties to literature see Evelyn Ender, *Sexing the Mind: Nineteenth-Century Fictions of Hysteria* (Ithaca, NY: Cornell University Press, 1995), or Janet L. Beizer, *Ventriloquized Bodies: Narratives of Hysteria in Nineteenth-Century France* (Ithaca, NY: Cornell University Press, 1994).

24. Yates, *Revolutionary Road*, 291.
25. Yates, *Young Hearts Crying*, 163.
26. Ibid. 171.
27. Ibid. 173.
28. Ibid. 185.
29. Ibid. 187.
30. Yates, *Revolutionary Road*, 287.
31. Ibid.
32. Ibid. 288.
33. Ibid. 165.
34. Ibid.
35. Ibid. 165-6.
36. See for instance David G. Schuster, *Neurasthenic Nation: America's Search for Health, Happiness, and Comfort, 1869-1920* (New Brunswick, NJ: Rutgers University Press, 2011); Tom Lutz, *American Nervousness, 1903: An Anecdotal History* (Ithaca, NY: Cornell University Press, 1991).
37. Wordsworth, 'Preface', in *Lyrical Ballads*, 95-116.
38. Fox, *The Widow's Children*, 48.
39. Ibid. 17.
40. Ibid. 18.
41. Ibid. 93.
42. Ibid. 58.
43. Ibid. 47-8.
44. Ibid. 158.
45. Ibid. 59.
46. Ibid.
47. Ibid. 50.
48. Ibid. 41.
49. Ibid. 50.
50. Ibid. 93.
51. Ibid. 215.
52. Ibid. 120-1.
53. Ibid. 50.
54. Ibid. 114.
55. Ibid. 196.
56. Ibid. 203.
57. Ibid. 178.
58. Ibid. 179.
59. Ibid. 88.
60. Ibid. 49.
61. Ibid. 89.
62. Ibid. 112.
63. Ibid. 51.
64. Ibid. 125.
65. See Plato, *Republic*, 82, 388a-b.

## Chapter 5

1. This position is omnipresent throughout a range of 'canonical' texts of psychedelic literature, notably Aldous Huxley, *The Doors of Perception and Heaven and Hell* (New York: Harper Perennial, 1956); Tom Wolfe, *The Electric Kool-Aid Acid Test* (New York: Picador, [1968] 2008); Timothy Leary, *The Psychedelic Experience* (New York: Citadel Press, [1964] 1995).
2. Timothy Leary, *The Politics of Ecstasy* (Berkeley, CA: Ronin Publishing, [1980] 1998), 38–9.
3. Ibid. 39.
4. Michel Foucault, *The Birth of the Clinic* (London: Routledge, [1963] 1989); Canguilhem, *The Normal and the Pathological*.
5. For overviews of this question in the field of psychiatry see Bassam Khoury, Ellen J. Langer and Francesco Pagnini, 'The DSM: Mindful Science or Mindless Power? A Critical Review', *Frontiers in Psychology* 5 (2014), <http://doi.org/10.3389/fpsyg.2014.00602>, and Martyn D. Pickersgill, 'Debating DSM-5: Diagnosis and the Sociology of Critique', *Journal of Medical Ethics* 40 (2014): 521–5.
6. For a critique of both the pharmacological industry and the Diagnostic and Statistical Manual (DSM), see for instance Gary Greenberg, *The Book of Woe: The DSM and the Unmaking of Psychiatry* (New York: Blue Rider Press, 2013).
7. See Canguilhem, *The Normal and the Pathological*, 287.
8. For the broadest acceptation of the term 'psychotrope', we need only look to its Greek etymology as whatever 'turns' (*trepein, tropos*) the spirit or mind (*psyche*).
9. For the link between Cold War politics and the rise of the pharmaceutical industry see Dominique A. Tobbel, '"Who's Winning the Human Race?": Cold War as Pharmaceutical Political Strategy', *Journal of the History of Medicine and Allied Sciences* 64, no. 4 (2009): 429–73.
10. For the explicitly racialised aspect of this discourse, and of the enactment of American drug policy more generally, see Doris Marie Provine, *Unequal under Law: Race in the War on Drugs* (Chicago: University of Chicago Press, 2007); Deborah Small, 'The War on Drugs Is a War on Racial Justice', *Social Research* 68, no. 3 (2001): 896–903.
11. Dan Baum, *Smoke and Mirrors: The War on Drugs and the Politics of Failure* (New York: Little, Brown and Company, 1996), 11.
12. Plato, *Symposium*, trans. Robin Waterfield (Oxford: Oxford University Press, 1994).
13. Pliny the Elder, *The Natural History of Pliny*, vol. 3, trans. John Bostock and H. T. Riley (London: H. G. Bohn, 1855), Book XIV, 272.
14. Patricia Highsmith quoted in Andrew Wilson, *Beautiful Shadow: A Life of Patricia Highsmith* (London: Bloomsbury, 2010), 107.
15. See Arthur Rimbaud, 'Lettres dites du "Voyant"', in *Œuvres complètes* (Paris: Gallimard, Bibliothèque de la Pléiade, 2009), 344–6.
16. For further literary contexts on this shift see Matts G. Djos, *Writing under the Influence: Alcoholism and the Alcoholic Perception from Hemingway to Berryman* (New York: Palgrave Macmillan, 2010), or Thomas B. Gilmore, *Equivocal Spirits:*

*Alcoholism and Drinking in Twentieth-Century Literature* (Chapel Hill: University of North Carolina Press, 1987).
17. Peter Conrad, 'Medicalization and Social Control', *Annual Review of Sociology* 18 (1992): 209–32, 209.
18. For the use of medicalisation in sociological theory see Jesse R. Pitts, 'Social Control: The Concept', in *International Encyclopedia of Social Sciences*, vol. 14, ed. David Sills (New York: Macmillan, 1968), 381–96, or Peter Conrad, *The Medicalization of Society: On the Transformation of Human Conditions into Treatable Disorders* (Baltimore: Johns Hopkins University Press, 2007).
19. For post-war debates on the issue, highly prevalent in journals from the 1940s to the 1960s, see K. M. Bowman and E. M. Jellinek, 'Alcohol Addiction and Chronic Alcoholism', *Quarterly Journal of Studies on Alcohol* 2 (1941): 98–176, or Mark Keller, 'Alcoholism: Nature and Extent of the Problem', *The Annals of the American Academy of Political and Social Science* 315 (1958): 1–11. For a general history of alcoholism as a disease, see Alfonso Paredes, 'The History of the Concept of Alcoholism', in *Alcoholism*, ed. R. Tarter and A. Sugerman (Reading, MA: Addison-Wesley, 1976), 9–52.
20. Joseph W. Schneider, 'Deviant Drinking as Disease: Alcoholism as a Social Accomplishment', *Social Problems* 25, no. 4 (April 1978): 361–72, 363.
21. Leonore Tiefer, 'The Medicalization of Impotence: Normalizing Phallocentrism', *Gender and Society* 8 (1994): 363–77; Elizabeth Siegel Watkins, 'Medicalization of Stress in the Twentieth Century', *Medicine Studies* 4, nos. 1/4 (May 2014): 29–36; Simon Carter, 'The Medicalization of Sunlight in the Early Twentieth Century', *Journal of Historical Sociology* 25, no. 1 (2012): 83–105.
22. Paul Starr, *The Social Transformation of American Medicine: The Rise of a Sovereign Profession and the Making of a Vast Industry* (New York: Basic Books, 1982), 13.
23. Marty Roth, *Drunk the Night Before: An Anatomy of Intoxication* (Minneapolis: University of Minnesota Press, 2008), xvi.
24. Ibid. xviii.
25. F. Scott Fitzgerald, *The Great Gatsby* (London: Penguin, [1925] 2000), 48.
26. Truman Capote, 'La Côte Basque', in *Answered Prayers* (New York: Vintage, 2012), 120.
27. Saul Bellow, 'John Berryman (1973)', in *It All Adds Up: From the Dim Past to the Uncertain Future* (New York: Penguin, 1994), 270.
28. John Updike, *Rabbit Angstrom: A Tetralogy*, including *Rabbit, Run* (1960), *Rabbit Redux* (1971), *Rabbit Is Rich* (1981), *Rabbit at Rest* (1990) (New York: Alfred A. Knopf, 1995), 26.
29. Updike, *Rabbit Angstrom: A Tetralogy*, 211.
30. Ibid. 217.
31. Ibid. 217–18.
32. Ibid. 220.
33. Ibid. 221.
34. Ibid. 221–2.
35. Tony Tanner, 'The Sorrow of Some Central Hollowness', in *Critical Essays on John Updike*, ed. William R. Macnaughton (Boston: G. K. Hall, 1982), 71–4, 72. Critical moralising on the worthlessness of Updike's characters is a staple

of his critical reception. In an extreme example, D. Keith Mano wrote in 1974 that 'Updike's characters don't deserve an obituary, let alone a novel. They are pathetic folk; even the pathos is undistinguished.' D. Keith Mano, 'Doughy Middleness', in *Critical Essays on John Updike*, 74–6, 74.

36. Tanner, 'The Sorrow of Some Central Hollowness', in *Critical Essays on John Updike*, 72.
37. Updike, *Rabbit Angstrom: A Tetralogy*, 222–3.
38. Ibid. 223.
39. Ibid. 227.
40. Ibid. 1,101.
41. Raymond Carver, *Collected Stories* (New York: Library of America, 2009): 'Where I'm Calling From', 452–66; 'Kindling', 654–66; 'Vitamins', 426–40.
42. Ibid: 'Gazebo', 234–9, 237.
43. Ibid: 'What We Talk About When We Talk About Love', 310–22.
44. Ibid. 310.
45. Ibid.
46. Ibid. 310–11.
47. Ibid. 311.
48. Arthur F. Bethea, *Technique and Sensibility in the Fiction and Poetry of Raymond Carver* (New York: Routledge, 2001), 94.
49. Charles E. May, '"Do You See What I'm Saying?": The Inadequacy of Explanation and the Uses of Story in the Short Fiction of Raymond Carver', *The Yearbook of English Studies* 31 (2001): 39–49, 45.
50. Carver, 'What We Talk About When We Talk About Love', 311.
51. Ibid. 312.
52. Ibid. 313.
53. Ibid. 313–14.
54. Ibid. 314.
55. Ibid. 314–15.
56. Ibid. 315.
57. Ibid. 315–16.
58. Ibid. 316.
59. Ibid.
60. Ibid. 320.
61. Ibid. 321.
62. Ibid. 321–2.
63. This is the very problem which Deleuze underlines in the *Abécédaire* regarding the constant deferral of the 'last drink'. See *L'abécédaire de Gilles Deleuze*, interview by Claire Parnet, directed by Pierre-André Boutang and Michel Pamart (Paris: Éditions Montparnasse, 2004).

## Conclusion

1. See Henry David Thoreau, *Walden*, ed. Stephen Fender (London: Oxford World's Classics, [1854] 2009), and Ralph Waldo Emerson, *Nature and Selected Essays* (New York: Penguin, [1836] 2003), 39.

2. For a sample of the expanding corpus of articles on such claims across both science journalism and academic disciplines such as cognitive psychology, behavioural and neurosciences, see Keith Oatley, 'Meetings of Minds: Dialogue, Sympathy, and Identification, in Reading Fiction', *Poetics* 26 (1999): 439–54; Dan R. Johnson, 'Transportation into a story increases empathy, prosocial behavior, and perceptual bias toward fearful expressions', *Personality and Individual Differences* 52 (2012): 150–5; Francesca Kay, 'A literary cure for loneliness: Put your iPad down, ditch the phone and pick up a book. It could boost your circle of sympathy', *The Guardian* (17 January 2016), accessed 16 December 2021: <https://www.theguardian.com/lifeandstyle/2016/jan/17/a-literary-cure-for-loneliness-pick-up-a-book>; Gregory S. Berns, Kristina Blaine, Michael J. Prietula and Brandon E. Pye, 'Short- and Long-Term Effects of a Novel on Connectivity in the Brain', *Brain Connectivity* 3, no. 6 (2013): 590–600; Jen Christensen, 'Why reading is good for your health', *CNN* (25 April 2017), accessed 17 April 2023: <https://edition.cnn.com/2016/07/21/health/reading-fiction-health-effects/index.html>; Honor Whiteman, 'Five ways reading can improve health and well-being', *Medical News Today* (12 October 2016), accessed 12 July 2021: <https://www.medicalnewstoday.com/articles/313429.php>.
3. Ironically, many critiques of empathy in contemporary moral philosophy, rather than attempting to forge a less superficial vision of affect than that which is encouraged by models of emotional fusion, advocate a return to rationality. See for example Paul Bloom, *Against Empathy: The Case for Rational Compassion* (New York: HarperCollins, 2016).
4. Greenwald Smith, *Affect and American Literature in the Age of Neoliberalism*, 1.
5. Ibid. 2.
6. Ibid. 4.
7. See respectively Roth, *Sabbath's Theater*; Fox, *The Widow's Children*; Updike, *Rabbit Angstrom: A Tetralogy*.
8. Leo Tolstoy, *What Is Art?* (London: Bloomsbury, [1897] 2014), 57.
9. Patrick Colm Hogan, *What Literature Teaches Us about Emotion* (Cambridge: Cambridge University Press, 2014), 9.
10. Ibid. 2.
11. Even the title of Hogan's book, *What Literature Teaches Us about Emotion*, makes the dynamics of this interaction clear: literature is not a representational site of play for forces of emotional ambivalence, but is attributed a primarily pedagogical role.
12. F. Scott Fitzgerald, *F. Scott Fitzgerald On Writing*, ed. Larry W. Phillips (New York: Charles Scribner's Sons, 1986), 10, first recorded by Sheilah Graham in her autobiography *Beloved Infidel: The Education of a Woman* (New York: Henry Holt and Company, 1958), 260.
13. William Faulkner, 'Address upon Receiving the Nobel Prize for Literature, Stockholm, December 10, 1950', in *Essays, Speeches and Public Letters*, 2nd rev. edn, ed. James B. Meriwether (New York: Modern Library, 2004), 119–21, 119.
14. Ibid.
15. Percy, *The Moviegoer*, 220.

16. Daniel J. Singal, *William Faulkner: The Making of a Modernist* (Chapel Hill: University of North Carolina Press, 1997), 2.
17. Raymond Williams, *Politics of Modernism: Against the New Conformists* (London: Verso, 2007).
18. Hannah Arendt, *The Origins of Totalitarianism* (Orlando: Harcourt, [1951] 1994), 474.
19. Hannah Arendt, *The Human Condition* (Chicago: University of Chicago Press, [1958] 1998), 242.
20. Jane P. Tompkins, 'Criticism and Feeling', *College English* 39, no. 2 (1977): 169–78, 169.
21. F. R. Leavis quoted in Dennis Donoghue, *Walter Pater: Lover of Strange Souls* (New York: Alfred A. Knopf, 1995), 3. See also F. R. Leavis, *New Bearings in English Poetry* (London: Faber & Faber, 2008), especially chapter 3, 'T. S. Eliot', 60–100.
22. F. R. Leavis quoted in R. P. Bilan, *The Literary Criticism of F. R. Leavis* (Cambridge: Cambridge University Press, 1979), 100.
23. June Howard, 'What Is Sentimentality?', *American Literary History* 11, no. 1 (1999): 63–81, 75.
24. Cleanth Brooks and Robert Penn Warren, *Understanding Fiction* (New York: Appleton-Century-Crofts, [1946] 1959), 219.
25. Saul Bellow in Matthew C. Roudané, 'An Interview with Saul Bellow', *Contemporary Literature* 25 (1974): 265–80, 270; Glenday, *Saul Bellow and the Decline in Humanism*, 1.
26. Boxall, *The Value of the Novel*, 48.
27. Ibid. 140.
28. G. K. Chesterton, *The Collected Works of G. K. Chesterton* (San Francisco: Ignatius Press, 1986), 143.
29. Witold Gombrowicz, *Diary*, trans. Lillan Vallee (New Haven: Yale University Press, 2012), 291.
30. Ibid.

# BIBLIOGRAPHY

Abrams, M. H. 'Realism and Naturalism', in *A Glossary of Literary Terms*, 5th edn. San Francisco: Holt, Rinehart and Winston, 1988: 152–4.
Adorno, Theodor. *Aesthetic Theory*, translated by R. Hullot-Kentor. Minneapolis: University of Minnesota Press, [1970] 1997.
Adorno, Theodor. 'Commitment', in Theodor Adorno, Walter Benjamin, Ernst Bloch, Bertolt Brecht and George Lukács, *Aesthetics and Politics: The Key Texts of Classic Debate within German Marxism*, edited and translated by Ronald Taylor. London: Verso, 1977: 177–95.
Ahmed, Sara. *The Promise of Happiness*. Durham, NC: Duke University Press, 2010.
Allen, Brooke. 'The Adventures of Saul Bellow', *The Hudson Review* 54, no. 1 (2001): 77–87.
Allen, R. T. 'The Reality of Responses to Fiction', *British Journal of Aesthetics* 26, no. 1 (1986): 64–8.
Aquinas, St Thomas. *Summa Theologica*, vol. 2, part II. New York: Cosimo, 2007.
Arendt, Hannah. *The Human Condition*. Chicago: University of Chicago Press, [1958] 1998.
Arendt, Hannah. *The Origins of Totalitarianism*. Orlando: Harcourt, [1951] 1994.
Aristotle. *The Nicomachean Ethics*, translated by David Ross, revised with an introduction and notes by Lesley Brown. Oxford: Oxford University Press, 2009.
Aristotle. *Poetics*, translated by Anthony Kenny. Oxford: Oxford University Press, 2013.
Auerbach, Erich. *Mimesis: The Representation of Reality in Western Thought*. Princeton: Princeton University Press, [1953] 2003.
Bailey, Blake. *Cheever: A Life*. New York: A. A. Knopf, 2009.
Baker, Geoffrey. 'Introduction', in *Realism's Others*, edited by Eva Aldea and Geoffrey Baker. Newcastle: Cambridge Scholars Publishing, 2010: ix–xiv.
Baldwin, James. *Giovanni's Room*. London and New York: Penguin Books, [1956] 2001.
Baldwin, James. *Going to Meet the Man*. London and New York: Penguin Books, [1948] 1991.

Baldwin, James. *Nobody Knows My Name*. New York: Vintage Books, 1993.
Baldwin, James. *Notes of a Native Son*. Boston: Beacon Press, 1955.
Barthes, Roland. 'L'effet de réel', *Communications* 11 (1968): 84–9.
Baudrillard, Jean. *Simulations*, translated by Paul Foss, Paul Patton and Philip Beitchman. New York: Semiotext(e), 1983.
Baum, Dan. *Smoke and Mirrors: The War on Drugs and the Politics of Failure*. New York: Little, Brown and Company, 1996.
Beizer, Janet L. *Ventriloquized Bodies: Narratives of Hysteria in Nineteenth-Century France*. Ithaca, NY: Cornell University Press, 1994.
Bell, Michael. *Literature, Modernism and Myth: Belief and Responsibility in the Twentieth Century*. Cambridge: Cambridge University Press, 1997.
Bell, Michael. *Sentimentalism, Ethics and the Culture of Feeling*. New York: Palgrave Macmillan, 2000.
Bell, Michael. *The Sentiment of Reality: Truth of Feeling in the European Novel*. London: Allen & Unwin, 1983.
Bellow, Saul. *The Adventures of Augie March*. London: Penguin Books, [1953] 2001.
Bellow, Saul. *Conversations with Saul Bellow*, edited by Gloria L. Cronin and Ben Siegel. Jackson: University Press of Mississippi, 1994.
Bellow, Saul. *Dangling Man*. London: Penguin Books, [1944] 2007.
Bellow, Saul. *The Dean's December*. London: Penguin Books, [1982] 2012.
Bellow, Saul. *Herzog*. London: Penguin Books, [1964] 2003.
Bellow, Saul. *It All Adds Up: From the Dim Past to the Uncertain Future*. New York: Penguin, 1994.
Berlant, Lauren. *Cruel Optimism*. Durham, NC: Duke University Press, 2011.
Berlant, Lauren. 'The Subject of True Feeling: Pain, Privacy, and Politics', in *Cultural Studies and Political Theory*, edited by Jodi Dean. Ithaca, NY: Cornell University Press, 2000: 42–62.
Bernard, Claude. *Introduction à l'étude de la médecine expérimentale*. Paris: J. B. Baillière et Fils, 1865.
Berns, Gregory S., Kristina Blaine, Michael J. Prietula and Brandon E. Pye. 'Short- and Long-Term Effects of a Novel on Connectivity in the Brain', *Brain Connectivity* 3, no. 6 (2013): 590–600.
Bethea, Arthur F. *Technique and Sensibility in the Fiction and Poetry of Raymond Carver*. New York: Routledge, 2001.
Bilan, R. P. *The Literary Criticism of F. R. Leavis*. Cambridge: Cambridge University Press, 1979.
Bloom, Paul. *Against Empathy: The Case for Rational Compassion*. New York: HarperCollins, 2016.
Bonanno, George A. *The Other Side of Sadness: What the New Science of Bereavement Tells Us*. New York: Basic Books, 2009.
Bowman, K. M., and E. M. Jellinek. 'Alcohol Addiction and Chronic Alcoholism', *Quarterly Journal of Studies on Alcohol* 2 (1941): 98–176.
Boxall, Peter. *The Value of the Novel*. New York: Cambridge University Press, 2015.
Brauner, David. 'Fiction as Self-Accusation: Philip Roth and the Jewish Other', *Studies in American Jewish Literature* 17, 'The Resonance of Twoness: Ambivalent Faith in an Ambiguous World' (1998): 8–16.

Brent, Jonathan. 'The Unspeakable Self: Philip Roth and the Imagination', in *Reading Philip Roth*, edited by Asher Z. Milbauer and Donald G. Watson. New York: St. Martin's Press, 1988: 180–200.

Brooker, Peter, and Andrew Thacker, eds. *The Oxford Critical and Cultural History of Modernist Magazines, Volume II: North America 1894–1960*. Oxford: Oxford University Press, 2012.

Brooks, Cleanth, and Robert Penn Warren. *Understanding Fiction*. New York: Appleton-Century-Crofts, [1946] 1959.

Brooks, Peter. *Realist Vision*. New Haven: Yale University Press, 2005.

Buffon, Georges-Louis Leclerc de. *Histoire naturelle, générale et particulière, avec la description du Cabinet du Roi*, vols I–X, edited by Stéphane Schmitt. Paris: Honoré Champion, 2007–17.

Canguilhem, Georges. *Knowledge of Life*, edited by Paola Marrati and Todd Meyers, translated by Stefanos Geroulanos and Daniela Ginsburg. New York: Fordham University Press, 2008.

Canguilhem, Georges. *The Normal and the Pathological, with an Introduction by Michel Foucault*, translated by Carolyn R. Fawcett in collaboration with Robert S. Cohen. New York: Zone Books, 1991.

Cannon, Walter B. *The Wisdom of the Body: How the Human Body Reacts to Disturbance and Danger and Maintains the Stability Essential to Life*. New York: W. W. Norton, [1926] 1963.

Capote, Truman. *Answered Prayers*. New York: Vintage, 2012.

Carr, Karen Leslie. *The Banalization of Nihilism: Twentieth-Century Responses to Meaninglessness*. New York: State University of New York Press, 1992.

Carter, Simon. 'The Medicalization of Sunlight in the Early Twentieth Century', *Journal of Historical Sociology* 25, no. 1 (2012): 83–105.

Carton, Solange, and Daniel Widlöcher. 'Émotions et affects en psychanalyse', *Geriatr Psychol Neuropsychiatr Vieil* 10, no. 2 (2012): 177–86.

Carver, Raymond. *Collected Stories*. New York: Library of America, 2009.

Cary, Joyce. 'The Art of Fiction', *Paris Review* 7 (1954–55): 65.

Castronovo, David, and Steven Goldleaf. *Richard Yates*. New York: Twayne, 1996.

Cheever, John. *The Journals of John Cheever*. New York: A. A. Knopf, 1991.

Cheever, John. *The Stories of John Cheever*. London: Vintage, 2000.

Cheever, John. *The Wapshot Chronicle*. New York: Harper Perennial, [1954] 2003.

Cheever, John, and Annette Grant. 'John Cheever, The Art of Fiction no. 62', interview in *The Paris Review* 67 (Fall 1976), accessed 6 October 2021: <https://www.theparisreview.org/interviews/3667/john-cheever-the-art-of-fiction-no-62-john-cheever>.

Chernecky, William G. '"Nostalgia Isn't What It Used to Be": Isolation and Alienation in the Frank Bascombe Novels', in *Perspectives on Richard Ford*, edited by Huey Guagliardo. Jackson: University Press of Mississippi, 2000: 157–77.

Chesterton, G. K. *The Collected Works of G. K. Chesterton*. San Francisco: Ignatius Press, 1986.

Christensen, Jen. 'Why reading is good for your health', *CNN* (25 April 2017), accessed 17 April 2023: <https://edition.cnn.com/2016/07/21/health/reading-fiction-health-effects/index.html>.

Clarke, Suzanne. *Sentimental Modernism: Women Writers and the Revolution of the Word*. Bloomington: Indiana University Press, 1991.

Clements, James. ''Bottomless Surfaces: Saul Bellow's "Refreshed Phrenology"', *Journal of Modern Literature* 33, no. 1 (2009): 75–91.

Collins, Kathleen. *Whatever Happened to Interracial Love?* New York: HarperCollins, 2016.

Confucius. *The Analects*, translated by Raymond Dawson. Oxford: Oxford University Press, 2008.

Conrad, Peter. 'Medicalization and Social Control', *Annual Review of Sociology* 18 (1992): 209–32.

Conrad, Peter. *The Medicalization of Society: On the Transformation of Human Conditions into Treatable Disorders*. Baltimore: Johns Hopkins University Press, 2007.

Corber, Robert J. *Homosexuality in Cold War America: Resistance and the Crisis of Masculinity*. Durham, NC: Duke University Press, 1997.

Cunningham, Conor. *Genealogy of Nihilism*. London: Routledge, 2002.

Currie, Greg. *The Nature of Fiction*. Cambridge: Cambridge University Press, 1990.

Cvetkovich, Ann. *Depression: A Public Feeling*. Durham, NC: Duke University Press, 2012.

Davies, William. *The Happiness Industry: How the Government and Big Business Sold Us Well-Being*. London: Verso, 2015.

De Sousa, Ronald. *Emotional Truth*. New York: Oxford University Press, 2011.

Deleuze, Gilles. *L'abécédaire de Gilles Deleuze*, interview by Claire Parnet, directed by Pierre-André Boutang and Michel Pamart. Paris: Éditions Montparnasse, 2004.

Derrida, Jacques. *La Dissémination*. Paris: Éditions du Seuil, 1972.

Derrida, Jacques. *Dissemination*, translated by Barbara Johnson. Chicago: University of Chicago Press, 1981.

Deleuze, Gilles. 'Lucretius and Naturalism [1961]', translated by Jared C. Bly, in *Contemporary Encounters with Ancient Metaphysics*, edited by Abraham Jacob Greenstine and Ryan J. Johnson. Edinburgh: Edinburgh University Press, 2017: 245–53.

Descartes, René. *The Passions of the Soul*, translated by Michael Moriarty. Oxford: Oxford World's Classics, 2015.

Diderot, Denis. *Entretiens sur le fils naturel, de la poésie dramatique, paradoxe sur le comédien*. Paris: Gallimard, 2005.

Diderot, Denis. *The Paradox of Acting*, translated by Walter Herries Pollock. London: Chatto & Windus, 1883.

Djos, Matts G. *Writing under the Influence: Alcoholism and the Alcoholic Perception from Hemingway to Berryman*. New York: Palgrave Macmillan, 2010.

Donoghue, Dennis. *Walter Pater: Lover of Strange Souls*. New York: Alfred A. Knopf, 1995.

Dror, Otniel E. 'Dangerous Liaisons: Science, Amusement and the Civilizing Process', in *Representing Emotions: New Connections in the Histories of Art, Music and Medicine*, edited by Penelope Gouk and Helen Hills. Aldershot: Ashgate, 2005: 223–34.

Du Bois, W. E. B. *The Souls of Black Folk*. New York: Barnes & Noble, [1903] 2003.

Duchenne (de Boulogne), Guillaume-Benjamin. *Mécanisme de la physionomie humaine ou analyse électro-physiologique de l'expression des passions*. Paris: Renouard, 1862.

Dutoit, Thomas. 'Just . . . Mimesis: Jack Hitt's Act V', *Revue française d'études américaines* 135, 'Mimesis dans les lettres américaines', edited by Richard Anker (2013): 94–109.
Ehrenrich, Barbara. *Bright-Sided: How the Relentless Promotion of Positive Thinking Has Undermined America*. New York: Metropolitan Books, 2009.
Ekman, Paul, and Richard J. Davidson. 'Voluntary Smiling Changes Regional Brain Activity', *Psychological Science* 4, no. 5 (1993): 342–5.
Ekman, Paul, E. T. Rolls, D. I. Perrett and H. D. Ellis. 'Facial Expressions of Emotion: An Old Controversy and New Findings', *Philosophical Transactions: Biological Sciences* 335, no. 1,273 (1992): 63–9.
Eliot, George. *Middlemarch*, edited by Bert G. Hornback. New York: W. W. Norton, [1871–72] 2000.
Eliot, T. S. *The Sacred Wood: Essays on Poetry and Criticism*. New York: Alfred A. Knopf, 1921.
Ellison, Ralph. *Invisible Man*. London and New York: Penguin Books, [1952] 2001.
Ellison, Ralph. *The Selected Letters of Ralph Ellison*, edited by John F. Callahan and Marc C. Conner. New York: Random House, 2019.
Emerson, Ralph Waldo. *Nature and Selected Essays*. New York: Penguin, [1836] 2003.
Ender, Evelyn. *Sexing the Mind: Nineteenth-Century Fictions of Hysteria*. Ithaca, NY: Cornell University Press, 1995.
Fanon, Frantz. *Peau noire, masques blancs*. Paris: Éditions du Seuil, 1952.
Faulkner, William. 'Address upon Receiving the Nobel Prize for Literature, Stockholm, December 10, 1950', in *Essays, Speeches and Public Letters*, 2nd rev. edn, edited by James B. Meriwether. New York: Modern Library, 2004: 119–21.
Fetzer, John Francis. 'The Evolution of a Revolution: Romantic Irony', *The Comparatist* 11 (1987): 45–53.
Fitzgerald, F. Scott. *The Great Gatsby*. London: Penguin, [1925] 2000.
Fitzgerald, F. Scott. *F. Scott Fitzgerald On Writing*, edited by Larry W. Phillips. New York: Charles Scribner's Sons, 1986.
Flaubert, Gustave. *Correspondance, t. II: Juillet 1851–Décembre 1858*. Paris: Gallimard, Collection Pléiade, 1980.
Flaubert, Gustave. *The Letters of Gustave Flaubert: 1830–1857*, edited and translated by Francis Steegmuller. Cambridge, MA: Harvard University Press, 1980.
Ford, Richard. *Independence Day*. New York: Vintage, [1995] 1996.
Ford, Richard. *The Lay of the Land*. London: Bloomsbury, 2006.
Ford, Richard. *The Sportswriter*. New York: Vintage, [1986] 1995.
Forter, Greg. *Gender, Race, and Mourning in American Modernism*. Cambridge: Cambridge University Press, 2011.
Foster Wallace, David. *Infinite Jest*. Boston: Little, Brown, 1996.
Foucault, Michel. *The Birth of the Clinic*. London: Routledge, [1963] 1989.
Foucault, Michel. *The Foucault Reader*, edited by Paul Rabinow. New York: Pantheon Books, 1991.
Foucault, Michel. *The Order of Things: An Archaeology of the Human Sciences*. New York: Vintage, [1970] 1994.
Fox, Paula. *The Widow's Children*. New York: W. W. Norton, [1976] 1999.
Frank, Adam. *Transferential Poetics, from Poe to Warhol*. New York: Fordham University Press, 2015.

Frank, Adam, and Elizabeth A. Wilson. 'Like-Minded: A Response to Ruth Leys' "The Turn to Affect: A Critique"', *Critical Inquiry* 38, no. 4 (2012): 870–7.

Furst, Lilian R. *All Is True: The Claims and Strategies of Realist Fiction*. Durham, NC: Duke University Press, 1995.

Furst, Lilian R. *Fictions of Romantic Irony*. Cambridge, MA: Harvard University Press, 1984.

Galen. *Galen on the Natural Faculties*, translated by Arthur John Brock. London: Loeb Classical Library, 1952.

Gilmore, Thomas B. *Equivocal Spirits: Alcoholism and Drinking in Twentieth-Century Literature*. Chapel Hill: University of North Carolina Press, 1987.

Glenday, Michael K. *Saul Bellow and the Decline in Humanism*. London: Palgrave Macmillan, 1990.

Goffman, Erving. *The Presentation of Self in Everyday Life*. London: Penguin Books, [1956] 1990.

Gombrowicz, Witold. *Diary*, translated by Lillan Vallee. New Haven: Yale University Press, 2012.

Gorgias. 'On What Is Not, or On Nature', in *The First Philosophers: The Presocratics and Sophists*, translated by Robin Waterfield. Oxford: Oxford University Press, 2009: 222–41.

Graff, Gerald. *Literature Against Itself: Literary Ideas in Modern Society*. Chicago: University of Chicago Press, [1979] 1995.

Graff, Gerald. *Professing Literature: An Institutional History*. Chicago: University of Chicago Press, 1987.

Graham, Sheilah. *Beloved Infidel: The Education of a Woman*. New York: Henry Holt and Company, 1958.

Grant, Colin. 'Whatever Happened to Interracial Love? by Kathleen Collins Review – Black Power and Pathos', *The Guardian* (24 February 2017), accessed 1 November 2021: <https://www.theguardian.com/books/2017/feb/24/whatever-happened-to-interracial-love-by-kathleen-collins-review>.

Greenberg, Gary. *The Book of Woe: The DSM and the Unmaking of Psychiatry*. New York: Blue Rider Press, 2013.

Greenberg, Jonathan. *Modernism, Satire and the Novel*. Cambridge: Cambridge University Press, 2011.

Greenwald Smith, Rachel. *Affect and American Literature in the Age of Neoliberalism*. Cambridge: Cambridge University Press, 2015.

Greif, Mark. *The Age of the Crisis of Man: Thought and Fiction in America, 1933–1973*. Princeton: Princeton University Press, 2015.

Gribble, James. 'The Reality of Fictional Emotions', *The Journal of Aesthetic Education* 16, no. 4 (Winter 1982): 53–8.

Hayes, Patrick. *Philip Roth: Fiction and Power*. New York: Oxford University Press, 2014.

Healy, David. *The Creation of Psychopharmacology*. Cambridge, MA: Harvard University Press, 2004.

Heidegger, Martin. *Being and Time*, translated by John Macquarrie and Edward Robinson. New York: Harper Perennial, [1927] 2008.

Heidegger, Martin. *Contributions to Philosophy (Of the Event)*, translated by Richard Rojcewicz and Daniela Vallega-Neu. Bloomington: Indiana University Press, [1989] 2012.

Held, Virginia. *The Ethics of Care: Personal, Political, Global*. Oxford: Oxford University Press, 2006.

Hinderliter, Beth, and Steve Peraza, eds. *More Than Our Pain: Affect and Emotion in the Era of Black Lives Matter*. New York: State University of New York Press, 2021.

Hobson, Linda Whitney, and Walker Percy. 'The Study of Consciousness: An Interview with Walker Percy', *The Georgia Review* 35, no. 1 (Spring 1981): 50–60.

Hochschild, Arlie Russell. *The Commercialization of Intimate Life: Notes from Home and Work*. Berkeley: University of California Press, 2003.

Hochschild, Arlie Russell. *The Managed Heart: The Commercialization of Human Feeling*. Berkeley: University of California Press, [1983] 2003.

Hochschild, Arlie Russell. *The Outsourced Self: Intimate Life in Market Times*. New York: Metropolitan Press, 2012.

Hogan, Patrick Colm. *What Literature Teaches Us about Emotion*. Cambridge: Cambridge University Press, 2014.

Horwitz, Allan V., and Jerome C. Wakefield. *All We Have to Fear: Psychiatry's Transformation of Natural Anxieties into Mental Disorders*. Oxford: Oxford University Press, 2012.

Howard, June. 'What Is Sentimentality?', *American Literary History* 11, no. 1 (1999): 63–81.

Huxley, Aldous. *The Doors of Perception and Heaven and Hell*. New York: Harper Perennial, 1956.

Illouz, Eva, Daniel Gilon and Mattan Shachak. 'Emotions and Cultural Theory', in *The Handbook of the Sociology of Emotions*, vol. 2, edited by Jan E. Stets and Jonathan H. Turner. Dordrecht: Springer, 2014: 221–44.

Jacobs, Beth. *Writing for Emotional Balance*. Oakland, CA: New Harbinger Publications, 2005.

James, William. *Writings 1902–1910*. New York: Library of America, 1987.

Jarcho, Saul. 'Galen's Six Non-Naturals', *Bulletin of the History of Medicine* 44 (1970): 372–7.

Jefferson, Thomas. *Notes on the State of Virginia*, edited by Frank Shuffelton. New York: Penguin Books, [1785] 1999.

Johannessen, Lene M. *Horizons of Enchantment: Essays in the American Imaginary*. Hanover, NH: Dartmouth College Press, 2011.

Johnson, Dan R. 'Transportation into a story increases empathy, prosocial behavior, and perceptual bias toward fearful expressions', *Personality and Individual Differences* 52 (2012): 150–5.

Jung, Carl Gustav. *The Spirit in Man, Art and Literature*. London: Routledge, 2003.

Jung, Carl Gustav. *Two Essays on Analytical Psychology*, translated by R. F. C. Hull. London: Routledge, [1953] 1966.

Kalsched, Donald E., and Daniela F. Sieff. 'Uncovering the Secrets of the Traumatised Psyche', in *Understanding and Healing Emotional Trauma: Conversations with Pioneering Clinicians and Researchers*. London: Routledge, 2015: 11–25.

Kang, Minsoo. *Sublime Dreams of Living Machines: The Automaton in the European Imagination*. Cambridge, MA: Harvard University Press, 2011.

Katwan, Ron. 'The Affect in the Work of Jean-François Lyotard', *Surfaces* 3 (1993), <https://doi.org/10.7202/1065103ar>.

Kay, Francesca. 'A literary cure for loneliness: Put your iPad down, ditch the phone and pick up a book. It could boost your circle of sympathy', *The Guardian* (17 January 2016), accessed 16 December 2021: <https://www.theguardian.com/lifeandstyle/2016/jan/17/a-literary-cure-for-loneliness-pick-up-a-book>.

Kearns, Katherine. *Nineteenth-Century Literary Realism: Through the Looking Glass*. Cambridge: Cambridge University Press, 1996.

Keats, John. *Complete Poems and Selected Letters of John Keats*. London: Modern Library, 2001.

Keller, Mark. 'Alcoholism: Nature and Extent of the Problem', *The Annals of the American Academy of Political and Social Science* 315 (1958): 1–11.

Kelleter, Frank. 'Portrait of the Sexist as a Dying Man: Death, Ideology, and the Erotic in Philip Roth's *Sabbath's Theater*', *Contemporary Literature* 39, no. 2 (1998): 262–302.

Khoury, Bassam, Ellen J. Langer and Francesco Pagnini. 'The DSM: Mindful Science or Mindless Power? A Critical Review', *Frontiers in Psychology* 5 (2014), <http://doi.org/10.3389/fpsyg.2014.00602>.

Kierkegaard, Søren. *Concluding Unscientific Postscript*. Princeton: Princeton University Press, 1974.

Kittay, Eva Feder, and Ellen K. Feder, eds. *The Subject of Care: Feminist Perspectives on Dependency*. Oxford: Rowman & Littlefield, 2002.

Kobre, Michael. *Walker Percy's Voices*. Athens: University of Georgia Press, 2000.

Kremer, Lillian S. 'Philip Roth's Self-Reflexive Fiction', *Modern Language Studies* 28, nos. 3/4 (1998): 57–72.

Latour, Bruno. *Politics of Nature: How to Bring the Sciences into Democracy*, translated by Catherine Porter. Cambridge, MA: Harvard University Press, 2004.

Latour, Bruno. *We Have Never Been Modern*, translated by Catherine Porter. Cambridge, MA: Harvard University Press, 1993.

Leary, Timothy. *The Politics of Ecstasy*. Berkeley, CA: Ronin Publishing, [1980] 1998.

Leary, Timothy. *The Psychedelic Experience*. New York: Citadel Press, [1964] 1995.

Leavis, F. R. *New Bearings in English Poetry*. London: Faber & Faber, 2008.

Levine, George. *The Realistic Imagination*. Chicago: University of Chicago Press, 1981.

Levy-Hussen, Aida. *How to Read African American Literature: Post-Civil Rights Fiction and the Task of Interpretation*. New York: New York University Press, 2016.

Leys, Ruth. 'The Turn to Affect: A Critique', *Critical Inquiry* 37, no. 3 (Spring 2011): 434–72.

Lucretius. *De rerum natura*, edited and translated by Cyril Bailey. Oxford: Clarendon Press, 1963.

Lutz, Tom. *American Nervousness, 1903: An Anecdotal History*. Ithaca, NY: Cornell University Press, 1991.

Lyotard, Jean-François. *Des dispositifs pulsionnels*. Paris: Galilée, 1994.

Lyotard, Jean-François. *Le Différend*. Paris: Éditions de Minuit, 1983.

Lyotard, Jean-François. *Discours, figure*. Paris: Klincksieck, 1971.

McCarthy, Joseph R. 'Address to the Republican Women's Club of Wheeling, West Virginia, "Enemies from Within" (February 9, 1950)', in *Essential Documents of American History, Volume II: From Reconstruction to the Twenty-first Century*, edited by Bob Blaisdell. New York: Dover, 2016: 232–40.

McConnell, Frank D. *Four Post-War American Novelists: Bellow, Mailer, Barth, and Pynchon*. Chicago: University of Chicago Press, 1977.

Mano, D. Keith. 'Doughy Middleness', in *Critical Essays on John Updike*, edited by William R. Macnaughton. Boston: G. K. Hall, 1982: 74–6.

Marinetti, F. T. 'War, the Only Hygiene of the World', in *Futurism: An Anthology*, edited by Lawrence Rainey, Christine Poggi and Laura Wittman. New Haven: Yale University Press, 2009: 84–5.

Martina, Roy. *Emotional Balance: The Path to Inner Peace and Healing*. London: Hay House, 2010.

Massumi, Brian. 'The Autonomy of Affect', *Cultural Critique* 31, 'The Politics of Systems and Environments' (Autumn 1995): 83–109.

Massumi, Brian. *Parables for the Virtual*. Durham, NC: Duke University Press, 2002.

May, Charles E. '"Do You See What I'm Saying?": The Inadequacy of Explanation and the Uses of Story in the Short Fiction of Raymond Carver', *The Yearbook of English Studies* 31 (2001): 39–49.

Melville, Herman. *Moby Dick*, 3rd edn, edited by Hershel Parker. New York: W. W. Norton, [1851] 2018.

Menand, Louis. *Discovering Modernism: T. S. Eliot and his Context*. Oxford: Oxford University Press, 1987.

Merleau-Ponty, Maurice. *Phenomenology of Perception*, translated by Colin Smith. London: Routledge, 1965.

Metzl, Jonathan M., and Anna Kirkland, eds. *Against Health: How Health Became the New Morality*. New York: New York University Press, 2010.

Montebello, Pierre. *Métaphysiques cosmomorphes. La fin du monde humain*. Dijon: Les Presses du Réel, 2015.

Montebello, Pierre. *Nature et subjectivité*. Grenoble: Millon, 2007.

Mooney, Edward F. *Lost Intimacy in American Thought: Recovering Personal Philosophy from Thoreau to Cavell*. New York: Continuum, 2009.

Morton, Timothy. *Ecology without Nature: Rethinking Environmental Aesthetics*. Cambridge, MA: Harvard University Press, 2007.

Moskowitz, Eva S. *In Therapy We Trust: America's Obsession with Self-Fulfillment*. Baltimore: Johns Hopkins University Press, 2001.

Musil, Robert. *The Man without Qualities*, translated by Sophie Wilkins and Burton Pike. New York: Alfred A. Knopf, [1930–32] 1995.

Naddaf, Gerard. *The Greek Concept of Nature*. New York: State University of New York Press, 2005.

Ngai, Sianne. *Ugly Feelings*. Cambridge, MA: Harvard University Press, 2005.

Nietzsche, Friedrich. *Beyond Good and Evil*, edited and translated by Marion Faber. Oxford: Oxford University Press, 2008.

Oakes, Guy. *The Imaginary War: Civil Defense and American Cold War Culture*. Oxford: Oxford University Press, 1994.

Oatley, Keith. 'Meetings of Minds: Dialogue, Sympathy, and Identification, in Reading Fiction', *Poetics* 26 (1999): 439-54.

Olsen, Stein Haugom. 'The Discipline of Literary Studies', in *Literary Studies and the Philosophy of Literature*, edited by Andrea Selleri and Philip Gaydon. London: Palgrave Macmillan, 2010: 37-64.

Palmer, Tyrone S. '"What Feels More Than Feeling?": Theorizing the Unthinkability of Black Affect', *Critical Ethnic Studies* 3, no. 2 (2017): 31-56.

Paredes, Alfonso. 'The History of the Concept of Alcoholism', in *Alcoholism*, edited by R. Tarter and A. Sugerman. Reading, MA: Addison-Wesley, 1976: 9-52.

Penguin Random House, 'Teacher's Guide: *Invisible Man*', accessed 6 May 2022: <https://www.penguinrandomhouseaudio.com/teachers-guide/46131/invisible-man>.

Percy, Walker. *The Moviegoer*. London: Vintage, [1961] 1998.

Pfifer, Ellen. 'If the Shoe Fits: Bellow and Recent Critics', *Texas Studies in Literature and Language* 29, no. 4, 'Twentieth-Century Fiction' (Winter 1987): 442-57.

Pickersgill, Martyn D. 'Debating DSM-5: Diagnosis and the Sociology of Critique', *Journal of Medical Ethics* 40 (2014): 521-5.

Pitts, Jesse R. 'Social Control: The Concept', in *International Encyclopedia of Social Sciences*, vol. 14, edited by David Sills. New York: Macmillan, 1968: 381-96.

Plato. *Ion*, in *Early Socratic Dialogues*, translated by Trevor J. Saunders. London: Penguin, 1987: 39-68.

Plato. *Republic*, translated by Robin Waterfield. Oxford: Oxford University Press, 2008.

Plato. *Symposium*, translated by Robin Waterfield. Oxford: Oxford University Press, 1994.

Pliny the Elder. *The Natural History of Pliny*, vol. 3, translated by John Bostock and H. T. Riley. London: H. G. Bohn, 1855.

Pound, Ezra. 'A Retrospect', in *Literary Essays of Ezra Pound*, edited with an introduction by T. S. Eliot. New York: New Directions, [1935] 1968: 3-14.

Provine, Doris Marie. *Unequal under Law: Race in the War on Drugs*. Chicago: University of Chicago Press, 2007.

Rasberry, Vaughn. *Race and the Totalitarian Century: Geopolitics in the Black Literary Imagination*. Cambridge, MA: Harvard University Press, 2016.

Rather, L. J. 'The "Six Things Non-Natural"', *Clio Medica* 3 (1968): 337-47.

Riley, Kathryn. 'John Cheever and the Limitations of Fantasy', *CEA Critic* 45, nos. 3/4 (1983): 21-6.

Rimbaud, Arthur. *Œuvres complètes*. Paris: Gallimard, Bibliothèque de la Pléiade, 2009.

Robinson, Jenefer. *Deeper Than Reason: Emotion and its Role in Literature, Music, and Art*. Oxford: Clarendon Press, 2005.

Rorty, Amélie O. *Explaining Emotions*. Berkeley: University of California Press, 1980.

Rosset, Clément. *L'anti-nature. Éléments pour une philosophie tragique*. Paris: Presses Universitaires de France, [1973] 1986.

Roth, Marty. *Drunk the Night Before: An Anatomy of Intoxication*. Minneapolis: University of Minnesota Press, 2008.

Roth, Philip. *American Pastoral*. New York: Vintage, 1997.

Roth, Philip. *Sabbath's Theater*. London: Vintage, [1995] 1996.
Roudané, Matthew C. 'An Interview with Saul Bellow', *Contemporary Literature* 25 (1974): 265–80.
Salmela, Mikko. 'True Emotions', *The Philosophical Quarterly* 56, no. 224 (July 2006): 382–405.
Sander, David, and Klaus Scherer, eds. *Oxford Companion to Emotion and the Affective Sciences*. Oxford: Oxford University Press, 2009.
Scarry, Elaine. *The Body in Pain: The Making and Unmaking of the World*. Oxford: Oxford University Press, 1985.
Schehr, Lawrence R. *Figures of Alterity: French Realism and its Others*. Stanford: Stanford University Press, 2003.
Schneider, Joseph W. 'Deviant Drinking as Disease: Alcoholism as a Social Accomplishment', *Social Problems* 25, no. 4 (April 1978): 361–72.
Schuster, David G. *Neurasthenic Nation: America's Search for Health, Happiness, and Comfort, 1869–1920*. New Brunswick, NJ: Rutgers University Press, 2011.
Sedgwick, Eve Kosofsky. *Touching Feeling: Affect, Pedagogy, Performativity*. Durham, NC: Duke University Press, 2003.
Sedgwick, Eve Kosofsky, and Adam Frank, eds. *Shame and its Sisters: A Silvan Tomkins Reader*. Durham, NC: Duke University Press, 1995.
Sedgwick, Eve Kosofsky, and Adam Frank. 'Shame in the Cybernetic Fold: Reading Silvan Tomkins', *Critical Inquiry* 21, no. 2 (1995): 496–522.
Seligman, Martin. *Authentic Happiness: Using the New Positive Psychology to Realize your Potential for Lasting Fulfillment*. New York: Free Press, 2002.
Sharpe, Christina. *In the Wake: On Blackness and Being*. Durham, NC: Duke University Press, 2016.
Sherwood, Robert. *The Petrified Forest*. New York: Dramatists Play Service, 1948.
Shklovsky, Viktor. 'Art as Device (1917/1919)', in *Viktor Shklovsky: A Reader*, edited and translated by Alexandra Berlina. London: Bloomsbury, 2017: 73–96.
Shouse, Eric. 'Feeling, Emotion, Affect', *M/C Journal* 8 (December 2005), accessed 2 February 2021: <www.journal.media-culture.org.au/0512/03-shouse.php>.
Sim, Lorraine, and Ann Vickery. 'New Feelings: Modernism, Intimacy, and Emotion', *Affirmations: Of the Modern* 1, no. 2 (Spring 2014): 1–14.
Singal, Daniel J. *William Faulkner: The Making of a Modernist*. Chapel Hill: University of North Carolina Press, 1997.
Small, Deborah. 'The War on Drugs Is a War on Racial Justice', *Social Research* 68, no. 3 (2001): 896–903.
Smith, Brian A. *Walker Percy and the Politics of the Wayfarer*. London: Lexington, 2017.
Solomon, Robert Charles. *True to our Feelings: What our Emotions Are Really Telling Us*. Oxford: Oxford University Press, 2007.
Starr, Paul. *The Social Transformation of American Medicine: The Rise of a Sovereign Profession and the Making of a Vast Industry*. New York: Basic Books, 1982.
Stevens, Hugh. 'D. H. Lawrence: Organicism and the Modernist Novel', in *The Cambridge Companion to the Modernist Novel*, edited by Morag Shiach. Cambridge: Cambridge University Press, 2007: 137–51.
Stockwell, Peter. *Cognitive Poetics: An Introduction*. London: Routledge, 2002.

Tallis, Raymond. *In Defence of Realism*. Lincoln: University of Nebraska Press, [1958] 1998.

Tanner, Tony. 'The Sorrow of Some Central Hollowness', in *Critical Essays on John Updike*, edited by William R. Macnaughton. Boston: G. K. Hall, 1982: 71–4.

Taylor, Charles. *Sources of the Self: The Making of the Modern Identity*. Cambridge: Cambridge University Press, [1989] 2012.

Taylor, Julie. *Djuna Barnes and Affective Modernism*. Edinburgh: Edinburgh University Press, 2012.

Thoreau, Henry David. *Walden*, edited by Stephen Fender. London: Oxford World's Classics, [1854] 2009.

Thrailkill, Jane F. *Affecting Fictions: Mind, Body, and Emotion in American Literary Realism*. Cambridge, MA: Harvard University Press, 2007.

Tiefer, Leonore. 'The Medicalization of Impotence: Normalizing Phallocentrism', *Gender and Society* 8 (1994): 363–77.

Tobbel, Dominique A. '"Who's Winning the Human Race?": Cold War as Pharmaceutical Political Strategy', *Journal of the History of Medicine and Allied Sciences* 64, no. 4 (2009): 429–73.

Tolstoy, Leo. *What Is Art?* London: Bloomsbury, [1897] 2014.

Tompkins, Jane P. 'Criticism and Feeling', *College English* 39, no. 2 (1977): 169–78.

Tracy, Sarah J., and Angela Trethewey. 'Fracturing the Real-Self ↔ Fake-Self Dichotomy: Moving Toward "Crystallized" Organizational Discourses and Identities', *Communication Theory* 15, no. 2 (May 2005): 168–95.

Trilling, Lionel. *Sincerity and Authenticity*. Cambridge, MA: Harvard University Press, 1971.

Tsur, Reuven. *Toward a Theory of Cognitive Poetics*. Brighton: Sussex Academic Press, 2008.

Updike, John. *Rabbit Angstrom: A Tetralogy*, including *Rabbit, Run* (1960), *Rabbit Redux* (1971), *Rabbit Is Rich* (1981), *Rabbit at Rest* (1990). New York: Alfred A. Knopf, 1995.

Vicedo, Marga. 'Cold War Emotions: Mother Love and the War over Human Nature', in *Cold War Social Science: Knowledge Production, Liberal Democracy, and Human Nature*, edited by Mark Solovey and Hamilton Cravens. New York: Palgrave Macmillan, 2012: 233–51.

Vidal, Gore. *Rocking the Boat*. Boston: Little, Brown and Company, [1951] 1962.

Vogel, Steven. *Against Nature: The Concept of Nature in Critical Theory*. New York: State University of New York Press, 1996.

Watkins, Elizabeth Siegel. 'Medicalization of Stress in the Twentieth Century', *Medicine Studies* 4, nos. 1/4 (May 2014): 29–36.

Watt, Ian. *The Rise of the Novel: Studies in Defoe, Richardson and Fielding*. Berkeley: University of California Press, [1957] 2001.

Wehrs, Donald R., and Thomas Blake, eds. *The Palgrave Handbook of Affect Studies and Textual Criticism*. London: Palgrave Macmillan, 2017.

Whiteman, Honor. 'Five ways reading can improve health and well-being', *Medical News Today* (12 October 2016), accessed 12 July 2021: <https://www.medicalnewstoday.com/articles/313429.php>.

Wilhite, Keith. 'WASP Culture', in *American Literature in Transition, 1950–1960*, edited by Steven Belletto. Cambridge: Cambridge University Press, 2018: 103–16.

Williams, Raymond. *Politics of Modernism: Against the New Conformists*. London: Verso, 2007.

Wilson, Andrew. *Beautiful Shadow: A Life of Patricia Highsmith*. London: Bloomsbury, 2010.

Winnicott, D. W. *The Collected Works of D. W. Winnicott, Volume 6: 1960–1963*, edited by Lesley Caldwell and Helen Taylor Robinson. Oxford: Oxford University Press, 2017.

Winnicott, D. W. 'Ego Distortion in Terms of True and False Self', in *The Maturational Processes and the Facilitating Environment*. Madison: International Universities Press, 1987: 140–52.

Wolfe, Tom. *The Electric Kool-Aid Acid Test*. New York: Picador, [1968] 2008.

Woolf, Virginia. *The Essays of Virginia Woolf, Volume 4: 1925–1928*, edited by Andrew McNeillie. London: Hogarth Press, [1921] 1984.

Wordsworth, William, and Samuel Taylor Coleridge. *Lyrical Ballads: 1798 and 1802*. Oxford: Oxford University Press, 2013.

Wright, Richard. *The Man Who Lived Underground*. New York: Library of America, [1941] 2021.

Wyatt-Brown, Bertram. *The House of Percy: Honor, Melancholy, and Imagination in a Southern Family*. Oxford: Oxford University Press, 1994.

Yates, Richard. *Disturbing the Peace*. London: Vintage, [1975] 2008.

Yates, Richard. *Revolutionary Road*. London: Vintage, [1961] 2007.

Yates, Richard. *Young Hearts Crying*. London: Vintage, [1984] 2008.

Zola, Émile. *Le Roman naturaliste*, edited by Henri Mitterand. Paris: Le Livre de Poche, [1880] 1999.

# INDEX

Page numbers in *italics* indicate figures, and those with the suffix 'n' indicate notes (246n63). Fictional characters are indicated with * and filed by surname if they have one, or by given name if not.

Adorno, Theodor, 6, 47, 53
*The Adventures of Augie March*
    (Bellow), 9, 68, 73–7
affect
    conceptualisation, 14–18
    representation of, 49–53, 56, 79–80
    *see also* Black affect; original affect
affective absence
    Fox, 171, 172, 179–80, 184
    further mentions, 51, 186
affective artifice *see* artifice of affect, conceptualisation; false feeling
affective authenticity *see* emotional truth
affective intensity
    Bellow, 67, 74
    Cheever, 103, 107
    Ellison, 10
    Ford, 150
    Fox, 176, 177–8, 181, 183
    Percy, 60–1, 65
    Roth, 92, 95, 96, 99–100
    Updike, 203
    Yates, 160, 162, 166–71
    further mentions, 15, 37, 54, 159, 192, 195
    *see also* emotional excess
African American protagonists *see* Black affect
Alcmaeon, 156
alcohol
    Carver, 206–8, 209–16
    Updike, 195–200, 201–3, 205
    further mentions, 190–5, 217
alienation, 51, 53–4, 70, 134, 137, 142
Allen, Brooke, 68
alterity (otherness)
    introduction, 4, 8, 17
    Bellow, 73
    Collins, 131
    Fox, 177, 181–2
    Percy, 58
    further mentions, 45, 48–50, 90, 189, 217, 225–6
*American Pastoral* (Roth), 40, 148
American realism, 34, 40–2
anger
    Baldwin, 134, 136, 137–42
    Ellison, 9, 10, 11–12, 13

Fox, 178
Yates, 161, 164, 168–9
Angstrom, Becky*, 196, 203
Angstrom, Harry 'Rabbit'*, 195–7, 204, 222
Angstrom, Janice*, 196–203
Angstrom, Nelson*, 196, 199, 200, 202, 203
anti-naturalism, 15, 87–90, 91, 114, 204
anti-sentimentalism, 32–4, 38, 42, 133–4, 231
apathy, 36, 63, 107, 148, 173, 178–80
Arendt, Hannah, 228–9
Aristotle, 81–2, 115, 145, 155–6, 235
art, 65, 81, 84, 99, 222; *see also* literature
artifice, conceptualisation, 1–2, 20, 68, 75
artifice of affect, conceptualisation, 2, 5, 17–18
artificialising *see* anti-naturalism
athletes, 40, 66, 129, 148–9
Auerbach, Erich, 120, 142
authenticity, 20, 69–70, 157; *see also* emotional truth; true self

balance *see* equilibrium; stability
Baldwin, James
  *Giovanni's Room*, 128
  'Previous Condition,' 134–42
  further mentions, 116, 133
Balzac, Honoré de, 52, 74, 120
banality
  Baldwin, 139–40
  Carver, 213
  Collins, 130
  Percy, 56–7, 60–2, 65–6
  further mentions, 186, 191, 219
Barthes, Roland, 47, 116
Bascombe, Frank*, 143–53
Baudrillard, Jean, 7
Baum, Dan, 190
Bell, Michael, 33
Bellow, Saul
  *The Adventures of Augie March*, 9, 68, 73–7

*Dangling Man*, 66–7
*The Dean's December*, 69, 77–8
*Herzog*, 69–73
further mentions, 68, 195, 232
Berlant, Lauren, 5, 6
Bernard, Claude, 158
Bethea, Arthur F., 209
*Bildungsroman*, 10, 128
binaries *see* dualism
biological equilibrium (homeostasis), 85–7, 154, 158–9
Black affect
  Baldwin, 134–42
  Collins, 128–33
  Ellison, 9–13, 40, 131
  further mentions, 40, 116
bodies/the body
  Baldwin, 136
  Bellow, 71
  Cheever, 103, 107, 110
  Ellison, 11
  Faulkner, 226
  Ford, 151
  Fox, 175, 178
  mimesis, 117, 118, 119, 120, 121
  Yates, 122–3, 169, 170
  further mentions, 14–15, 81–91, 113–14, 234, 237
  *see also* humourism; smiles/smiling; tears/crying
Bolling, Jack 'Binx'*, 56–66
Boxall, Peter, 54–5, 234
Brent, Jonathan, 246n63
Brooks, Cleanth, 231

Campbell, Shep*, 122, 123–6
Canguilhem, Georges, 89, 187, 188
Cannon, Walter Bradford, 158
capitalism
  Updike, 202, 204–5
  further mentions, 21–2, 36, 74, 158, 195, 220–1
  *see also* pharmaceutical industry
Capote, Truman, 194
Cartesian dualism, 14, 71, 89, 121

Carver, Raymond
  'Gazebo,' 206
  'What We Talk About When We Talk About Love,' 206–17
Cary, Joyce, 33
Cheever, John
  'The Geometry of Love,' 102–11, 112–13
  interview in *The Paris Review*, 111
  *The Journals of John Cheever*, 110–11
  'The Swimmer,' 126–8
  *The Wapshot Chronicle*, 111
  further mentions, 82, 116
Chernecky, William, 152
Chesterton, G. K., 235
civil rights movement, 13, 34, 36, 134
Clapper, Clara*, 171, 176, 179–80, 182–3
Clapper, Desmond*, 174
Clapper, Laura Maldonada*, 171–80, 182, 183, 184, 222
class, 38, 63, 65, 67, 122, 134
Clement, James, 67
cocaine, 203–4
cognitive poetics, 83–4
cognitive processes, 3, 83–7, 90, 223–4
coherency, 3, 22–3, 45, 103, 110, 211; *see also* formal coherency; harmony; unified self; unity
Cold War, 27, 34–6, 158, 226, 228, 234
Collins, Kathleen
  'The Uncle,' 128–32, 133
  'Whatever Happened to Interracial Love?' 132
  further mentions, 116
colonialism, 132
Communism, 35–6
conformity
  Bellow, 66
  Ellison, 10, 11, 12
  Fox, 176
  Percy, 61, 63
  smile experiments, 31–2
  Yates, 122, 160
  further mentions, 8, 23, 26, 41, 53–4, 157

consciousness
  affect's relation to, 49–50, 51
  Baldwin, 136
  biological equilibrium, 86
  Carver, 208, 209
  Ford, 144
  meta-consciousness, 87, 90–1
  pre-consciousness, 14–18
  psychotropes, 186, 188, 189
  Roth, 92, 94, 102
  self-consciousness, 54, 92, 131, 198
  unconsciousness, 16, 48–9, 53, 208
  Updike, 198
contamination, 123, 145, 177, 187, 188
corporality *see* bodies/the body
corporality-textuality binary, 82–4, 91
countercultures, 34, 36, 186–7, 190, 193
crying *see* tears/crying
Cutrer, Emily (Aunt Emily)*, 63–5, 227

*Dangling Man* (Bellow), 66–7
Davenport, Lucy*, 165–6
Davenport, Michael*, 162–3
David* (*Giovanni's Room*), 128
De Sousa, Ronald, 18–19
*The Dean's December* (Bellow), 69, 77–8
death
  Carver, 210, 216
  Collins, 128, 130–3
  Ford, 143
  Fox, 171–5, 179, 180
  Percy, 58
  Updike, 203
  Yates, 123
  further mentions, 7
Derrida, Jacques, 55, 116, 143
Descartes, René *see* Cartesian dualism
determinism
  Ford, 150
  Roth, 93
  Yates, 122, 165
  further mentions, 31, 82, 83, 86, 88, 226, 237

Diderot, Denis, 97, 98
disruption
  Baldwin, 140
  Carver, 210
  Cheever, 105
  corporality, 84, 85–6, 187, 189, 190, 217
  Ford, 145
  Fox, 180
  literature as disruption, 221, 222–3
  Percy, 56, 60, 65
  Updike, 199, 201, 203
  Yates, 160, 168–70
  further mentions, 17, 24, 52, 53, 54–5, 80, 229
dissimulation and simulation
  Baldwin, 135
  Bellow, 69
  Carver, 216
  Cheever, 127
  Ford, 143
  Fox, 181, 183
  Updike, 199, 200, 202
  further mentions, 7, 25–7, 159
*Disturbing the Peace* (Yates), 160–2
domestic sphere
  Carver, 207, 208
  Updike, 196–203
  Yates, 122, 124, 166–7, 169–70
  further mentions, 30, 34, 155, 163
domestic violence, 164–5, 177, 194, 197, 202–3, 208–9
double-consciousness, 131
doubling, 117–19, 199
Dror, Otniel E., 85
Du Bois, W. E. B., 131
dualism
  introduction, 3, 5, 14–18
  Baldwin, 136
  Bellow, 68–9, 71, 75
  Carver, 207, 209, 214, 216
  Cheever, 104, 113
  Ellison, 11, 40
  Fox, 173
  Percy, 65

Roth, 97–9, 101
  Updike, 200, 203, 205
  further mentions, 25–30, 236–7
Duchenne (de Boulogne), Guillaume-Benjamin, 27–9, *28*, *29*
Dutoit, Thomas, 118

ecstasy, 12, 26, 68, 144, 168, 186
egotism, 7, 148, 171, 173
Eliot, George, 37
Eliot, T. S., 32, 70, 230
Ellison, Ralph, *Invisible Man*, 9–13, 40, 128, 131
emotion, conceptualisation, 14–16, 81–2
emotion of truth, 73–4, 77–8
emotional control
  Cheever, 110
  Ford, 148–9
  Fox, 182–3
  Roth, 97–9, 100
  Yates, 161, 164, 165
  further mentions, 35, 154–5, 156, 158–9, 226, 233
emotional equilibrium
  Fox, 175–6, 180
  and oppression/repression, 154–5, 157, 185
  Updike, 201
  Yates, 161–2, 164–6, 168, 170
emotional excess
  Baldwin, 134, 137–8, 141
  Collins, 128–30, 131–2, 133
  Fox, 171, 172, 174–9, 180–4
  Roth, 96, 98
  Updike, 203
  Yates, 164–70
  further mentions, 5, 154, 156, 159, 185
  *see also* affective intensity
emotional truth
  introduction, 1–9, 18–20, 32–40
  as criterion of value, 3, 20–5, 33, 41–2, 230, 236–7
  Ellison, 9–13
  Faulker, 225–7

emotional truth (*cont.*)
  utilitarian approaches to literature, 8, 218–24
empathy
  Baldwin, 138
  Bellow, 70–1
  Cheever, 107–8
  Fox, 171, 180, 181
  Updike, 199
  further mentions, 53–4, 219–22, 224, 226, 229, 233
Enlightenment, 34, 86, 112, 121
enslavement, 11, 13, 132, 183, 199
epiphany
  Bellow, 71, 77–8
  Cheever, 104, 127
  Ellison, 9–13
  Ford, 147
  Fox, 184
  Percy, 56
  Roth, 100
  Updike, 200
  Yates, 170
  further mentions, 191, 219, 221
equilibrium
  biological, 85–7, 158
  geometrical, 105
  *see also* emotional equilibrium
essentialism
  introduction, 3, 6, 20, 21, 23, 26
  Bellow, 73
  Carver, 207, 208–9, 212, 215
  Cheever, 108, 110, 112
  Duchenne smiles, 30–1
  Faulkner, 226, 227
  Ford, 151–2
  Fox, 176–7, 184
  nature, 87, 88
  Roth, 95
  Updike, 201
  Yates, 125–6
  further mentions, 41, 51, 188, 218, 236–7
Euclid, 107, 108
events
  Baldwin, 141
  Cheever, 105, 107, 111
  Ford, 147
  Fox, 173, 174
  Percy, 59, 62, 65
  further mentions, 6, 54, 81
everydayness *see* banality

facts, 62–3, 73, 107, 108, 127, 172
false feeling
  Baldwin, 134
  Bellow, 68–9, 73
  conceptualisation, 4–5
  further mentions, 11, 23, 42, 70, 226, 231
  *see also* artifice of affect, conceptualisation
false self, 25–7, 31, 40, 102
Faulkner, William, 225–7
feeling, conceptualisation, 16
femininity
  Cheever, 103
  and emotional truth, 32
  Roth, 96, 100
  Updike, 199, 200
  Yates, 161, 164–8
feminist theory, 21, 33, 38–9
fictionality, 113–14, 118, 124, 153, 236, 237
Fitzgerald, F. Scott
  alcohol, depictions of, 192, 194
  Ford, comparison with, 144
  *The Great Gatsby*, 9, 194
  *On Writing*, 225
Flaubert, Gustave
  letters, 48, 49
  *Madame Bovary*, 49, 99–100, 164
  modern realism, 120
Ford, Richard
  introduction, 116
  *Independence Day*, 143
  *The Sportswriter*, 143–53
formal coherency, 41, 50, 52, 60, 79
Formalism, 15, 47, 84, 230, 231
Foucault, Michel, 6, 116, 187
Fox, Paula, *The Widow's Children*, 171–84, 222

Freud, Sigmund, 25, 27, 162, 240n47
Furst, Lilian, 48

Galen, 150, 156
'Gazebo' (Carver), 206
gender *see* femininity; masculinity
'The Geometry of Love' (Cheever), 102-11, 112-13
ghosts, 59-60, 93
*Giovanni's Room* (Baldwin), 128
Givings, Helen*, 169
Givings, John*, 168-9
Glenday, Michael K., 68, 232
God, 3, 35-6, 48, 58, 88, 107, 209
Gogol, Nikolai, *Dead Souls*, 201
Gombrowicz, Witold, 235-6
*The Great Gatsby* (Fitzgerald), 9, 194
Greenberg, Jonathan, 32
Greenwald Smith, Rachel, 5, 221
Greif, Mark, 75
grief
   Collins, 128, 130, 132, 133
   Ford, 143
   Fox, 171-2, 179, 181
   Roth, 92-3, 94, 95
   Yates, 124, 125, 126
   further mentions, 22-3, 26-7

harmony
   Baldwin, 140
   Carver, 213
   Roth, 97
   and unity, 3, 5, 52, 213
   further mentions, 155, 157, 221, 229
   *see also* coherency; unified self; unity
Hayes, Patrick, 99
Hemingway, Ernest, 144, 192, 194
Hendricks, Pamela*, 160-1
*Herzog* (Bellow), 69-73
Herzog, Moses S.*, 67, 70-3
heteronormativity, 34-5, 38-40
Highsmith, Patricia, 191-2
Hinderliter, Beth, 133
Hippocrates, 150, 156
Hochschild, Arlie, 21
Hogan, Patrick Colm, 223

homeostasis (biological equilibrium), 85-7, 154, 158-9
homosexuality, 38-9, 180-2
Howard, June, 231
humourism, 150, 156
hysteria, 96, 100, 103, 161, 164-8

identity
   Baldwin, 134
   Bellow, 68, 76
   Collins, 128
   Ellison, 10, 12, 13
   Fox, 171, 172, 175
   further mentions, 4, 25-6, 36, 38-40, 116, 155, 185
*Iliad*, 81
*imitants* (imitator/copy), 117, 149
*imité* (imitated/original), 117
incoherence *see* coherency
*Independence Day* (Ford), 143
insanity, 168-9
intensity *see* affective intensity; emotional excess
*Invisible Man* (Ellison), 9-13, 40, 128, 131
irony
   Bellow, 69
   Cheever, 103, 105, 112
   Collins, 133
   Ellison, 9
   Ford, 145-6, 147, 153
   Fox, 181-2
   Percy, 64
   further mentions, 194, 230

Jack* (*Young Hearts Crying*), 165-6
James, William, 6
Jefferson, Thomas, 11, 13
Jewishness, 40, 134, 139, 141
Johannessen, Lene M., 148
Joseph* (*Dangling Man*), 67
Joyce, James, 147
Jung, Carl Gustav, 25

Kalsched, Donald E., 26-7
Kang, Minsoo, 97

Katwan, Ron, 52
Keats, John, 160
Kierkegaard, Søren, 58, 62
Kobre, Michael, 59

language
   affect's relation to, 50, 51–3, 56, 79–80
   Baldwin, 137–8, 142
   Bellow, 67
   Carver, 209, 213, 214, 215
   Ford, 150, 151, 152
   Percy, 59–60, 62–3
   Roth, 96
   further mentions, 14, 88, 90–1, 114, 195
Latour, Bruno, 88
laughter, 28, *28*, 29, 164, 177
Laura* ('What We Talk About When We Talk About Love'), 213
Lawrence, D. H., 33, 99
Leary, Timothy, 186
Leavis, F. R., 231
Levy-Hussen, Aida, 132
linguistics, 13, 15, 60, 83, 209
literary modernism
   Bellow, 70
   Faulkner, 226–7
   Ford, 143
   further mentions, 48, 53, 120, 224–5, 234
literary realism
   introduction, 47–55, 79–80, 119–20, 217, 233–4
   post-war American realism, 34, 40–2
literature
   utilitarian purpose of, 8, 218–24
   writing process, depictions of, 144–7, 149, 151, 166–7
   *see also* nineteenth-century realism; Romanticism
love
   introduction, 7–9
   Bellow, 71–2
   Carver, 207–17
   Cheever, 112

Ford, 150, 151–2
Yates, 123, 124
further mentions, 34, 35–6, 37, 186, 226–7, 228–9
Lyotard, Jean-François, 51, 52

McCarthy, Joseph, 35–6
McConnell, Frank D., 68
McGinnis, Mel*, 207, 208, 209–15, 216
*Madame Bovary* (Flaubert), 49, 99–100, 164
Maldonada, Carlos*, 171, 172, 180–2
Maldonada, Eugenio*, 171, 172, 177
Maldonada, Laura*, 171–80, 182, 183, 184, 222
Mallory, Charlie*, 102–11, 112–13
Mallory, Mathilda*, 103, 105, 107–8, 109–10
Mano, D. Keith, 258n35
Marinetti, F. T., 32
marionette (puppet) metaphor, 97–9, 202
market capitalism *see* capitalism
Marx, Karl, 35–6
masculinity
   Bellow, 67
   Cheever, 103
   Collins, 128–9
   and emotional truth, 32, 39
   Fox, 181
   Yates, 123, 161–2, 163, 164–5, 167–8
masks
   Baldwin, 134
   Carver, 216
   Cheever, 112, 128
   Ellison, 40
   Ford, 148
   Fox, 171, 176
   Roth, 102
   Yates, 123, 128
   further mentions, 7, 25, 30, 69, 82, 228
Massumi, Brian, 14–15, 50, 53
medical profession, 27–30, 186, 188, 192–5, 207; *see also* psychiatry

Merleau-Ponty, Maurice, 87-8, 90, 113
Merrill, Ned*, 126-7
meta-consciousness, 87, 90-1
meta-representation, 86-7
metaphysics
  Cheever, 104-5, 107, 111
  Ford, 143
  Percy, 60, 61, 63, 65
  Yates, 124
  further mentions, 88, 117, 218, 235
metatextuality, 41, 60, 74, 102, 142, 153
mimesis
  Aristotelian mimesis, 81-2, 115, 145
  Baldwin, 134, 142
  Ford, 143, 144, 146-50, 152
  original affect, absence of, 116-21, 153
  Platonism, 116-17, 121
  Yates, 122, 125
  further mentions, 41, 233-4
misogyny, 96, 103
modernism, 32-4; *see also* literary modernism
modernity, 3, 48, 161, 185, 219, 230; *see also* capitalism
Montebello, Pierre, 88
Mooney, Edward F., 22-3
Morton, Timothy, 88, 91
*The Moviegoer* (Percy), 56-66, 227

narcissism, 152, 173
narrators
  Baldwin, 128
  Bellow, 66
  Carver, 207, 214
  Collins, 128, 129-30, 131, 132
  Ellison, 9-13, 128, 131
  Ford, 144, 145-6, 148-9, 151
  Fox, 175, 180-1
  Roth, 94, 97
  Yates, 125, 126, 167
  further mentions, 41, 49, 50, 51, 52, 54-5
natural-artificial binary
  Roth, 92-102

further mentions, 21, 30, 81-91, 113-14, 236-7
*see also* psychotropes
naturalist framework
  Bellow, 69
  Cheever, 103, 104, 107, 113
  Naturalism, 41, 120
  Percy, 60
  further mentions, 82-3, 86-90, 114, 153
neoliberalism, 221
neuroscience, 30, 87, 220
New Criticism, 230-2
Ngai, Sianne, 5
Nick* ('What We Talk About When We Talk About Love'), 206-7, 208, 214, 215
Nietzsche, Friedrich, 87, 90
nihilism, 68, 70, 93, 101, 111-12, 144
nineteenth-century realism
  examples and elements of, 49, 52, 74, 120, 222, 233
  modernism defined in relation to, 33, 41, 53, 142
  Percy, 66
  Yates, 164
Nixon, Richard, 189-90
normality
  Collins, 133
  Fox, 175
  Percy, 60
  Updike, 196
  further mentions, 23, 36, 40, 84, 86, 185, 187-9
normativity/normalisation
  introduction, 5, 8, 23-5, 32
  Collins, 129-31
  Fox, 180
  heteronormativity, 34-5, 39, 40
  Percy, 61
  psychotropes, 163-4, 190-1
  Updike, 198, 199-200, 201
  WASPs (White Anglo-Saxon Protestants), 34-5, 38-40
  Yates, 160, 161, 165, 168-70

normativity/normalisation (*cont.*)
  further mentions, 80, 85–6, 91, 155–6
novel, as literary form, 33, 75, 235

Oakes, Guy, 35
objectivity, 32, 47, 49, 57–9, 62, 110–11
objects
  Bellow, 69, 78
  Cheever, 111
  Percy, 57–9, 62
  further mentions, 81–4, 89, 90, 115
omniscience, 41, 47, 50, 52, 55–6, 167
oppression
  introduction, 2, 5, 18, 39
  Arendt, 228
  Baldwin, 135, 138, 140
  Bellow, 67, 71–3, 76
  Ellison, 11
  Updike, 199, 203
  further mentions, 154–5, 185, 227, 233, 234
  *see also* normativity/normalisation; repression
ordinariness *see* banality
original affect
  absence of, 115–21, 125–6, 128, 130, 153
  access to, 135, 144, 149, 151
*ostranenie* (defamiliarisation), 56, 84
otherness *see* alterity (otherness)

parody, 103, 111, 132, 182, 199, 200, 206
Peraza, Steve, 133
Percy, Walker, *The Moviegoer*, 56–66, 227
performativity
  introduction, 4–5, 23
  Baldwin, 134–6, 141–2
  Bellow, 73, 75
  Carver, 214, 216
  Fox, 171, 172, 175–8, 180, 182, 184
  Roth, 93–102
  smiles/smiling, 7, 27–32, *28*, *29*, 61, 141, 172, 175

Updike, 199, 200–1, 202, 203
Yates, 123, 161, 165–6
further mentions, 55, 118, 233–4, 236–7
*see also* masks
Peter* ('Previous Condition'), 134–42
Pfifer, Ellen, 69
pharmaceutical industry, 163–4, 188, 189, 215
Plato and Platonism
  balance, 155, 156–7, 185
  Baldwin, 137
  Carver, 207–8
  Cheever, 104
  Ford, 144
  mimesis, 116–17, 121, 191, 236
Pliny the Elder, 191
poetry, 32, 83, 84, 117, 192
polarities *see* dualism
positivism
  Carver, 207
  Cheever, 103, 105, 113
  further mentions, 114, 120, 159
  Percy, 59, 66
  further mentions, 32
post-war America, overview, 34–8
post-war American realism, 34, 40–2
postmodernism, 41, 55, 79, 91, 103, 143, 232
Pound, Ezra, 32
'Previous Condition' (Baldwin), 134–42
psychedelic drugs, 186, 190
psychiatry, 105–6, 163, 168, 188
psychotherapy/psychology, 25–30, 37, 162–4, 220, 223–4; *see also* cognitive processes
psychotropes, 186–7, 189–90, 191, 202, 203–5, 215, 217; *see also* alcohol; pharmaceutical industry
puppet metaphor, 97–9, 202

quest
  Carver, 212
  Cheever, 103, 106, 109, 111, 113
  Percy, 56, 61, 65

*Rabbit at Rest* (Updike), 203–5
*Rabbit, Run* (Updike), 195–203, 222
race *see* Black affect; Whiteness
racial violence, 134, 136
rationalism, 34, 36, 59, 112, 232
rationality, 191, 199, 203, 206, 207–10, 232; *see also* facts; 'The Geometry of Love' (Cheever)
realism, 41; *see also* literary realism; nineteenth-century realism; postwar American realism
reality
  Baldwin, 135
  Bellow, 67, 71–2, 76–8
  Carver, 212, 213–14
  Cheever, 104–5, 107, 110–11, 128
  Ford, 147
  Fox, 173
  Updike, 198, 202
  further mentions, 20, 82–3, 89–90, 228, 232, 237
reason
  Cheever, 105–6, 111
  Percy, 65
  Updike, 199, 200, 203
  further mentions, 3, 157–8
relativism, 94, 144, 177, 209, 211, 237
representation
  affect's relation to, 49–53, 56, 79–80
  Bellow, 75, 76, 77
  Ford, 148–9, 151–2
  meta-representation, 86–7
  Roth, 92, 94–5, 97, 101
  further mentions, 223, 228, 233–7
  *see also* mimesis
repression
  introduction, 2, 18, 34, 37
  Bellow, 66
  Carver, 206
  Cheever, 127
  Collins, 128
  Ford, 143
  Fox, 172, 174, 179, 183
  psychotropes, 163–4, 190
  Updike, 198, 199, 201, 205
  Yates, 167
  further mentions, 154–5, 157, 185, 232
  *see also* normativity/normalisation; oppression
*Revolutionary Road* (Yates), 122–6, 160, 164–5, 168–70
Rice, Peter*, 171, 173, 177–84
rituals, 129–30, 131, 211, 213
Robinson, Jenefer, 89
Romanticism, 32, 34, 37, 97, 121, 145, 167, 218–19
Rorty, Amélie O., 86
Rosset, Clément, 88, 89
Roth, Marty, 193
Roth, Philip
  introduction, 82
  *American Pastoral*, 40, 148
  *Sabbath's Theater*, 92–102, 222
  Zuckerman novels, 246n63
Russian Formalism, 15, 47, 84, 230, 231

Sabbath, Mickey*, 92–102, 222
*Sabbath's Theater* (Roth), 92–102, 222
Scarry, Elaine, 89
Schneider, Joseph, 193
science, 11, 85, 207, 218, 224, 232; *see also* facts; 'The Geometry of Love' (Cheever); medical profession; neuroscience; objectivity; positivism
screaming, 137, 177
searching *see* quest
Sedgwick, Eve Kosofsky, 16–17
self *see* false self; identity; true self; unified self
self-consciousness, 54, 92, 131, 198
self-control *see* emotional control
self-help, 25, 137, 154, 155, 218–20
self-invention, 74–8
self-reflexivity
  Bellow, 71
  Cheever, 113
  Ellison, 10–11, 13
  Ford, 148, 151–2
  Yates, 122, 125

self-reflexivity (*cont.*)
   further mentions, 4, 86, 91, 120, 158, 217, 236
   *see also* solipsism
Seligman, Martin, 27–8, 29, 30–2
senses/sensations, 73, 77–8, 95, 137, 222
sentimentality
   anti-sentimentalism, 32–4, 38, 42, 133–4, 231
   further mentions, 25, 36, 64–5, 72, 126
sexual violence, 197
Sharpe, Christina, 130
Shelley, Percy, 231
Shklovsky, Viktor, 56, 84–5
Shouse, Eric, 50
Sieff, Daniela F., 26–7
simulation *see* dissimulation and simulation
Singal, Daniel J., 227
smiles/smiling, 7, 27–32, 28, 29, 61, 141, 172, 175
Smith, Brian A., 61
social class, 38, 63, 65, 67, 122, 134
social homeostasis, 158–9
social order, 34, 65, 159
solipsism
   Bellow, 68, 71
   Carver, 213
   Ford, 148
   Percy, 60
   further mentions, 4, 22, 42, 120, 191, 233
   *see also* self-reflexivity
Solomon, Robert Charles, 24–5
Spanish identity, 176, 178, 180, 182–3
*The Sportswriter* (Ford), 143–53
stability
   Carver, 211, 214
   Cheever, 105, 109, 112, 126
   Ford, 152, 154–5
   Fox, 172
   social homeostasis, 158–9
   Updike, 200, 202
   Yates, 126, 162–3, 167
   further mentions, 184–5, 189, 234–5
Stanislavsky, Konstantin, 37
Starr, Paul, 193
Stevens, Hugh, 32–3
Stockwell, Peter, 83
Stoicism, 87, 90, 143, 181–2
*A Streetcar Named Desire* (Williams), 165
Structuralism, 15, 230
suburbia
   Cheever, 126
   Percy, 59
   Updike, 196, 198
   Yates, 122–4
   further mentions, 34, 38, 40
suicide, 100, 107, 210
'The Swimmer' (Cheever), 126–8

Tanner, Tony, 201
Taylor, Charles, 156, 157
tears/crying
   Cheever, 103, 126–7
   Collins, 128–30, 131–2, 133
   Fox, 180–1
   Roth, 92, 96, 98, 100
   Updike, 200–1
   Yates, 122, 124–5, 169
   further mentions, 121–2, 231
Temperance movement, 192–3
temporality
   Carver, 212, 216
   Cheever, 104, 106, 110–11, 126–7
   Fox, 172, 174
   Percy, 57, 59–60, 62
   psychotropes, 188
   Updike, 202
Terri* ('What We Talk About When We Talk About Love'), 208, 209, 210–11, 212, 214, 215
theatrical settings, 57, 124, 165, 173
theatricality *see* performativity
Thrailkill, Jane, 94
Tolstoy, Leo, 52, 164, 222
Tompkins, Jane P., 230
totalitarianism, 25, 228

Index / 285

totality, 43, 47, 52, 86, 89, 209
Tracy, Sarah, 21, 25
transcendence, categories of, 20
transparency, 41, 47, 77, 120, 146, 182, 198
Trethewey, Angela, 21, 25
Trilling, Lionel, 68
true feeling *see* emotional truth
true self
  Bellow, 67-8
  Du Bois, 131
  Ford, 152
  Fox, 176
  Roth, 95
  further mentions, 6, 25-7, 31, 40, 185, 218, 232
truth, category of, 6, 20, 88, 156-7, 228; *see also* emotion of truth; emotional truth; objectivity
Tsur, Reuven, 83, 84

'The Uncle' (Collins), 128-32, 133
unconsciousness, 16, 48-9, 53, 208
unified self
  Ellison, 11
  Ford, 145, 150
  Fox, 175, 182
  Roth, 95, 99
  further mentions, 8, 22, 36, 39, 114, 155
United States of America
  post-war overview, 34-8
  post-war realism, 34, 40-2
unity
  community, 34, 36, 39-40
  and harmony, 3, 5, 52, 213
  love, concept of, 208
  *see also* coherency; harmony; unified self
universalism
  Arendt, 229
  Baldwin, 139, 141
  Carver, 209-10
  Cheever, 106
  Collins, 128, 132-3
  Faulkner, 225-7

New Criticism, 232
Roth, 93, 96
utilitarian approaches to literature, 218, 220-1, 223-4
  further mentions, 35, 36, 48, 233, 235, 237
Updike, John
  *Rabbit at Rest*, 203-5
  *Rabbit, Run*, 195-203, 222
utilitarianism
  Bellow, 71
  Carver, 211
  Ellison, 12
  value of literature, 8, 218-24
  Yates, 123, 126
utopianism, 69-70, 105, 142, 229, 234

Vicedo, Marga, 34
Victorian literature, 32, 37, 218, 220, 235
Vidal, Gore, 37
violence *see* domestic violence; racial violence

*The Wapshot Chronicle* (Cheever), 111
Warren, Robert Penn, 131
WASPs (White Anglo-Saxon Protestants), 34-5, 38-40
well-being, 30, 32, 155, 156, 158, 205
'What We Talk About When We Talk About Love' (Carver), 206-17
'Whatever Happened to Interracial Love?' (Collins), 132
Wheeler, April*, 122-4, 160, 164-5
Wheeler, Frank*, 122-3, 160, 164-5, 168-9
whiteness
  Baldwin, 134, 136, 137, 138, 140, 141-2
  Collins, 129
  Fox, 176
  normativity, 34-5, 38-40, 116, 131, 133
*The Widow's Children* (Fox), 171-84, 222
Wilder, John*, 160-2

Wilhite, Keith, 39
Williams, Raymond, 227
Williams, Tennessee, *A Streetcar Named Desire*, 165
Winnicott, D. W., 26
Wordsworth, William, 'Preface', 170, 242n77
Wyatt-Brown, Bertram, 65

Yates, Richard
   introduction, 116, 159–60
   *Disturbing the Peace*, 160–2
   *Revolutionary Road*, 122–6, 160, 164–5, 168–70
   *Young Hearts Crying*, 162–3, 165–8

Zola, Émile, 74, 120

EU representative:
Easy Access System Europe
Mustamäe tee 50, 10621 Tallinn, Estonia
Gpsr.requests@easproject.com

www.ingramcontent.com/pod-product-compliance
Lightning Source LLC
Chambersburg PA
CBHW050209240426
43671CB00013B/2272